AMERICAN
ENVIRONMENTAL
POLITICS

AMERICAN ENVIRONMENTAL POLITICS

David Howard Davis
University of Toledo

Nelson-Hall Publishers/Chicago

Project editor: Steven M. Long
Typesetter: Precision Typographers
Printer: McNaughton & Gunn, Inc.
Cover photograph: *Bald Eagle* by Daniel J. Cox, Natural Exposures, Inc.

Library of Congress Cataloging-in-Publication Data

Davis, David Howard.
    American environmental politics / David Howard Davis.
       p. cm.
    Includes bibliographical references and index.
    ISBN 0-8304-1518-1
    1. Environmental policy—United States. 2. Environmental
movement—United States. 3. Environmental protection—United
States.
    I. Title.
    GE180.D38   1998   97-24488
    363.7'00973—DC21   CIP

Manufactured in the United States of America

10 9 8 7 6 5 4 3 2 1

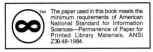

The paper used in this book meets the
minimum requirements of American
National Standard for Information
Sciences—Permanence of Paper for
Printed Library Materials, ANSI
Z39.48-1984.

to Jill and Greg

CONTENTS

PREFACE

My first goal has been to write a book you will enjoy reading. I hope you will find it interesting, provocative, and fun, whether your background is political science or ecology. Politics fascinates people because it is about power and money, and environmental politics adds controversial issues of philosophy, religion, and collective action. Moreover, it calls on other disciplines in the natural and social sciences. Our modern industry and technology has caused many of our environmental problems, and science may not be able to solve them. The policy choices offer the thrill of a gamble, because if we are wrong, the greenhouse effect, the ozone hole, or toxic chemicals may kill us. To a degree greater than for other issues, environmental politics cannot be understood without considering economics, history, biology, and other disciplines. Within the realm of political science, no single approach can explain all aspects, which is the reason this book uses four approaches: mass movements, interest groups, political parties, and governmental procedures. Although this book is about the American situation, it examines international aspects such as the Chernobyl nuclear reactor explosion, endangered rain forests in Latin America, and, more ominously, population growth in Africa and Asia.

I began teaching environmental policy in spring 1972. By the end of the semester, I had decided to write a textbook, but was sidetracked by writing *Energy Politics*, now in its fourth edition. (A popular book can be a curse as well as a blessing.) After a mere quarter of a century, I got back on track. Much of the material comes from my employment in the Environmental Protection Agency, the Department of the Interior, and other jobs in government and business. Over the years I have visited many of the places mentioned in this book, and have interviewed and enjoyed the friendship of people in government, environmental groups, and business.

After my sophomore year in college, I got a summer job sorting garbage at the incinerator in Yosemite National Park—an ironic mixture of environmental themes. In 1973, I went to Washington, D.C., to work at the EPA and returned to the Capital a few years later to positions in the General Accounting Office and the Library of Congress. These three jobs taught me about the inner workings of the bureaucracy and Congress. When I held a political appointment in the Department of the Interior, I got a view from the top, which differs in many ways. The perspective of a departmental secretary or assistant secretary is much more like the interest group model of political science than the view from within the bureaucracy, I hope my practical experience flavors the book.

On the academic side, I have tried to bring out the major issues and theories and to balance the pros and cons. Problems of air, water, and hazardous waste fit together because they are pollution—unwanted soot, chemicals, and germs dumped into the air, rivers, or landscape, over which the EPA has the primary responsibility. Radiation is a pollutant also, but Congress decided to leave responsibility with the Atomic Energy Commission and the Nuclear Regulatory Commission. The politics of protecting endangered species, wilderness areas, parks, and other land differs greatly from those of controlling pollution. The policy has evolved over a longer time span, and involves many agencies, interest groups, and all three levels of government.

I have tried to avoid bias and hope that my writing about various issues presents both sides, and allows you to draw your own conclusions. Environmentalists, in my opinion, are sometimes too zealous, and industry sometimes cannot look beyond the costs to see the benefits. Some writers on this topic, unfortunately, allow partisan bias to creep into their analysis, painting a negative view of the Republican party. Although the Reagan administration was obviously unfriendly toward the environment (and a bit of that attitude continues in Congress), other Republicans have been favorable. President Richard Nixon supported the movement strongly, establishing the EPA in 1970 and backing the Clean Air Act and other early laws. Heads of the EPA like William Ruckelshaus, Russell Train, and William Reilley were dedicated to a clean environment, and members of Congress like Senator Robert Stafford stood up to the Reagan administration attempts to weaken the Clean Air Act. President George Bush strongly supported amendments to the Clean Air Act to deal with acid rain and the ozone hole.

Ordinary citizens have played a bigger part in the environmental politics than in other arenas. Lois Gibbs was a mother who did not want to send her son to the elementary school built over the chemicals dumped into the Love Canal, David Brower joined the Sierra Club so he could climb mountains, before he mobilized nationwide opposition to a dam in Dinosaur National Monument. Rachel Carson was a government scientist who wrote books in her spare time, including *Silent Spring*, which alerted the nation to the dangers of DDT. The stories of these citizens, politicians, scientists, and bureaucrats make up the full story of American environmental politics.

CHAPTER 1
INTRODUCTION

Environmental politics today is far more complex than when it bounded onto the national scene in 1970. Earth Day makes a convenient date of birth for this new aspect of politics. On April 22, 1970, twenty million Americans rallied in cities, campuses, and schools across the country demanding the government to pass laws protecting the air, water, and land. Rallies drew up to twenty-five thousand participants in New York, San Francisco, Washington, Chicago, and Philadelphia. The demonstrations copied, in a less angry form, those against the Vietnam War and for civil rights that had torn the United States apart during the 1960s. In fact, President Richard Nixon and members of Congress were eager to cooperate with the demands, which seemed easier to achieve than saving the South Vietnamese government or ending racial bigotry. Within eight months Congress passed the Clean Air Act and Nixon established the Environmental Protection Agency (EPA). In 1972, Congress passed the Clean Water Act, and followed with many more laws.

Nearly thirty years later, however, the hopes of the Environmental Decade are still not achieved. Although auto exhaust and factory smoke are cleaner, more automobiles and more factories keep the air dirty. While Congress set a goal of making all rivers and lakes fishable and swimmable by 1985, this section of the Clean Water Act is now considered ridiculously optimistic. In 1970, people did not anticipate the difficulties with ending pollution. Scientists did not know that chemicals used in refrigerators and air conditioners caused holes in the ozone layer in the stratosphere or that burning coal and oil threatened to warm the earth

1

like a greenhouse. Many of the problems are more subtle than these. For example, the great expense of controlling pollution raises the issue of whether the best method is to set strict standards or to offer financial rewards for a good job. A bigger issue is to determine the optimal level of pollution to balance good health and life against the cost.

The environmental burst gave common features to the new laws and agencies established during the 1970s. The Clean Air Act, the Clean Water Act, the Resource Conservation and Recovery Act (RCRA), and the Surface Mining Act are all national laws delegated to the states for implementation. Congress and Presidents Nixon and Jimmy Carter believed that Washington was taking on too much, so the national government set standards and general policies then told the state governments to implement them. These implementations contrast with earlier national programs like social security pensions and land management, but copy programs like social welfare. The method was for Congress (in the law) and the EPA (in regulations) to establish standards, usually in great detail. Factories, automobile manufacturers, and sewage plants were required to comply with the exact limits and received no reward for doing any better. Critics labeled environmental policy "command and control," pointing out its rigidity and inefficiency. Perhaps more seriously, they found fault with the amount of regulation, arguing that it was excessive, hurt the total economy, and infringed on the rights of citizens and companies.

The election of Ronald Reagan nearly reversed the programs of the Environmental Decade. The chief change was to reduce the rigor of enforcement. Reagan won in 1980 with the promise "to get the government off the backs of the American people." He downgraded the authority of the EPA, reduced the enforcement effort, and cut its budget. At the Department of the Interior, he diminished its environmental mission and told it to sell and give away land to private owners or to state governments, a response to the so-called Sagebrush Rebellion. In general, the Reagan administration was much more pro-business than either the Carter or Nixon administrations. While Reagan's extreme anti-environmental policies moderated after 1983, the EPA and the Interior Department remained favorable to business.

BACKGROUND

The environmental movement, however, did not spring out of the ground on Earth Day, 1970. Momentum had been building during the 1960s and events of the previous three decades prepared the way. Franklin Roosevelt's New Deal presaged many aspects, and his personal commitment was strong. As a boy growing up on his wealthy father's estate at Hyde Park, he played at damming up streams, planting trees, and stringing wire for a homemade telephone. Many say that, as president, he just did this on a larger scale by damming the Missouri River at Fort Peck, planting millions of acres of trees, and establishing the Rural Electrification Administration (REA). During the 1930s, the Agricultural

2

Table 1.1 Environmental Groups

Group	Founded	Budget	Staff	Members	Headquarters
Sierra Club and its Legal Defense Fund	1892	$42 million	325	550,000	San Francisco, office in Washington, DC
National Audubon Society	1905, (1886, 1896)	$40 million	315	542,000	New York City, office in Washington, DC
National Parks and Conservation Association	1919	$11 million	43	400,000	Washington, DC
Izaak Walton League of America	1922	$2 million	23	53,000	Washington, DC area
The Wilderness Society	1935	$16 million	136	293,000	Washington, DC
National Wildlife Federation	1936	$83 million	608	4 million	Washington, DC
The Nature Conservancy	1951	$278 million	1,150	708,000	Washington, DC area
World Wildlife Fund	1961 (1948)	$61 million	244	1 million	Washington, DC
Friends of the Earth	1969	$2.5 million	45	50,000	Washington, DC
Environmental Defense Fund	1967	$17 million	110	250,000	New York City, office in Washington, DC
Natural Resources Defense Council	1970	$20 million	128	170,000	New York City, office in Washington, DC
Greenpeace Fund, Inc. (formerly Greenpeace USA)	1971	$21 million in U.S., $157 million internationally	65	400,000 in U.S., 4.5 million worldwide	U.S.: Washington, DC World: Amsterdam 250 offices in 30 countries

Adjustment Administration (AAA) restored topsoil eroded by poor farming, the Civilian Conservation Corps (CCC) built trails and shelter houses in parks, and the Rural Electric Administration (REA) strung electric lines to remote farms. The Tennessee Valley Authority (TVA) built a half-dozen dams to control floods and generate electricity, manufactured fertilizer for soil depleted by the cotton industry, and taught the mountaineers how to organize cooperative action. On the Great Plains, where the winds of the Dust Bowl had literally blown away farms,

3

On September 18, 1996, with the Grand Canyon as a backdrop, President Bill Clinton in the company of Vice President Al Gore signed a bill declaring 1.7 million acres of southern Utah's red-rock cliffs and canyons as Grand Staircase-Escalante National Monument. Since 1832, the federal government has set aside lands of exceptional natural interest for protection.

the U.S. Department of Agriculture bought millions of acres of wind-swept property to become National Grasslands. The president ended uncontrolled homesteading and Congress reined in grazing cattle and sheep on the public domain. In the Blue Ridge Mountains of Virginia, the government established the Shenandoah National Park. In Pennsylvania, the Works Progress Administration (WPA) sealed abandoned coal mines that were leaching acid into creeks. The New Deal, of course, was not confined to the environment. It fought the unemployment of the Great Depression, brought the stock market under control to prevent another crash like Black Monday in 1929, began the social security pen-

Rachel Carson's *Silent Spring* created wide-spread public awareness of the pesticide DDT's lethal effects on birds.

sions, and rescued the bankrupt state welfare programs. The New Deal changed the national government from little to big and set the pattern of Washington attacking the biggest problems.

World War II prepared the way for the environmental movement in its own fashion. Government became even bigger. To manufacture guns, tanks, ships, and airplanes, the nation doubled its industry. Manufacturers sent smoke into the air and pollution into the rivers. Miners reopened the abandoned coal mines sealed by the WPA. The Army and Navy sent soldiers and sailors to ports and camps far from home. Many saw for the first time the beauty of the mountains and the sea. The Pacific campaign sent soldiers, sailors, and factory workers to California, Oregon, and Washington state. Thousands went to Alaska by ship or the newly built highway through Canada. Once the war ended, the veterans felt they had earned the right to direct the country, entering politics and business with determination and confidence. To help them along and thank them for their sacrifice, Congress passed the GI Bill paying them to go to college and providing cheap loans for houses.

The economy after 1945 was far different than before the war. In 1940, the Great Depression gave way to the war boom and never reappeared. Economic growth from 1945 to 1969 was the greatest before or since. The stock market crash of 1929 and the Great Depression had discredited the old system of business. After the war, the big corporations that came to dominate were conscious of their need to be good citizens. Companies and labor unions began to cooperate, with wages rising along with profits. With prosperity, millions of Americans had the time and money to camp in the mountains, buy a boat for the lake, or travel to a national park in their new station wagon. The automobile and chemical industries were the most vigorous. This period earned the nicknames of both the Automobile Age and the Chemical Age. Beginning in 1956, the national government invested billions in Interstate highways. All these new factories, automobiles, and chemicals polluted the air and water. The twenty-year period following 1945 also witnessed better education and information. Service in the military had been an education in itself. The government paid for college for veterans; in turn, the veterans' higher incomes paid for college for their children. Inspired by wartime accomplishments in science, technology, and health, the government spent millions on scientific research. Magazines with high quality photographs like *Life, Look, Colliers,* and *National Geographic* stimulated interest in nature. It was a period of optimism and of faith in government—science could harness the atom, technology could crack petroleum, physicians could cure diseases, and the government could manage the economy.

Not all the events were positive, however. Commuters could see the smog as they drove to work from the suburbs. Cities like Gary, Cleveland, and Pittsburgh struggled to reduce smoke from steel mills. Fish died in the Mississippi River and Lake Erie turned a sickly green in the summer. In Donora, Pennsylvania, twenty people died and 40 percent of the population became sick during an air inversion in 1948. In 1952, four thousand died in London from a killer smog, a tragedy widely publicized in the United States. Rachel Carson's book *Silent Spring* crystallized opposition to DDT. A biologist by profession, she explained in lay terms how this chemical, designed to kill mosquitoes, ended up poisoning birds. She warned that spring would no longer have the joyous sound of songbirds, and the bald eagle—the symbol of the Republic—would die out.

In Her Own Words: Rachel Carson
U.S. Fish and Wildlife Service scientist and author of *Silent Spring*

Over increasingly large areas of the United States, spring now comes unheralded by the return of the birds, and the early mornings are strangely silent where once they were filled with the beauty of bird song. . . .[1] Like the robin, another American bird seems to be on the verge of extinction. This is the national symbol, the eagle. Its populations have dwindled alarmingly within the past decade. . . .[2]

For the first time in the history of the world, every human being is now subjected to contact with dangerous chemicals, from the moment of conception until death.[3]

1. Rachel Carson, *Silent Spring* (Boston: Houghton Mifflin, 1962), 103.
2. Ibid., 118.
3. Ibid., 15.

FOUR APPROACHES

From the mid-1950s to the 1970s, the environmental movement grew and changed rapidly. It began with the ideas and concerns of a few men and women who convinced many others of the dangers. The public began to realize the problems were not confined to Pittsburgh, the Green River, or the California mountains; dirty air and water were a difficulty throughout the country. DDT was killing birds everywhere. Membership in the Sierra Club, the Wilderness Society, and National Wildlife Federation doubled and tripled. From its founding in 1892 until 1952, Sierra Club membership stayed below seven thousand; by 1968, it increased to seventy thousand, and currently, its members number half a million. As popular attention increased, political leaders recognized the problems and moved to take action. Environmental groups lobbied Congress, and business groups countered with their own concerns about expense. After debating all sides, Congress passed laws and presidents reorganized the government. The EPA began to implement the new laws, state governments took on new responsibilities, and corporations conformed to the new regulations.

By the end of the 1970s, the dynamic stage drew to an end. Environmental policy became more stable and the basic framework was in place. In this mature stage, environmental and business groups now lobbied for amendments to the laws and for the EPA to issue regulations favorable to their side. National and state agencies developed programs and learned to work together. Once corporations recognized that the regulations were permanent, they began to cooperate with the government. In the colorful words of a Colorado native, "the companies just needed to be housebroken."

Analyzing the dynamic and stable features in the development of environmental policy calls for four different approaches: (1) mass movements, (2) interest groups, (3) political parties, and (4) governmental procedures. Each illuminates different facets, issues, and time periods. Theories of mass movements explain environmentalism in terms of a cycle of growth. By its very definition, a mass movement cannot be the same at the end as at the beginning. As the original ideas inspire the crusade, they spread and others join. The innovation of environmentalism is diffused to gain acceptance. Once this happens, theories about mass movements no longer can explain the mature phase that is stable, not dynamic. This stable situation calls for theories about interest groups, parties, and bureaucratic procedures. Each of these four approaches has a different view about the purpose of government, who should participate, the role of Congress, courts and the bureaucracy, timing, and the future.

Mass Movements

Popular concern about the environment swept the country quickly in the late 1960s and into the 1970s. Its wide scope and sudden emergence shared many features with other mass movements of the 1960s and 1970s like civil rights, the

Vietnam War protests, women's liberation, and anti-abortion as well as earlier ones like abolition of slavery, women's suffrage, trade unions, and the prohibition of liquor. And, further in history, from 1750 on, the idea of liberty swept the American colonies.

Although the term "mass movement" correctly focuses on the people at the grass roots, political scientists speak of "setting the agenda" for government decision making. Before Congress passes a law, a presidential candidate promises changes, or a governor proposes a new program, the ideas are shapeless. After a while, certain ideas bubble up to the surface, while elected officials, candidates campaigning for office, and others form them into proposals, platforms, and bills. They are then on the agenda for debate and decision. Unfortunately, this phase is poorly understood. Most analysts prefer to examine a movement after it has acquired structure. Even those who specialize in mass movements tend to begin after the amorphous blob becomes organized. Moreover, most political scientists consider a mass movement just an interest group in its early stage. As such, the movement is in a transitional status.

One of the most troublesome problems in understanding a mass movement is the question of its timing. Why were the 1970s the Environmental Decade instead of the 1950s or the 1920s? A solution may be to compare it to other innovations and how they diffused. Television is a good case study. Social scientists believe that innovations diffuse for four reasons: technical, economic, structural, and educational. Television broadcasts could not begin until scientists invented transmitters and receivers. The pattern of a station serving a single city emerged because the electronic signal only carried thirty to forty miles. The industry could not expand beyond the three stations in New York City until 1945 because World War II preempted the engineering talent, the raw materials, and the entertainers. After 1945, however, prosperity gave consumers the money to buy television sets and the products advertised on them. National networks like CBS and NBC were natural developments because of the efficiency of programming and the sponsors' desire to advertise their brand names all across the country. The industry developed as private companies regulated by the Federal Communications Commission because that was the pattern for radio. In the case of television, the educational requirements for the viewers were minimal (some would say negative).

For the environmental movement, the technical aspect of its diffusion was not its own, but that of its adversaries. Starting during World War II, the revolution in chemicals poured millions of tons of hazardous waste into the air, water, and soil. DDT was the most notorious. Scientists were not aware of many of the dangers until the 1960s. The economic depression of the 1930s had kept the United States far less polluted prior to World War II than it became once the war began in Europe. Factories sitting idle during the Depression did not produce smoke or waste. Few people could afford an automobile. After the war ended, however, production went from two million cars per year to nearly seven million in sixteen years. Today, the number of new cars sold is nine million per year. The total number of cars went from thirty million to eighty million in 1960. Today, it is nearly two hundred million.

For the environment, perhaps the greatest blessing of the prosperity from 1945 through the 1960s was people's increased leisure time. The governmental structural factors included Veterans' Administration (VA) mortgages that encouraged suburban sprawl, the interstate highway program, and big government that focused policy at the national level. The GI Bill, and later high incomes, enabled many Americans to attend universities where they learned science, engineering, and organizing skills. Federal laboratories and grants for scientific research led to the discovery of environmental dangers.

Besides these background factors, innovations diffused due to talent, resources, leadership, esprit de corps, and missionary effort. From its beginning, the environmental movement benefitted from scientific talent. Indeed, many of its concepts originated from governmental and academic experts. Aldo Leopold, who popularized the concept of ecology, was a U.S. Forest Service employee and later a biology professor at the University of Wisconsin. Bob Marshall was a Forest Service employee as well. The discoverer of DNA, James Watson, later led opposition to the Shoreham nuclear plant. Barry Commoner taught biology at Washington University in St. Louis. Environmentalists have been able to mobilize resources more easily than the average citizen. Besides scientific talent, many have been trained in law, journalism, and politics. They also tend to be wealthier than average Americans. Some, like the Rockefellers and the Pews, have been extremely wealthy.

Good leadership explains much of the success of the movement. In 1954, the executive director of the Sierra Club, David Brower, alerted the members of the Interior Department's plan to flood Echo Park Canyon. In 1968, he founded the Friends of the Earth and, in 1982, founded the Earth Island Institute. Environmentalists truly believe in their cause. They work long hours at the mimeograph machine and on the telephone. They travel to mountain tops and to Washington, D.C., and may go to the extremes of climbing fences at electric generating plants and lying down in front of bulldozers. Many devote themselves to being missionaries, preaching against evil, and traveling in search of converts. Environmentalists have the advantage adherents to other causes may lack. The natural beauty they seek to protect refreshes their spirits, while hikes and evenings around the campfires strengthen their devotion and fellowship.

Approaching the environmental movement in terms of the diffusion of innovation offers the advantage of understanding when and why the movement began. Background factors like changes in the chemical industry and increased numbers of automobiles address its timing and emergence. Factors of resources and leadership are harder to evaluate. Many other movements have had these same attributes, yet never emerged or were less successful.

Mass movements start at the grass roots. Perhaps social scientists should coin the term "small movements" to explore the beginning stages. Furthermore, they need to explain citizens gathering together to protest a new incinerator, a spill of

In His Own Words: David Brower
Director of the Sierra Club, Founder of Friends of the Earth, League of
Conservation Voters, and the Earth Island Institute

Henry Voge, indeed, talked me into joining the Sierra Club to learn how to climb more
safely than he thought I had. On Berkeley and Mount Diablo rocks and in Pinnacles
National Monument we climbed, either with the club's rock-climbing section or by our-
selves. . . .[1]

The club's serious concern [about damming Echo Park Canyon in Dinosaur National
Monument] began in 1950 and it became my principal concern at the close of 1952, when
I became the club's first executive director and was swallowed by Dinosaur. . . .

Testimony before the House Committee on the Interior
January 26, 1954

I am the Executive Director of the Sierra Club, a national conservation organization of
eight thousand members founded in 1892 by John Muir, Warren Olney, and colleagues to
explore, enjoy, and protect the nation's scenic assets. . . . Deplorable is a mild word to
describe what would happen to the scenery in Dinosaur were we to permit these dams to
be built there. The Echo Park project alone calls for a dam 525 feet high, backing up 107
miles of reservoir, inundating the intimate, close-up scenes and living space with nearly
6½ million acre-feet of water. . . . The pinion pines, the Douglas firs, the maples and cot-
tonwoods, the grasses and other flora that line the banks, the green living things that shine
in the sun against the rich colors of the cliffs—these would all go. The river, its surge and
its sound, the living sculptor of this place, would be silent forever, and all the fascination
of its movement and the fun of riding it, quietly gliding through these cathedral corridors
of stone—all done in for good.[2]

1. David Brower, *For Earth's Sake* (Layton, Utah: Gibbs Smith, 1990), 30.
2. Ibid., 328–329.

a chemical into a river, or a petitioning for a neighborhood park. These grass roots
movements, the smaller versions of mass movements, are the building blocks of
environmentalism. Certainly, the fact that millions of Americans rallied to the side
of nature is a unique feature. At the same time, the phenomenon owes its success
to thousands of small collective actions. Just like mass movements, their timing
depends on technical, economical, structural, and educational factors. Talent,
resources, and leadership also determine their success or failure. For every David
Brower, a thousand local entrepreneurs exhort, organize, and fight.

Movements are dynamic and emotional, with a life cycle starting with
grievances, evolving limited structure, and ending in triumph, failure, or dissipation. Members agree on the identity of their antagonists, speak with a common vocabulary, and recite their own narrative history. They are self-conscious
and both participants and outsiders name the movement. Participants identify
the cause as their own. Their feeling is intense, emotional, and even spiritual.

Some are zealots, while the most salient members are ordinary people who adhere to the cause. Leaders, commonly labeled activists, emerge from the rank and file. As the movement grows, it sets up chapters, either spontaneously or with planning.

As the early spontaneity matures into formal organization, the movement employs techniques to recruit new members. It rehearses its grievances into a litany and makes people conscious of the problem in face to face meetings, which may be small groups or large rallies. Indeed, mass meetings are characteristic. Techniques to mobilize are both conventional ones of writing letters, petitioning, voting, picketing, and more unconventional actions such as sit-ins, climbing fences, confronting corporate managers, and even sabotage. The movement uses television, street theater, and newspapers to communicate with the general public, and newsletters and telephone trees to communicate with its own members. The Freedom of Information Act and the Community Right to Know Act give a wedge. Lawsuits against government and industry are a favorite technique. A movement can be as big as the environmental movement or as small as neighbors objecting to a garbage incinerator. By definition, a movement is dynamic and fluid; if it succeeds, it is no longer called a movement.

On the other hand, a movement is not the casual drift of public opinion over time, or consumer preference for red cars instead of blue ones. It is not an interest group of highly organized, narrowly focused lobbyists prowling the Capitol or Department of the Interior. A mass movement must have extensive membership, typically with little structure, yet be dynamic and fluid. Its activists truly believe in their cause. It must be considered to be a movement by both its participants and the general public.

Social science attention to mass movements was at its height from 1930 to 1950 in response to the appeal in Europe of Naziism, fascism, and communism. Psychology, a new and dynamic discipline at the time, offered an interpretation. The explanations stressed grievances, deprivation, and the breakdown of the social order and ideology. Psychologists saw mass action beginning with spontaneous crowd response and developing into publics attuned to the problem. At first, communication was crude, by contagion, rumor, and diffusion. The fascist and communist parties exploited spontaneous popular responses with their propaganda, secrecy, and indoctrination. The Nazis excelled in manipulation by wearing uniforms, staging rallies at night, parading with flags, and singing military songs. The three movements recruited members from deprived classes in society. Social scientists who analyzed Naziism, fascism, and communism nearly always opposed these mass movements; they were not neutral and dispassionate investigators, but researchers of the enemy, trying to learn its causes and strategies. The other mass movement attracting attention in the 1930s was labor unions, which social science analysts were quite favorable towards, even though trade unions displayed similar features with fascist and communist organizations such as capitalizing on popular grievances, mass rallies, and propaganda.

The theories of the 1930s and 1940s, however, could not explain the American Civil Rights movement. Grievances and deprivation did not explain much since blacks had been deprived since the end of Reconstruction and were slaves prior to the Civil War. These movements, plus the anti-war and environmental movements, drew their leadership and many participants from the well-educated middle class, hardly a deprived strata of society. Unlike prior protests, these flowed into the political mainstream. Unlike prior mass movements, those of the 1960s and 1970s were decentralized, which contrasted with the trade union organizing of the 1930s. Grass roots support of nature needed little cultivation. The goals of the new movements included personal involvement and new personal identities. They also shared the older goals of solidarity. In contrast to social scientists who studied fascism and communism, those who have studied the civil rights and environmental movements tend to be favorable.

Social scientists believed analyzing the resources of a movement would give a better explanation than the old ways of analysis. Tangible resources were money, mimeograph machines, telephones, office space, and volunteer labor. Intangible ones were skills in organizing, lawyering, and technology. Even less tangible were legitimacy, the support of key politicians, and public attention. The treat of disruption, such as a public demonstration, was a resource. Responding to the question of timing for the civil rights crusade, readiness was also seen as a resource. Readiness, in turn could be explained in terms of background such as increased education. In an analogy to the way a business mobilizes resources, movements needed entrepreneurs who could exploit a situation to the profit of the cause. These entrepreneurs could mobilize resources and use their understanding of the policy "marketplace." They would polish and shape their raw materials, even occasionally manufacturing grievances.[1] Martin Luther King, Jr., ranks as one of the greatest leaders in mobilizing his resources, which appeared insignificant when he first volunteered to run the mimeograph machine for the 1955 bus boycott in Montgomery, Alabama.

While most collective protests must struggle against opposition, other movements find broad consensus. Mothers Against Drunk Drivers (MADD) serves as an example. It grew rapidly and achieved success in toughening laws and educating young people. Like other consensus movements, MADD expanded by franchising chapters, aligning with existing organizations like schools and churches, winning government grants from the Federal Highway Administration, and gaining endorsement from newspapers, television, and the general public. In the long run, however, consensus movements may be less successful than ones that protest. Although protest movements have a tougher task in recruiting members and finding money, once established they are stronger. Support for consensus movements may be shallow, evaporating as members turn their attention elsewhere and grant money dries up.[2]

The environmental movement makes certain assumptions, the major premise being that government should take the lead in cleaning the environment. This role is seen as one of government's major purposes. More generally, the government should empower people by giving citizens input into licensing nuclear reactors or toxic waste dumps, for example, and all citizens should participate. While collective action is important, everyone should help individually, for instance, by recycling aluminum cans and commuting by mass transit. Still, leaders recognize that people may not understand the problem, may need to become more conscious of the scope, and may need to learn how to remedy pollution. While adherents of a movement look to government as the savior, they tend to have little faith in political parties. This contrasts the civil rights leaders who enthusiastically allied with the Democrats. Environmentalists believe Congress and state legislatures have a duty to do right, by which they mean to pass favorable laws. They also believe Congress often blocks good programs due to "special interests." The movement sees the courts as especially useful and often more favorable than Congress, a belief similar to that for Civil Rights. From the perspective of the environmental movement, the role of government agencies is also to do right, although it may exaggerate the power and expertise of executive branch agencies.

Social scientists who take the mass movement approach on environmental politics have their own assumptions. First, a movement exists and is important. The correlate is that interest groups are not as important, that the interaction between certain groups and certain companies are secondary maneuvers to the grand scheme, which has essentially only two sides. Second, mass movement theory assumes a life cycle. It will start with vague discontent spread widely, evolve as many people become conscious of their shared grievances, organize more and more widely, and finally move on to triumph, failure, or dissipation. A third, perhaps biased, assumption is that the mass movement is not fully efficient, in part because it is a less mature stage. In the mature stage, formal groups emerge that can lobby, persuade, and motivate voters. With respect to the future, participants are optimistic of success. Indeed, membership increases greatly when success seems imminent.[3]

Interest Groups

When a mass movement becomes more structured, it evolves into an interest group. Two explanations address the bridge between a mass movement and an interest group. The first maintains that groups only appear because of a disturbance like a drop in farm prices or damming the Green River in Dinosaur National Monument. Typically, the new group merely wants to stop the disturbance and return to the old situation, at least as they remember it.[4] The second explanation argues that this is not enough, holding that disturbance theory ignores the question of timing: when a movement organizes and when it withers away. Also, many disturbances occur without bringing forth organized groups. The second explanation suggests that the key is an entrepreneur who produces benefits for the members in exchange for benefits to him- or herself. The group succeeds if a leader can provide the members with benefits of jobs, lower taxes, better prices, warm friendships, and ideological satisfaction. In exchange, the

13

leader gets a high salary, prestige, and personal satisfaction. If no leader can provide benefits, the group disappears.[5]

Pro-environmental groups like Friends of the Earth, Greenpeace, and the Audubon Society are far more structured and discrete than the environmental movement as a whole. While, obviously, the mass movement and interest group approaches to analyzing policy aim at different levels, the two are not necessarily compatible. On one hand, interest group theory considers a mass movement an earlier stage before groups fully organize, but the movement perspective does not honor interest groups in a reciprocal fashion. This side may view the groups as part of the problem, the "establishment" bent on defending its position, while the movement seeks an overall improvement.

The group approach is popular among political scientists; more of them believe this theory more than any other single theory. An alternative name is pluralism, reflecting that many groups exist. Its central belief is that society will inevitably form into groups to promote their common political interests. They will both compete with other groups and cooperate with them for their mutual benefit. Politics is a continuous struggle of one interest with another. The framers of the Constitution assumed this conflict and sought to put it to work by using one group to balance another. In *The Federalist No. 10*, James Madison lists a series of antagonistic groups such as those who own property and those who do not. He then argues that they will each limit the aggrandizement of the others, resulting in compromise and cooperation. Pluralism tends to be amoral; it does not consider one side to be right, but that each seeks to advance itself. This theory contrasts with a common opinion of a movement's adherents—for a movement to succeed in accomplishing its goals, the goals have to be good for society.

The most successful groups have narrow interests, such as not to spend too much money cleaning up water from a factory before discharging it into a river. A company in this position will focus completely on this goal. In contrast, the general interest by many members of the public to have clean water in the river is diffuse. The river has many miles of shoreline needing protection and a single individual only swims or fishes in the river once in a while. The rule, almost a cliche, is that a small group with a narrow interest is more effective than a large group with diffuse interests.

As with a mass movement, the resources of an interest group are a key to its strength. Money is an easy resource to measure; a group needs it to hire professional staff, to rent offices, and to buy newspaper advertisements. While some interest groups (especially environmental ones) use volunteers, full-time paid directors, lawyers, and lobbyists are more effective. Generally, a group resource may be prestige (the Audubon Society), size (five hundred thousand members of the Sierra Club), and expertise (lawyers and scientists). Good leadership strengthens a group. David Brower became a hero for leading the Sierra Club in the fight to block the Echo Park Dam. When the Internal Revenue Service took away the club's tax-free status in crude retaliation, he established a separate Legal Defense Fund and later the Friends of the Earth to continue the crusade. Similarly, an interest group's tangible resources are money, copier machines, telephones, office space, and volunteer labor. Intangible resources are skills in organizing, lawyering, and technology. Even less tangible are legitimacy, the support of key politicians, and public attention.

While mass movements may evolve into interest groups, a typical interest group is smaller and more structured. On one hand, a few groups like the National Wildlife Federation, with four million members, are certainly large, but in this case, its sixty years of existence, its decentralization into state and local chapters, and its lobbying function make it more like an interest group than a mass movement. Inevitably, a group this large has features of a mass movement. On the other hand, a single company probably should not be considered an interest group. However, if that company is General Motors lobbying for amendments to the Clean Air Act, it may deserve to be considered as a group in itself.

Interest groups are not temporary like a movement, nor do they have a life cycle. Social scientists do not believe they will evolve and develop due to internal dynamics. Instead, a group may well continue indefinitely (subject to all the vicissitudes of demand and resources). The U.S. Chamber of Commerce remains the same today as when it was founded over a century ago. An interest group differs from a political party by not seeking to place people in an elected office. As such, neither government agencies nor congressional committees are an interest group. In the 1940s and 1950s, American political scientists propounded the virtues of an interest group's give-and-take as an antidote for fascism and communism. Pluralism, to use its other name, offered the merit of checks and balances to protect all segments of society. It strengthened democracy and had American roots from the days of the Constitution and Bill of Rights.

The alternative explanation popular at the time was elite theory. Its backers did not praise its virtues, but claimed the elite theory was the most realistic answer. Its basic tenet is that people who run America have their power because they are wealthy and usually were born to wealthy families. Besides enjoying inherited wealth, they also advance themselves by taking advantage of good educations and personal connections with others who are rich and powerful. Elite theory does not suggest that those in powerful positions like a senator, company president, or secretary of the interior are an elite merely for occupying those powerful positions, for this would be a tautology. Instead, this theory claims that the wealthy elite controls policy because its members are more likely to hold those positions due to their head start in life, and because the elite pull the strings from behind. John D. Rockefeller IV won election as governor of and later senator for West Virginia largely because of his wealth, prep school connections, and education. Although his father, John D. Rockefeller III, neither ran a big corporation directly nor held an important political post, he donated millions of dollars to charity, parks, and political candidates, while managing the family fortune. Also, two of the senator's uncles (both rich, of course) were governors. This example of the Rockefellers—father, son, and uncles—illustrates the power of the elite.

Interest group theory, even the groups themselves, considers that the purpose of government is to form the arena in which the interests compete. The court decision on protecting Storm King Mountain on the Hudson River describes the regulatory commission as a baseball umpire calling the balls and strikes. The plaintiffs, who finally won on appeal, wanted the agency to make a positive effort to preserve the mountain, instead of being neutral. Pluralists believe the leaders and professional staff of groups are best able to understand the situation, promote their interests, and make the deals necessary; and ordinary citizens, the heroes of mass movements, are best confined to contributing money and writing their members of Congress when asked. This belief is not arrogance, but appreciation of the experts who are most effective—as well as more efficient and practical. Members of Congress and government officials are there to be pressured. Political parties are crucial because they are the most important single link between the groups and Congress. Groups both align with one party and keep their connections with the other party. Environmentalists chiefly favor the Democrats, yet they also cultivate the Republicans. After all, the Republicans have won the presidency in five of the last eight elections and won both houses of Congress in 1994 and 1996. Interest groups consider courts a useful source of leverage, but recognize they are a two-edged sword. Lawsuits are a means of blocking an oil refinery, dam, or nuclear plant, but the courts are passive. They are not good for cleaning up the air, a river, or radioactivity.

Overall, pluralism exalts the political process itself rather than the outcome. While its champions from James Madison to the present day praise this process as a virtue, its critics are concerned with the actual results. Pluralism's view of the future is that the groups will readjust continually, instead of winning a final victory or suffering a final defeat. The political accommodation will be endless.

Political Parties

In spite of the decline of partisanship in the twentieth century, political parties continue to explain many aspects of environmental politics. In 1969, Nixon realized he could attract voters to the Republican party by cleaning the air and water. On the Democratic side, Senator Edmund Muskie, who had been the Democratic nominee for vice president and had chaired the subcommittee responsible for air pollution control, had his eye on the 1972 nomination for president. As Congress held hearings and debated a clean air act, Nixon and Muskie goaded each other to make the bill stronger and bolder. In a complete reversal, by 1980 the Republicans switched to opposing environmental regulation.

The political science theory of partisanship is simple; it explains policy in terms of party—the Democrats have one view and the Republicans have another. Building on this truism, it elaborates factors of competition between the parties, underlying ideology, connections between Democrats (or Republicans) in Congress and a Democratic (or Republican) president, between the national and

Edmund Muskie was an early voice for environmental concerns. Here in 1970, as chairman of a Senate public works subcommittee on air and water pollution, he announces approval of a bill to set up national air quality standards and mandate the production of a non-polluting car.

state governments, and so forth. Parties differ from interest groups in that their goal is to win elections. Their commitment to particular policies is only a tool. If they win, they are obligated to implement those policies, but at the time of the next election (especially if they are out of power), they are free to put other policies in their platform. And, parties, like interest groups are stable. They will be around for the next election, and do not grow and evolve like a mass movement.

Granting that parties have declined, partisanship nevertheless explains much of environmental policy. The Republican party is strong in the west from the Great Plains to the Sierra Nevada Mountains. (California swings between the Republicans and Democrats.) These western states tend to elect Republicans to the Senate, where they gravitate to positions on the Committee on Energy and National Resources, which is responsible for land, minerals, and water. The small populations of the western states mean they have few representatives in the House, but each have two in the Senate giving them power disproportionate to their populations. The western states faithfully deliver their vote to Republican candidates for president, entitling them to rewards when one is elected.

17

Environmentalists from the west are more likely to be Democrats. During the 1980s, the term "Sagebrush Rebellion" captured the dissatisfaction of the west with Washington regulation. Now the term "War on the West" expresses the same complaint. The Grand Old Party (GOP) is also strong in the south, a region with the lowest level of support for environmental protection.

Republicans and Democrats differ in their ideologies and styles. Following their New Deal heritage, the Democrats are more likely to intervene in business, to regulate directly, to experiment, and to concentrate power in Washington. Like Franklin Roosevelt, they believe that government should be active. Republicans are more likely to trust the market to correct problems of private businesses (and less likely to consider a situation as a problem). When Republicans do regulate, they are critical of "command and control." At the same time, as the parties perpetuate their ideologies and styles of the past, they can occasionally change policy abruptly. Their purpose is to win elections, not to maintain the faith. For example, in May 1996, the Republicans, who controlled both the House and Senate, reversed their year long opposition to the EPA; public opinion polls showed the voters wanted the EPA to control pollution.

With his ideological flexibility and creative genius, Nixon recognized that he and his party could win the votes of the middle class who supported cleaning the air and water. These were the people who had the money to do more than just buy the necessities and the education to understand the technical issues. These were also voters who no longer supported his conduct of the Vietnam War. The environment would distract them. In 1972, the country gave him a landslide victory of 61 percent. Eight years later, Reagan took the opposite tack in his campaign. He won the GOP nomination through appeals to the most conservative side of the party. His close advisors tended to be self-made businessmen who despised regulation. Many were westerners like Paul Laxalt from Nevada and Joe Coors from Colorado.

The fact that American politics are fragmented is an axiom, and parties are at the top of the list for this characteristic. The national party is to a large extent fifty state parties. For example, six weeks before the 1996 election President Bill Clinton could declare 1.7 million acres of southern Utah to be a national monument in defiance of the wishes of the Senators and Representatives of the Beehive State because they were all Republicans. Clinton knew that he could not win Utah under any circumstances and that Republicans in other states did not consider it an important issue. Power in Congress is also fragmented. Reforms put in place in 1970 decreased the power of the chairmen of the full committees in favor of the subcommittees, thus fragmenting power. Under the prior system, parties were stronger because twenty committee chairmen could cooperate and trade votes more easily than one hundred subcommittee chairmen.

To compensate for the fragmentation of American politics, parties link within Congress, between Congress and the executive branch, and between Washington and the state capitals. Party membership still plays a big part in how a member of Congress votes, even if its influence is less than a generation ago.

Members of the president's party carry the flag for agencies in hearings and debates, and, in turn, the members involve themselves deeply in the affairs of the agency. Elected officials in the states often contact members of their own party in Congress to lobby for or against a bill, and the members alert the officials to its progress. Members frequently solicit the opinions of party leaders back home. Not all the contacts, however, are within the same party just because partisan links are stronger than those across party lines. At the state level, legislators, governors, and appointed officials follow a similar pattern of links based on their party. Many career bureaucrats find partisanship distasteful, believing it often prevents rational decisions. One of the few partisan politicians with whom bureaucrats identify is Vice President Albert Gore, who has a long standing commitment to environmental values, is the author of *Earth in the Balance*,[6] and has a love of technology and problem solving.

Governmental Procedures

Governmental procedures explain much of what actually happens in environmental policy, in particular, how a certain procedure leads to a certain result. For example, it illuminates why the Congressional Joint Committee on Atomic Energy retarded protection from radioactivity or why U.S. Forest Service Advisory Committees contribute to deterioration of forests and streams. All branches of government, legislative, judicial, and executive, have and follow extensive rules when making and implementing decisions. Procedures for Congress and courts are better known than those for the executive branch, and the operations of the national government are better known than those at the state level. Some governmental procedures are actual rules published in the *Federal Register* or manuals. Others are ways of operating like a congressional compromise or a judge's reluctance to accept evidence based on statistical inference.

When Congress passed the Surface Mining Act, it placed the Office of Surface Mining in the Department of the Interior rather than in the EPA, which would have been a logical home. The reasoning behind this decision was guided by a rule of the House of Representatives regarding committee jurisdiction for oversight. Each committee is assigned certain departments and agencies. The Interior Committee oversees the Department of the Interior, but not the EPA. The bill originated in the Interior Committee and its chief sponsor, Representative Morris Udall who chaired the committee, wanted to keep the new agency within his jurisdiction.

Procedures with the executive branch are less well known. Although they are not secret, the problem is that they are so extensive and detailed. Moreover, inertia slows action and favors the existing situation.

Besides formal procedures, the bureaucracy operates in ways that affects its results. Agencies are specialized, autonomous, and technical. Like all good bureaucrats, those in the EPA believe pollution is a problem to be solved rather than a political issue suitable for continued bargaining and adjustment. The

19

agency sits at the center of the cleanup, which it will accomplish by directing programs like the Superfund or the regulation for clean air and water, and constructing sewage treatment plants. Congress or a state legislature may pass laws, but only bureaus can implement them. The bureaucracy has the technical expertise, the full-time staff, and the connections with companies and other agencies to turn the noble sentiments of the laws into actual programs. Unfortunately, the skills, resources, and power of bureaus have a negative side. Agencies can overconform to rules, block new ideas, displace their original goals, and simply move slowly.

Looking at environmental policy from the bureaucratic perspective assumes a series of "problems," which, in turn, assumes solutions. Engineering, planning, and regulation are the techniques. This view is a bit antiseptic, ignoring the fact that different groups may not agree on what the problem is or even that a problem exists, let alone the technique for solving it. Another assumption, not so strongly held as in the past, is that the solution will be through regulation rather than through the marketplace. Critics argue that economic incentives are superior to command and control, which they believe is repressive and inefficient. A fourth assumption is that the bureaucracies are powerful. For environmentalists to persuade Congress to pass a law is only the beginning because how the EPA implements it is crucial.

The bureaucratic perspective typically concentrates on implementation, but the traditional picture of Congress passing laws and the bureaucracy executing them is too simple. The agencies themselves play a role in setting the agenda for discussion, drafting the legislation sent to Congress, interpreting the laws, filling in the gaps with regulations, defending the laws and regulations in court, and so forth. Agency officials tend to see interest groups as players in the game of government. The groups can simplify the political environment, give technical advice, serve as liaisons with Congress, and become allies. Bureaucrats often consider the public at large (e.g., "the environmental movement") difficult to work with because it is too distant and unstructured.

Agency officials rarely work with political parties directly because (1) law restricts it, (2) bureaucrats have many direct means of access to Congress and its committees so they do not need a link as interest groups do, and (3) the party's policies on a topic like the environment are too vague to be useful. In fact, virtually always a bureaucrat holds a negative view of political parties for lacking detailed knowledge and merely promoting some narrow point for an individual company or person. Agency officials hold similar negative views of some members of Congress who seem to be "busybodies" poking into the agency to cause trouble. To avoid this and to maintain their autonomy, agencies try to manage Congress by coordinating with the committee chair, and liaison with key staff to coopt them into a lenient attitude toward the agency's mission and programs. Also, agencies consider lawsuits a major hindrance. Litigation throws off their timing, distracts them from their real work, and upsets priorities. Judges are prone to second guess the agencies.

Agencies consider themselves the hub of their policy area because they have the expertise, permanency, and narrow focus. Because bureaucrats specialize and work full-time on a program, they are the people best informed on their topics. In addition, they may control information by deliberately withholding it. Bureaucrats consider process important for efficiency and accountability, often reciting, "We are a government of laws, not men." Being specialists, bureaucrats get a worm's eye view, not a bird's eye view.

The bureaucratic work of solving problems proceeds at its own pace according to technical and funding capabilities. It lacks the drama of an Earth Day rally or the climax of Congress passing a major bill. Administrators view the future as a series of problems to address; when the present ones are taken care of or abandoned, new ones will appear. Their relationships with other agencies and with interest groups need to be managed for the long term; no great turning point will appear. Their permanency is a strength. This is not to say that situations cannot get worse or get better. The election in 1994 of many conservative Republicans to Congress, who were unfriendly to the environment, distressed the EPA staff, who consoled themselves by saying: "We are the B Team; we will Be here when they are gone."

MOVING FORWARD

Choosing four theories inevitably means not choosing others. While the choice is not arbitrary, it does rule out using alternative explanations in depth. The rationale for these four theories is that they address the most important political aspects, although others may be useful to understand particular situations.

Explanations of environmental policy based on science, technology, risk, and economics are important, but this book concentrates on politics. For the first three—science, technology, and risk—the question is how do they affect decisions about the environment. Meteorologists discover that holes have appeared in the ozone and physicians warn that more ultraviolet rays will increase cancer. Back on earth, engineers build a better electrostatic machine to scrub the sulfur as it goes up a smokestack. Statisticians calculate the risk if a refinery releases a hundred gallons of benzene into a river.

Economics works both ways. Like science, technology, and risk, it informs decision makers about the pros and cons of a policy. On the other hand, the decision will affect the economics. Senators and Representatives debating a bill may well consider how a provision will effect the level of pollution and the cost to comply. Economists are quick to criticize the inefficiency of traditional regulation. For example, once a factory has reduced its emissions into the air to the official standard, it has no incentive to do more, even if further actions would be cheap; a steel manufacturer may keep an obsolete smelter in operation because a replacement would have to meet a higher requirement. An economic perspective asks whether the benefits outweigh the costs, a question passionate environmentalists dislike. Comparing costs to benefits may show business has to spend $100 million to save a single life, money that could pay for twenty thousand children living in homeless shelters. Within the environmental area, comparing the cost to

NATIONAL ENVIRONMENTAL LAWS

General

National Environmental Policy Act, 1970

Pollution Prevention Act, 1990

Engangered Species, Parks, and Land

Wilderness Act, 1964

General Mining Law, 1872

Mineral Leasing Act, 1920

Federal Coal Leasing Amendemnts Act, 1976

Homestead Act, 1862

Kinkaid Act, 1906

Taylor Grazing Act, 1934

Federal Land Policy Management Act, 1976 (FLMPA)

National Forest Management Act

Multiple Use Sustained Yield Act, 1960

Surface Mining Control & Reclamation Act, 1977 (SMCRA)

Resource Planning Act, 1974

Alaska National Interest Lands Conservation Act, 1980

National Park Service Organic Act, 1916

Endangered Species Act, 1973

Bald and Golden Eagle Protection Act

Migratory Bird Treaty Act

Antiquties Act, 1906

Wild and Scenic Rivers Act

National Historic Preservation Act

Air

Clean Air Act, 1970, 1977, 1990

Water

Refuse Act, 1899

Clean Water Act, 1972, 1977, 1987 (originally called the Federal Water Pollution Control Act)

Safe Drinking Water Act, 1974, 1986

Marine Mammal Protection Act, 1972

Coastal Zone Management Act

Ocean Dumping Act, 1988

Fisheries Conservation and Management Act, 1976

National Ocean Pollution Palnning Act

Outer Continental Shelf Lands Act

Omnibus Water Act, 1992

Solid, Hazardous, and Toxic Waste

Resource Conservation and Recovery Act, 1976, 1984 (RCRA)

Solid Waste Disposal Act 1978 and 1980 amendments

Used Oil Recycling Act, 1980

Federal Insecticide, Fungicide, and Rodenticide Act

Toxic Substances Control Act, 1976

Comprehensive Environmental Response, Compensation, and Liability Act 1980 (Superfund)

SARA, 1986

Radiation

Atomic Energy Act of 1946, 1954, 1974

Low-Level Radioactive Waste Policy Act, 1980, with later amendments

Nuclear Waste Policy Act, 1982, 1987

Uranium Mill Tailings Reclamation Act

the benefit may show that $1 million spent to prevent one case of cancer from a nuclear plant would prevent twenty cases if spent on decreasing a toxin in the air.

Five factors make environmental policy more interesting than other issues such as energy or housing. The first factor is that popular concern has continued at a high level. A recent Gallup Poll found 63 percent called themselves "an environmentalist" and 29 percent called themselves "a strong environmentalist." Although the movement emerged suddenly in the 1970s, it was not a fad that disappeared. Second, environmental politics bring forth emotions, even passions, rarely encountered for other issues. Environmentalists truly believe in their cause. This passion touches a religious chord by recalling the Garden of Eden, Moses leading the Hebrews in the wilderness, and Jesus wandering in the desert. The question of endangered species triggers feelings deep within the psyche. Humans feel a connection with other animals that goes beyond rational thought. The saying "extinction is forever" sums up the despair that a species will never exist again. The beauty of mountains, the sea, an ancient oak, or a sunset triggers similar emotions.

The third factor of fascination is its collective aspect. To have the air clean for one person means it must be clean for everyone; for one Los Angeleno to breathe clean air while his or her neighbor's air is polluted is physically impossible. Sewage dumped into a river pollutes it for everyone downstream. Risk is the fourth factor. Wrong policies about pollution present risk to health. Dirty air aggravates lung and heart disease, and can even cause death. At the extreme, wrong environmental policies may make all life on earth extinct due to the ozone holes and the greenhouse effects. Polluting the air amounts to a gamble with high stakes. Finally, environmental policy demands understanding and managing advanced technology. Before the industrial revolution, the air was pure and the streams were clean. Science may be unable to explain the phenomenon or offer solutions; moreover, research is always advancing so the scientific answers of one year may change over time.

This book concentrates on major questions about environmental policy: How did it originate? How does it work? Curiosity about origins is natural. It is why people are fascinated by astronomy, evolution, and human fossils. It is why Americans revere George Washington and political scientists devote so much attention to the Constitutional Convention of 1787. This book examines environmental policy in the next eight chapters, beginning with air pollution control. Each chapter first examines the policy's background, the major laws, programs, and agencies, then probes issues, and finishes with a look at international aspects. It combines general issues with the most suitable chapter, for instance, air is a collective good, meaning it cannot be provided for one person and not for another. Water has some collective features and solid waste has almost none. On the other hand, spiritual and emotional aspects fit best in chapter 6 on the wilderness.

Air pollution comes first because it is expensive, causes ill health, and is a collective good. The Clean Air Act was the first of the new environmental laws Congress passed. Water follows in chapter 3 because it is also expensive, threatens health, is partially a collective good, and was the second environmental law established. Chapter 4 focuses on hazardous, solid, and toxic wastes. All three programs share similar laws passed in the 1970s, the EPA jurisdiction, detailed regulation, and delegation to the states. Radiation control, covered in chapter 5, is not an EPA program, but falls, instead, under the jurisdiction of the Atomic Energy Commission (AEC) and its successors: the Nuclear Regulatory Commission and the Department of Energy (DOE). With one exception, its control is exclusively at the national level. Chapter 6 investigates policies of endangered species and wilderness areas, and addresses unique topics with worldwide implications and philosophical ramifications. Extinction cannot be outlawed by Congress and forbidden by the EPA. Management of parks and land is fragmented, spanning the national, state, and municipal levels of the federal system. Some programs are centralized and others are delegated. For the national parks, forests, and lands, the number of specific laws exceeds one hundred and involves at least six bureaus in two departments. The scope of parks and lands means dividing it into two chapters: 7 and 8. Chapter 8 also considers the importance of privately owned land, which is, after all, the most common situation in America. Chapter 9 covers the related issues of population control, the consumer movement, and Green parties, then draws conclusions.

NOTES

1. Margit Mayer, "The Career of Urban Social Movements in West Germany" in Robert Fisher and Joseph Kling, eds., *Mobilizing the Community* (Newbury Park, CA: Sage, 1993), 63–65.
2. Aldon D. Morris and Carol McClurg Mueller, eds., *Frontiers in Social Movement Theory* (New Haven, CT: Yale University Press, 1992), 207.
3. Morris, 214.
4. David B. Truman, *The Governmental Process* (New York: Knopf, 1951).
5. Robert Salisbury, "An Exchange Theory of Interest Groups," *Midwest Journal of Political Science* 13 (1969): 1–32.
6. Albert Gore, *Earth in the Balance* (Boston, MA: Houghton Mifflin, 1992).

CHAPTER 2
AIR POLLUTION CONTROL

Nearly all American cities suffer from air pollution. The worst is Los Angeles, where the sunshine cooks the auto exhaust into smog and the mountains on the east trap it. The Los Angeles basin violates air quality standards one-hundred days a year, and its neighbors like Bakersfield, Fresno, and San Diego are nearly as bad. Denver, located in a valley with bright sunshine, has its Brown Cloud in the winter and its smog in the summer. New York City has less sunshine and no mountains or hills to the east, but its residents cluster together more densely, which makes them violate air quality standards sixty days a year. Chicago, Philadelphia, and Baltimore are also polluted. Nationwide, sixty-two million people live where pollution exceeds safe levels. In spite of this gloom, the air is cleaner than in 1970. Particulates are down 50 percent; sulfur, 32 percent; carbon monoxide, 25 percent; and lead, 98 percent.[1] This improvement occurred even though Americans drive three times as many miles and their industries produce nearly twice as much. The EPA estimates clean air costs $20 billion a year, but yields benefits of $400 billion a year, a figure critics consider exaggerated.[2]

Air pollution causes illness. Unlike water and other forms of pollution, this endangers health. The American Cancer Society estimates as many as sixty four thousand people may die prematurely from air pollution. In the most polluted cities, death comes a year or two sooner than in clean locations as dirty air leads to lung cancer, heart disease, emphysema, bronchitis, and tuberculosis. The increase of asthma, now afflicting thirteen million Americans, perplexes medical researchers, since it has increased dramatically at the same time as pollution has decreased.

Smog obscures the Los Angeles skyline. The smog is produced by sunlight cooking the emissions from automobiles, power plants, factories, and refineries, and is trapped by mountains on the east. Although southern California has the worst air in the nation, it has improved.

BACKGROUND

The Industrial Revolution gave birth to air pollution with its wood, charcoal, and coal for smelting, forging, power, and heating. Crowding workers into cities and mill towns made conditions worse. Before the age of factories and mines, only the biggest cities suffered. In the fourteenth century, the Crown forbid coal fires in London while the Parliament was sitting. By 1661, at the cusp of the Industrial Revolution in England, the rain was already acidic from burning coal. By the nineteenth century in America as well as England, smoke polluted the cities. Railroad locomotives coughed it out even in small towns. Coal mining valleys and steel towns in Pennsylvania and Virginia were among the worst. In 1860, Pittsburgh forbid locomotives from burning bituminous coal or wood (only anthracite was allowed), but it was unable to enforce the ordinance. On his American tour, Charles Dickens described the city as "Hell with the lid lifted."[3] By the turn of the century, cities were enacting and enforcing laws. Toledo established its Smoke Control Office in 1906. This period was the Gilded Age when "Captains of Industry" like Andrew Carnegie and Henry Frick forged giant corporations. The number of factories in the United States doubled and tripled. Smoke became the symbol of prosperity: "Smoke means jobs." Not to see smoke meant workers were laid off.

Factories continued to increase burning coal until the Great Depression temporarily brought an end to prosperity, but when the war in Europe brought orders for guns, tanks, planes, ships, and ammunition, the factories started burning coal at a more intense rate. King Coal, the most polluting of all fuels, continued to increase in tonnage until it reached its first peak in 1947. With the end of the war, automobiles resumed spewing their exhaust as the number of cars on the road nearly tripled over the next sixteen years. Two government policies promoted the automobile. The Veterans Administration mortgages encouraged construction of detached, single family houses, which were usually in the suburbs beyond the reach of streetcars and bus lines. Families who wanted a mortgage for an older house closer to downtown jobs and stores found banks reluctant to loan the funds. Second, government began to build more and bigger roads. The apex came in 1956 when Congress enacted the interstate highway system. The Federal Highway Administration paid 90 percent of the cost of construction. Total investment in highways was less than $1 billion in 1947, $4 billion in 1962, $40 billion in 1980, and $90 billion today. Both of these programs, housing and highways, put more cars on the road. World War II also began the Chemical Revolution. Industry dramatically increased its use and manipulation of chemicals. In 1939, the Du Pont company had invented nylon, named for its two research laboratories in New York and London. Refineries became more efficient at making gasoline and diesel and produced plastic from the waste product.

Pittsburgh and St. Louis pioneered the control of smoke in 1940. In Pittsburgh, the Civic Club, Medical Society, and League of Women Voters led the crusade. The new City Smoke Commission forbade "dense smoke," required clean anthracite coal, regulated new manufacturing plants, and extended regulation of residences. At the end of the war, the mayor and businessmen joined forces to renew the effort. The driving force was Richard King Mellon, scion of the family that owned the Gulf Oil Company and the Mellon Bank. He was also a director of the Pennsylvania Railway Company; when the railroad balked at reducing smoke from its locomotives, Mellon got the company to cooperate. The city council organized an advisory committee with members from the steel, coal, and chemical companies, railroads, trade unions, and other industries and businesses. City leaders realized that the cleanup had to extend beyond the city boundaries to encompass all of Allegheny County so the county established a coordinated program in 1949.[4]

Citizens organized GASP—Group Against Smog and Pollution. The spur was a 1969 hearing on the proposed state ambient air quality standards, which the group considered too lenient. Previously, only a few industry representatives would show up, but this time four hundred fifty attended. Only one out of the fifty speakers favored the proposal. GASP's chair was Michelle Madoff, who had a flair for organizing, lobbying, and getting on television. GASP awarded the Dirtie Gertie prize to polluters and sold cans of clean air. Although it was a grass roots group, GASP solicited members who were physicians, scientists, engineers, and labor leaders.[5]

In terms of geography, Los Angeles faces the double problem of bright sunshine and the San Gabriel, San Bernadino, and Santa Ana Mountains to the east.

The Spanish explorer who discovered the Los Angeles basin, Juan Rodríguez Cabrillo, observed that the mountains trapped the smoke from the American Indian campfires. The Golden State remained lightly populated and mostly agricultural until World War II brought factories for war matériel. In summer 1943, Los Angeles experienced severe smog, which the residents incorrectly blamed on a synthetic rubber plant. Automobile exhaust, however, was the real cause. Despite a municipal Bureau of Air Pollution established in 1944, the smog grew more frequent. In 1947, the city suffered fifty-seven days from polluted air, yet people still thought the cause was factory smoke. Within a few years, however, engineers from California Institute of Technology demonstrated that auto exhaust was to blame. To counter that conclusion, the American Automobile Manufacturers' Association sent seven experts who claimed the smog came from factories and garbage incinerators. In spite of this rearguard defense, the guilt of the automobiles, trucks, and buses became increasingly clear. The city's answer was to detail police Captain Fuller from the motorcycle command to the smog patrol. His policemen ticketed diesel trucks emitting smoke.[6] In fact, the cause of the smog was invisible fumes from automobiles. Not until 1976 did Los Angeles County combine with Orange, Riverside, and San Bernadino counties to form the South Coast Air Quality Management District with jurisdiction over the entire basin.

In spite of the smog and soot, air pollution did not rank as a political problem prior to the late 1960s. Matthew Crenson calls this the "un-politics" of air pollution. Government and the public never brought the issue onto the agenda. Crenson examined the problem in Gary and East Chicago, Indiana, two steel towns adjoining Chicago to the south, where he found evidence that the U.S. Steel and the Inland Steel corporations applied subtle pressure on the mayor and council members to avoid addressing the problem, because the costs to cleanup emissions would be high. Crenson emphasizes the importance of a "nondecision," that is, keeping a problem off the political agenda.[7]

COLLECTIVE GOODS

The necessity for St. Louis, Pittsburgh, and Los Angeles to enlist all governments in their metropolitan areas comes from the physical characteristics of air pollution. It extends across city and county boundaries throughout its entire airshed. Air cannot be clean for one person if it is not clean for everyone. The pollution affects everyone in the region. The social science term for this concept is "collective good." (Economists use the term "public good," but political scientists refrain from using this word, because it is too easy to confuse "public" with "governmental.") Whether or not a good is collective depends on its physical properties, not whether government provides it. Examples are defending the United States against nuclear missiles launched over the North Pole or immunity from an infectious disease. For any single person, the costs of the Air Force or for an injection are high, considering that he will get the same protection even if he does not pay money or get the needle in the arm. It is too easy to take a free ride. Consequently people will not contribute their fair share. They either will not provide any or not enough of it; the quantity will fall short of the optimum.[8]

When a good is collective, only two solutions exist. One is to exploit the fact that small groups will cooperate when large ones will not. Thus, St. Louis joined with its suburbs and Pittsburgh joined with Allegheny County; it was not a million residents in the metropolitan areas but St. Louis and four towns nearby or Pittsburgh and Allegheny County. When a group gets larger than six or seven, this altruism ceases to operate. The second solution is coercion. Because many American citizens will not make voluntary contributions to the Air Force, the IRS forces them to pay their taxes. Because many people, especially children, will not volunteer to be injected with vaccine, the government requires vaccination before a child can enroll in school. As such, Pittsburgh did not expect industry to reduce emissions voluntarily, but by coercion instead. The fact that clean air is a collective good is its curse; an individual person or company does not have an incentive to reduce pollution unless all others do the same.

POLLUTION AS MORE THAN A LOCAL PROBLEM

In 1948, Pittsburgh witnessed a vivid display of the dangers of air pollution twenty miles to the south at Donora on the Monongahela River. In its narrow mountain valley, the city of twelve thousand people had thirteen open hearth furnaces, two blast furnaces, a zinc smelter, a sulfuric acid plant, and three mills. On October 25, dense smoke prevented seeing across the street and the sulfur dioxide smell was strong enough to taste. When the wind died down on that wet, raw night, the smog settled onto the town. Residents choked, vomited, and wheezed. They suffered from belly aches, headaches, and even coughed up blood. Before the wind finally blew away the smog the following week, twenty people had died and five thousand were sick. Across the Atlantic four years later, London suffered a worse disaster when smog killed four thousand. Because London is the capital of the Mother Country and the international hub of newspapers and radio, Americans got a full report of its misfortune.

By the 1960s, municipal governments realized that they could not solve the whole problem. First, they could not be fully effective in coercing industry. When they cooperated over an entire airshed as in St. Louis, Pittsburgh, and Los Angeles, industries might simply move away to a different jurisdiction that would be more lenient. Corporations that stayed often decided against expansion, choosing to build their new factories where cities did not regulate pollution. Municipalities could not afford to lose the tax revenue and jobs. Cities and even states could not stand up to the threats of industry. Moreover, a number of metropolitan airsheds straddled two or three states, making cooperation harder. New York, Philadelphia, and Cincinnati are in this situation. Second, automobiles were becoming more of a pollution problem. The auto industry was national in scope; any state with a smaller population than California found it hard to force General Motors, Ford, or Chrysler to build cleaner engines. The auto makers did not want to segment their market.

The federal government had a kernel of concern. In 1949, President Harry S. Truman convened a conference of experts which recommended an advisory council, but declared the responsibility for corrective action belonged locally. A 1956 law set up an interagency committee chaired by the surgeon general of the Public Health Service and again declared the responsibility was local. When the House of Representatives considered a bill to set standards in 1959, the Public Health Service testified against it. The service envisioned its mission as medical research, not implementation. Its scientists had little interest in policy and feared partisan politics. Its relationships with state health departments were to gather statistics, investigate epidemics, and promote immunization. To enforce pollution standards would upset their cooperation and would require additional personnel who did not conduct research.[9] At that time cities recognized they needed help. The U.S. Conference of Mayors lobbied for national standards, while the Automobile Manufacturers Association lobbied against them.

The Kennedy administration took more interest in pollution. It supported legislation aimed at gathering more data and assisting states to plan; Congress enacted this bill in 1963 as the Clean Air Act. In the long term, the act's chief contribution was its title, because in 1970 Congress recycled the name for the major new scheme that, in fact, had nearly nothing in common with the modest legislation passed seven years earlier. By 1965, the Public Health Service had established an air pollution division, which later became the National Air Pollution Control Administration. Its research demonstrated that auto emissions did harm health, and that motor vehicles contributed half the pollution. The solution would require redesigning engines.[10]

Interest about air pollution increased on Capitol Hill as well. Senator Edmund Muskie, an ambitious Democrat from Maine, chaired a new subcommittee on air pollution. Muskie took the subcommittee on tour to Los Angeles, Denver, Chicago, Boston, New York, and Tampa to hear firsthand about the problem. The senators learned that while California was ready to demand automobiles be equipped to reduce emissions, the other states were not. The auto companies were reluctant to cooperate, blaming the extra cost. Their greatest objection was to different standards in different states, which would segment their marketing. Uniform national requirements were more acceptable. For stationary sources of pollution like factories and electric generating plants, however, the rationale for uniform national standards was weaker. Unlike motor vehicles, they were not designed and marketed nationally. Nor did they travel from state to state. Nevertheless, top leadership at the Department of Health, Education, and Welfare promoted the idea, in part because it believed cities and states lacked the courage to take on industry.

With growing popular awareness of dirty air, both Congress and President Lyndon B. Johnson's administration felt pressure to act, even though which direction to take remained unclear. Data was scarce, the Public Health Service avoided the responsibility, and Congress did not know what sort of a bill to propose. In 1967, Congress passed the Air Quality Act (sometimes referred to as the National Emissions Standards Act), which directed the national government to set standards, but not enforce them. This curious compromise resulted from the administration's urge to solve problems from Washington and Senator Muskie's wariness of Washington infringing on the rights of the states. It was the acme of Johnson's Great Society. In the tradition of Franklin Roosevelt's New Deal, Johnson believed government could solve social problems. The National Emissions Standards Act set national requirements for new motor vehicles—requirements that could be enforced, not just recommended. For automobiles, the national scope of marketing and driving justified the uniformity.[11] Muskie won praise for shepherding the bill through Congress, one of many reasons the Democratic party nominated him to run for the vice presidency in the 1968 election.

THE CLEAN AIR ACT OF 1970

By 1970, public anxiety about dirty air showed the need for a stronger national effort. As "Mr. Clean Air" in the Senate, Muskie held a key position. He was running for reelection in Maine that year and had his eye on the 1972 Democratic nomination for president. President Nixon, too, sought to capitalize on public demands to control air pollution. In his State of the Union address in January 1970, he asked Congress to pass legislation setting strict standards and strengthening enforcement for both automobiles and factories. The environmental issue appealed to Nixon's political instincts. Opinion polls showed strong support, especially from middle-class voters who were the core of the Republican party. It deflected interest away from the Vietnam War, the president's chief cross to bear. Nevertheless, by his nature Nixon was a problem solver; air pollution appeared to be solvable.

Muskie soon realized that Nixon challenged his own role as a leader in cleaning the air. The Nixon administration sent a draft bill to Congress giving the national government authority to set enforceable standards while Muskie still opposed them. Moreover, on the other side of the Capitol, the House Commerce Committee was working on a "tough bill." Ralph Nader, the leader of the consumer movement and crusader for auto safety, sharply criticized Muskie for failing to push hard enough. Not wanting to give up his reputation for protecting the environment, Muskie augmented his bill to make it tougher than the president's proposal or the House bill. It told auto companies to install engines nearly free of pollution within five years. General Motors and Ford said this was technically impossible. Amoco said refining the gasoline was chemically impossible, the Sun Oil Company said refineries could not meet the standards, and the National Coal Association said cleaning emissions from smokestacks was not feasible. Supporters rebutted that setting the standards for the future would force industry to invent new technologies. Critics said this was mere speculation.

Two political scientists consider the Clean Air Act pivotal in defining governmental function. Focusing on Congress, Charles O. Jones labels the phenomenon "speculative augmentation." For reasons of partisan competition, the two sides augmented the proposed standards at the same time as they speculated (contrary to engineering data) that the law could force industry to comply. He concludes that government tried to implement policy beyond its capability.[12] While

---

Scorecard for AIR POLLUTION CONTROL

LAW
Clean Air Act 1970, amended in 1977 and 1990

POLLUTANTS

Ozone (smog)   Down 23%   Source: Auto and truck exhaust
Causes respiratory illness, damages lungs, and is especially bad for asthmatics. Damages crops, forests, and buildings and reduces visibility.

Sulfur dioxide   Down 32%   Chief source: Factories and electric power plants
Causes respiratory illness, damages lungs, and is especially bad for asthmatics. Causes acid rain.

Carbon monoxide   Down 23%   Chief source: Auto and truck exhaust
Damages lungs, causes circulation problems.

Nitric oxides   Up 14%   Chief source: Factories and electric power plants
Damages lungs and causes respiratory illness.

Particulates   Down 78%   Chief source: Factories and electric power plants
Damages lungs and causes premature death.

Lead   Down 98%   Source: Auto exhaust
Damages the brain, especially for children.

CONGRESS
House Committee on Commerce, subcommittee on Health and the Environment
Committee on Transportation and Infrastructure, subcommittee on Water Resources and Environment
Committee on Science, subcommittee on Energy and the Environment
Senate Committee on Environment and Public Works, subcommittee on Clean Air

AGENCIES
Environmental Protection Agency (EPA)
State environmental agencies
South Coast Air Quality District in southern California

INTEREST GROUPS
American Lung Association   Electric and auto industries
Clean Air Coalition   Natural Resources Defense Council (NRDC)

Source: EPA 1994 National Air Quality and Emissions Trend Report.

the irresponsibility of speculative augmentation is common in environmental legislation, it afflicts other policy arenas too, especially ones involving science.

Using the term "regulatory regime," George Hoberg believes that the act marked a major turning point in the place of interest groups. The old regime, dating back to the New Deal, was for the agency to cooperate with the industry and make decisions case by case. It was decentralized and informal. The goal was economic efficiency. The government lacked strong authority to enforce its rules and the courts rarely intervened. The laws were short and general; Congress gave the agencies broad discretion to use its technical expertise. In a paternalistic fashion, the agency represented the public interest. The new regime, which he labels pluralist, is centralized and formal. Its goal is to improve the quality of life. Government has authority and personnel to enforce its rules and courts intervene frequently. The laws are long and detailed; Congress gives the agencies limited discretion. The agency can no longer take a paternalistic role, but becomes the center of the struggle between interest groups.[13]

The Clean Air Act of 1970 set in place a comprehensive program reversing the prior national policy of not interfering in decisions made by the states. It went far beyond the halfway measures of earlier laws confined to research and exhortation. The law set nationwide standards for the ambient air, that is, air already in the atmosphere that people breathe. Primary standards affect health and secondary standards affect property and the environment. The EPA was to set standards only for seven pollutants that matched the criteria in Sections 108–109. Thus, these "criteria pollutants"—particulates, carbon monoxide, sulfur dioxide, nitrogen dioxide, hydrocarbons, ozone, and lead—were the only ones regulated. If a pollutant was not on the list, it was not officially a pollutant.

The law controlled emissions from new factories or electric generating plants, but not from existing ones. Congress believed that to retrofit existing factories and plants would be expensive and provoke strong opposition. New facilities would be less polluting anyway, because engineering had improved and, by incorporating emission control right from the beginning, construction would be cheaper. The 1970 law did not require permits for existing facilities, an omission later regretted. A number of states, however, required permits. With bright optimism, the law declared the deadline for all this was 1975, only five years away.

Automobiles would have cleaner exhaust at the tailpipe and gasoline would be purer. Faced with the inevitable demand for regulation, Detroit preferred to have uniform national standards rather than different ones in each state. In fact, the act set two standards: a strict one for cars sold in California and a moderate one for the other forty-nine states. Gasoline companies consoled themselves that uniform requirements would leave them in the same relative position as their competitors, albeit with each gallon costing more. Other companies stood to gain or lose a lot. The Corning Glass Company, which would profit from the introduction of the catalytic converter, established a permanent office in Washington to lobby for it. The Ethyl Company, which man-

33

ufactured virtually all of the lead additive, stood to lose. The congressman from Richmond, Virginia, the location of Ethyl Company's headquarters, was among the bill's most bitter opponents.

Implementation was by the states, not the national government. If a state wanted to manage its own program, it applied to the EPA with a proposed State Implementation Plan (SIP) for stationary sources like factories and electric power plants and another for mobile sources. The incentive for the state to cooperate was a grant of money to fund the work. Congress chose to delegate the implementation for three reasons: (1) there was deference to state sovereignty; (2) the act extended the (largely ineffective) 1967 law that tried to have the states take the full responsibility, which provided the image of gradualism to a major change; and (3) Washington did not have the personnel to staff the program and the abhorrence of swelling the bureaucracy to do so. Although the Roosevelt administration had conducted many programs like social security and the WPA at the national level, the Johnson and Nixon administrations wanted to keep the number of national employees small. In view of laws passed during the Environmental Decade, the Clean Air Act delegated in a more fragmented manner than later laws that were more systematic in their delegation.

When Congress passed and the president signed the Clean Air Act in December 1970, the EPA was only one month old. Nixon, who prided himself on good administration, recognized environmental programs needed their own home. The Council on Environmental Quality, established in January (roughly a full year prior to the act's signing), was supposed to coordinate government wide. Within months its inadequacy was obvious. It was too small and lacked authority. Nixon chose to create the EPA using his administrative authority rather than ask Congress to pass a law. It was faster and he did not have to reach agreement with the Democrats who had majorities in both the House and Senate. His legal basis was the Reorganization Act. Since Roosevelt, Congress has passed a reorganization act that permits each president to shift bureaus from one department to another, without creating or abolishing a department. Nixon moved the National Center for Air Pollution Control out of the Department of Health, Education, and Welfare into the new EPA. The other big bureau was the National Water Quality Administration. Like the Air Center, the Water Administration originated in the Public Health Service and then became a separate bureau in the Department of Health, Education, and Welfare. In 1966, it moved to the Department of the Interior before being reestablished as an independent agency in the executive branch. These two bureaus became the bulk of the EPA. Nixon also added a small radiation office from the Atomic Energy Commission.

To be the EPA's first administrator, Nixon appointed William Ruckelshaus, who proved to be a dynamic leader with influence at the White House and respect on Capitol Hill. He began his political career in the Indiana House of Representatives, then came to Washington as assistant attorney general. Impressed with his intelligence and leadership, Nixon appointed him to head the

Figure 2.1 Department of the Interior

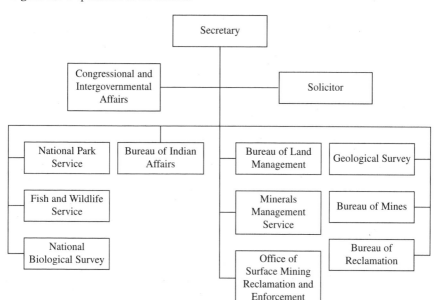

newly established Environmental Protection Agency, in spite of Ruckelshaus's lack of environmental background. Ruckelshaus infused the agency with his energy and dedication. He quickly won the respect of the personnel from the Air Control Center and the Water Administration. He recruited additional staff who were energetic and dedicated. Ruckelshaus also got along well with Congress, environmentalists, and business leaders.

Indeed, Nixon considered him so talented that as the Watergate scandal closed in on him, he moved Ruckelshaus from the EPA to head the FBI, which was in turmoil with accusations of mismanagement and favoritism. When the president's problems grew worse, he moved Ruckelshaus to the second ranking position in the Department of Justice. Archibald Cox, the special prosecutor appointed to investigate the Watergate scandal, was moving closer to the White House and the president. On the evening of Saturday, October 20, 1973, Nixon became aware that Cox was about to implicate him. He telephoned the Attorney General and ordered him to fire Cox. The Attorney General refused and resigned immediately. Nixon then telephoned Ruckelshaus, who automatically became Acting Attorney General, and told him to fire Cox. Ruckelshaus refused to obey the president's command and was fired.

When Ruckelshaus left for the Justice Department in 1973, Nixon appointed Russell Train in his place. Unlike his predecessor, Train had been an environmentalist for years, at first as an amateur. While serving as a judge on the Tax Court and inspired by travel in Africa, he had founded the African Wildlife

Figure 2.2 Environmental Protection Agency

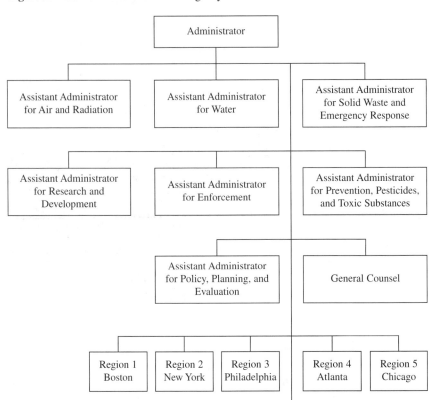

Foundation. He decided to give up his judgeship to become president of the Conservation Foundation. When the National Environmental Policy Act established the Council of Environmental Quality, Nixon appointed him as its first chair.

The Clean Air Act was designed to set and enforce standards, much like criminal law. The system resembled traffic laws; if the speed limit was fifty-five miles per hour, the police stopped those who drove faster. The EPA set the limits and punished those who violated them; moreover, it did not reward a company that emitted less than the limit. The act declared that a company was to use "the best available technology" (BAT). Exactly what this declaration meant still remains unclear. Besides being vague and changeable, BAT failed to consider

William Ruckelshaus was the first administrator of the EPA and returned to that position midway through the Reagan administration to repair the damage to the agency.

costs. Whether pollution control cost $100 or $1 million made no difference. Once the EPA set its standards, companies had to comply. The law also introduced a novel feature of citizen suits. In order to prod the government to enforce the law, Section 304 enabled private citizens to sue in court. These citizens, usually environmental organizations, but sometimes industry, could sue polluters, potential polluters, or the EPA. They did not have to wait for the government to take action. Moreover, they could collect attorney fees and pay expert witnesses. The Clean Air Act, which removed the barrier of expense for environmentalists (since the industry already had money), was the first law to permit citizen suits on a wide scale.

The EPA Promulgates Regulations

In the first year or two after the act became law, the EPA promulgated hundreds of pages of regulations to implement the new legislation. In accordance with the Administrative Procedures Act, the agency held public hearings, accepted written comments, and consulted with experts on its own staff, in other government agencies, and in industry. With this information, it first published proposed regulations in the *Federal Register* and after further comments, hearings, and modifications, the EPA then published the final regulations. Those detailed regulations turned general directives in the law into specific programs and filled the gaps that Congress left vague in the law. For example, Section 108 of the Clean Air Act did not declare which pollutants harmed health; it directed the EPA to weigh the scientific and medical evidence. The EPA determined that seven met the criteria: particulates, carbon monoxide, sulfur dioxide, nitrogen dioxide, hydrocarbons, ozone, and lead. Section 110 directed the EPA to approve or disapprove a State Implementation Plan within four months; while the plan obviously had to conform to the law, Congress gave the agency the discretion to decide, according to its regulations and procedures. When a citizen or a corporation affected by the regulations objected but could not persuade the EPA, the Administrative Procedures Act gave that citizen or corporation the right to sue in court.

After reading the final regulations on air pollution, environmentalists became troubled about a missing piece. The rules did nothing to protect the quality of air that already existed. The mammoth Four Corners generating plant was reducing visibility in New Mexico and the utility company planned another large plant in Utah. The EPA proposed nothing to keep air quality from deteriorating so long as it met the bare minimum. The agency's position was that the law did not give it authority to disapprove state plans on this basis. In 1972, the Sierra Club took the EPA to court, three days before the agency was scheduled to publish the air regulations. The club sued Ruckelshaus, the administrator, arguing that while the Clean Air Act did not have a particular section addressing this point, the EPA had the duty according to the statement of purpose in Section 101 at the beginning of the law which read: "The purposes of this title are to protect and enhance the quality of the Nation's air resources. . . ." To most experts, the Sierra Club contention seemed outlandish. Up until then, no one took these provisions seriously; they were considered pious fluff. The U.S. District Court, however, took Section 101 seriously—the EPA was ordered to promulgate regulations for the prevention of significant deterioration (PSD). The Appeals Court upheld the decision without writing an opinion, a highly unusual step. The Supreme Court split 4–4 so the decision stood, and the Sierra Club had won. When Congress amended the law in 1977, it incorporated the provisions in the Clean Air Act.

With respect to reducing emissions from stationary sources like factories and electric generating plants, the EPA and industry soon recognized the economic inefficiency of Clean Air Act provisions. An obvious way to increase efficiency, for example, was to require that when a facility had several smokestacks, all of the smokestacks could be combined for a net calculation. The goal was to clean the air, not to conform in an arbitrary fashion. In an instance of bureaucratic creativity, the EPA devised "the bubble," allowing a company to put an imaginary bubble over its entire facility and reduce the total amount of pollution without worrying about which emission came from which smokestack. The advantage was that a company could then reduce emissions where it was cheapest. Perhaps it could make a big improvement at one point that would make up for excessive emissions at another point. The Armco steel plant at Middletown, Ohio, was supposed to reduce particulates from its blast furnace at $12,000 per ton. Instead, the company proposed to reduce particulates by paving roads, oiling dirt roads, and planting grass on bare ground. The expense would only be a fraction as much. Not everyone at the EPA liked the bubble proposal, however. The enforcement division believed it would encourage violations. The compromise left the regulations so stringent that the bubble was not worth industry effort. Eventually, the EPA was able to develop a system that balanced clean air with less cost.

The bubble emerged out of a branch of the agency established to analyze problems from the perspective of economics and operations research. Ruckelshaus set up the Planning Division after criticism by management experts, who believed the lawyers were too powerful.[14] Previously, the EPA's mentality was to enforce the law and regulations without considering the consequences. Even the act itself takes this tactic, by ordering states to submit plans and industry to control emissions. After all, a third of the members of Congress are lawyers and only a handful are economists.

Command and control fits the lawyer's objectives of "enforcement" and the traditional attitude of courts. The EPA lawyers and judges like its simplicity. Moreover, this simplicity fits the attitude of engineers and scientists. Economists, on the other hand, believe its simplicity makes it a crude way to control pollution. Offering incentives like the negotiable rights or rewarding for cleaning up more than the minimum would allow for a greater chance of success. A typical conflict within the EPA about proposed regulations has the lawyers and engineers on one side and the economists on the other. The EPA's attempt to regulate automobile driving in order to reduce air pollution totally collapsed. Unlike preventing significant deterioration, the law specifically demanded regulations. Senator Muskie wanted automobile regulations, and, in 1973, the court ordered it become a high priority. The EPA demanded that the most polluted cities drastically reduce auto traffic. Los Angeles was to reduce it by 90 percent. When the driving public screamed its outrage, the EPA retreated and abandoned its plan.

By this time the auto manufacturers were trying to produce a vehicle that burned more efficiently and cleaned its exhaust in a catalytic converter. The other aspect was the fuel itself. Lead was the worst pollutant. This common natural element, at substantial levels, causes mental retardation, especially in a fetus or toddler. When children who live near busy highways play in their backyards, they can ingest lead when they put their fingers in their mouths or eat dirt. As the level of lead increases within their bodies, these children risk a greater chance for permanent brain damage. Trying to stop children from sucking on their fingers or eating dirt is a daunting task, because they like the sweet taste of the metal, which tastes like candy. While removing the lead from gasoline helps, most of the poison is already in the ground. The traffic of the past haunts the present. When lead was common and mileage was only ten miles a gallon, a busy intersection might have received as much as four or five tons a year. That lead is still there in the soil.

Carol Browner was appointed to head the Environmental Protection Agency in 1993 by President Bill Clinton. She previously headed the Florida Department of Environmental Protection.

Most of the EPA staff in the early 1970s were enthusiastically dedicated to environmentalism. Personnel from its predecessors, the Center for Air Control and the Water Administration, were for the most part personally dedicated, and for new staff, the agency attracted young, ambitious, and well-educated lawyers, economists, and managers. A number came to the EPA after working as volunteers or paid staff for groups like the Sierra Club or the Wilderness Society. Older staff members came from backgrounds in state parks, water commissions, and land management. Many were from the west. While none were so old as actually to have worked for New Deal agencies, many were cast in that mold and admired the Roosevelt years. Young or old, most believed the national government should intervene in industry and state government when necessary.

The political turmoil of the Watergate scandal had little effect on the EPA. Nixon had, of course, established the agency, supported the Clean Air Act, and courted the environmental movement. Once up and running with laws enacted, the EPA proceeded on its own. Party politics was not important. The new president, Gerald Ford, gave a general blessing to environmental programs. He spent his time, however, on greater worries of foreign policy, inflation and his 1976 presidential campaign.

THE CARTER ADMINISTRATION

Ford's Democratic opponent, Jimmy Carter, campaigned for strong environmental protection. Once elected, Carter appointed Douglas Costle to head the EPA. Costle had directed the Connecticut EPA and later was an assistant director of the Congressional Budget Office. With the regulations and state plans in place, Costle emphasized enforcement. As assistant administrator for air, he appointed David Hawkins who had been an attorney for the Natural Resources Defense Council (NRDC). This appointment put a prominent advocate from a committed interest group in the key position. By 1975, Congress recognized the need to revise the Clean Air Act. The Arab oil embargo and so called energy crisis of 1973 argued for relaxing standards that decreased auto efficiency. Industry blamed part of the 1974 economic recession on pollution control expenses. In spite of congressional speculation that tough standards would force industry to develop new technology, the arbitrary deadline of 1975 was recognized as unreasonable. The amendments finally enacted in 1977 proved to be extensive and complex. With 180 pages, the law was three times as long as the original. The environmentalists were better organized than five years before, having established an umbrella of the National Clean Air Coalition. Friends of the Earth, the Sierra Club, American Lung Association, and the American Public Health Association were the core. The League of Women Voters and the United Steelworkers of America participated. Although not an official member, the NRDC coordinated its lobbying. On the other side, the United Auto Workers lobbied against provisions harmful to auto manufacturers.

The biggest issue was how and at what level to protect areas with clean air from deterioration due to new factories and electric generating plants. In deciding the Sierra Club lawsuit in 1972, the court ordered the EPA to promulgate regulations to prevent significant deterioration. The Prevention of Significant Deterioration regulations, however, were based on a slender reed, the "goals" of Section 101. Congress, which strongly supported the program, recognized it needed to address the problem squarely and put language into the law before future presidents or other court decisions could weaken the regulations.

Environmental groups proposed that all stationary sources be required to scrub their emissions. Coal was the fuel for nearly all of them, with sulfur being the worst problem. As smoke goes up the smokestack, electrostatic machines remove the pollution. The proposal was to reduce the pollution by 90 percent. Surprisingly, coal mine operators in the midwest and east liked the plan. Although the proposal would increase the cost of burning their coal, it would increase expenses even more for western coal, which is much cleaner. If the regulations merely required an absolute level of pollution, factories and utility companies would switch to buying from Wyoming and Montana. When it became apparent in 1976 that they could not prevail, senators from western states killed the bill with a filibuster. It did not pass for another year. On behalf of Ohio coal companies, Senator Howard Metzenbaum advocated even more than scrubbing.

He proposed that when a factory or utility company could not find enough low sulfur coal in its own state, it would be exempt from the requirement. Even after becoming part of the law, it retained the name of "the Metzenbaum Amendment." In the final count, the environmentalists and the midwestern and eastern coal producers accomplished their objectives. Besides western coal producers, the losers were factories and electric generators, although utility companies could pass on their higher costs to consumers.

ADMINISTRATOR GORSUCH AND REPRESENTATIVE DINGELL

The election of Ronald Reagan reversed the trend toward increasing support of environmental goals. The California governor had campaigned on the basis of reducing regulation. Put positively, the Republican candidate wanted to ease the burden of regulation to permit the economy to grow. He wanted to get government out of responsibilities that the private sector could handle more efficiently and to move decisions closer to the people by delegating responsibility to the states.

Once in the White House, Reagan appointed officials dedicated to his goals of deregulation and decentralization. Portentously, he determined that the EPA should operate under the direction of the Cabinet Council for Natural Resources and the Environment chaired by the secretary of the interior. Senator Paul Laxalt of Nevada, a close friend of Reagan and early supporter of his presidential campaign, recommended James Watt, who was eventually appointed secretary of interior by Reagan. A Wyoming native and attorney, he had served in the Interior Department during the Nixon administration. More recently, Watt had directed the Rocky Mountain Legal Foundation at its Denver headquarters. The foundation was a conservative, pro-business group of lawyers committed to protecting property owners and the free enterprise system. A proud conservative, Watt wanted to reduce government to the bare minimum. Later on, he would champion the Sagebrush Rebellion.

As might be expected for a president unconcerned about the environment, Reagan had trouble identifying an administrator for the EPA. During the campaign he had declared that air pollution had been "substantially controlled." He also announced that the explosion of Mount St. Helens had spewed out more sulfur dioxide "than has been released in the last ten years of automobile driving or things of that kind that people are so concerned about." Reagan also stated: "Growing and decaying vegetation in this land are responsible for 93 percent of the oxides of nitrogen." The actual facts were that Mount St. Helens released five hundred to two thousand tons of sulfur dioxide a day compared with eighty-one thousand tons a day from manmade sources and that the bacteria that decompose vegetation release nitrous oxide (N_2O), rather than nitrogen dioxide (NO_2), which is the source of acid rain. Reagan finally settled on Anne Gorsuch—a Republican

In His Own Words: James Watt
Secretary of the Interior 1981 to 1983

The position of secretary of the interior carries with it tremendous responsibilities. . . . Service as a steward of much of the nation's vast resources and its environmental values, coupled with the obligation and duty to carry out statutory mandates of Congress that are not always compatible, is a great challenge. . . . The tremendous complexities . . . fill that job with conflict and controversy. . . .[1]

I am a concerned westerner—a concerned American. I want the federal and state governments to strike a balance between the development and protection of our natural resources.[2]

For many years the environmental movement championed great projects and had a healthy impact on legislation. Then, beginning in the late 1960s, the politicization of the movement began. By September of 1980, that process was formalized when the paid leadership of the largest and most active conservation/environmentalist groups marched lockstep into the Rose Garden of the White House and endorsed Carter's reelection bid. They came out in total opposition to Governor Reagan. Again, in 1984 they opposed President Reagan.[3]

1. Senate Committee on Energy and Natural Resources, *Hearings on the Nomination of James Watt*, January 7–8, 1981, 27.
2. Ibid., 30.
3. James G. Watt, *The Courage of a Conservative* (New York: Simon and Schuster, 1985), 40.

member of the Colorado legislature[15] (where she was a leader of a group of conservative representatives known as the Crazies because of their beliefs)—to be the new EPA administrator. From the White House perspective, she combined strong conservative values, a western background and past elective office. She and Watt were already friends from Colorado politics.

One of the first changes in environmental policy in the Reagan administration came, not from the EPA, but from the new Task Force on Regulatory Reform chaired by Vice President George Bush. In April, the Task Force proclaimed that easing regulations on gasoline would save consumers $4 billion and auto manufacturers $800 million, over the following five years. The recommendation fit the new administration's orientation toward big corporations and against regulation. Like previous presidents, not just Republicans, Reagan discovered his control over issuing regulations could accomplish what the law and agency expertise did not. An agency like the EPA was not allowed to promulgate regulations until the Office of Management and Budget (OMB) approved them. Consequently, OMB simply would withhold its approval. This power of delay served the Reagan team well because its goal was negative. It did not want government to act but to restrain itself. As of 1981, the EPA had a backlog of regulations on diesels, hazardous pollutants, acid rain, and leaded gasoline left over from the Carter administration. They simply sat on the shelf for years.

When Congress passed the Clean Air Act Amendments in 1977, it left some aspects unfinished, such as toxics, trucks, buses, and acid rain. In order to postpone the conflict, it appointed an air quality commission to study the intractable problems and report in three years when Congress might be more able to reach agreement. When 1980 arrived, everyone in Washington recognized the impossibility of passing such a controversial bill during a presidential campaign so they postponed the report another year.

Thus, in 1981, the House Committee on Energy and Commerce and the Senate Committee on Public Works and the Environment expected to begin serious work. Reagan's victory had brought enough Republicans into the Senate to elect a Republican majority for the first time since 1952. The House remained Democratic. John Dingell, a Democrat from the suburban cities down river from Detroit, chaired the House committee. As a young man, he had worked five summers as a ranger for the National Park Service. He strongly favored protecting the environment if it meant parks and forests; on the other hand, his district had many automobile manufacturers and employees. Although he chaired the whole committee, he did not see eye-to-eye with the chair of the subcommittee on health and the environment, Henry Waxman. Waxman, who represented Los Angeles, wanted the strictest standards possible. In the Senate, the chair was Robert Stafford of Vermont who came from the moderate wing of the Republican party.

According to custom, the EPA would send "the Administration bill" to the Hill and the two committees would use this as their basis for discussion. But no bill came. Dingell found the agency's lack of cooperation annoying and insulting. In fact, the EPA career staff had a draft bill that incorporated recommendations of the air quality commission. At first, Gorsuch was about to send the draft to Congress, but upon reflection and advice, she determined it was tainted by connections to the Carter administration so she decided to keep hold of it. (Mysteriously the press got a copy of the draft bill and wrote articles criticizing the Reagan administration for suppressing it. Presumably a disgruntled career employee had leaked it to the press.) Dingell continued to push the EPA for a draft to work on. Finally in August the EPA sent Dingell's committee a two-page memorandum of the "Eleven Basic Principles." Dingell was outraged that the EPA did not consider his committee worthy of a serious effort.

Polling data taken that summer put the Reagan administration in a quandary. It showed that Americans did not want to lower standards for clean air. The Eleven Basic Principles were, in Gorsuch's mind, an attempt at conciliation. After vetting his frustration, Dingell introduced his own bill in December, which was expectedly lenient toward the auto industry. The Motor Vehicle Manufacturing Association lobbied for it, as did the National Association of Manufacturers and the U.S. Chamber of Commerce. Environmentalists opposed it, calling it the "Dirty Air Act." Even Dingell's own committee refused to back it. The following year Senator Stafford introduced his version. As a moderate Republican, he supported a clean environment. The result was a stalemate. The EPA seemed paralyzed, Senator Stafford could not move forward, and Representative Dingell was stymied. In this manner, the Clean Air Act revisions began a nine-year impasse. Neither side could muster the votes for changes and both were afraid to upset the delicate balance.

Lack of cooperation on clean air was not Dingell's only quarrel with the EPA. Gorsuch ran into trouble managing the EPA as well as meeting Dingell's demands. Top political appointees lacked skill and experience. A scandal in the Superfund to clean up toxic waste proved the worst. Career employees referred to this period as the "Time of Troubles," adapting the name from the strife in Northern Ireland. In late 1982 with support of the White House, Gorsuch fired virtually all of her political appointees and replaced them with experienced careerists from other departments in Washington. Yet, even this dramatic shakeup proved inadequate. When the EPA refused to turn over documents that Dingell and another committee chair had subpoenaed, the House of Representatives voted that Gorsuch was in contempt of Congress. But before the Sergeant at arms arrested her, the contempt vote was too much even for the feisty Anne Gorsuch; she resigned.

Reagan needed to turn the calamity around, the public wanted the EPA to do its job, and Congress was displeased. The happy solution was that William Ruckelshaus, the first administrator, was willing to return. This time he held the position for two years, rehabilitating the agency. Ruckelshaus's return marked a turning point for the Reagan administration, both at the EPA and in other departments throughout Washington. The zealots who wanted less regulation and more opportunities for business lost momentum. The public wanted a less extreme course.

However, the right wing "cowboys" discovered managing the government and gaining Congressional cooperation was hard to do. Secretary of the Interior James Watt resigned under pressure in October 1982 after nineteen months in office. Ruckelshaus also resigned after turning the EPA over to Lee Thomas, a practical manager who lacked an environmental background. Thomas began his career working for the South Carolina government in criminal justice, then moved to safety and emergency relief for four years. Thomas arrived in Washington during the Reagan administration to carry out an assignment with the Federal Emergency Relief Administration. Before long, he moved to the EPA to run the Superfund program shortly before the time of Gorsuch's troubles and resignation.

ACID RAIN

During the 1980s, scientists came to understand the problem of acid rain. The phenomenon was not new, just the understanding. Historically, the problem was recognized three hundred years ago and named in 1872. In the 1960s, Scandinavians realized some of their lakes were sterile; millions of plants and fish were killed by the acidic water. In the 1970s, Canadians noticed the same problem near Sudbury, Ontario, and throughout Quebec. Lakes in northern New England and the Adirondack Mountains of northern New York suffered as well.

45

The immediate cause was acidic rain and snow that drained into the lakes, while other acid fell as a dry powder or in fog. For the most part, it was sulfuric acid although nitric acid was also common.

The dual mystery was the acid's source and why one lake could be afflicted and not others. Except for those near nickel smelters in Sudbury, the lakes were remote from industry. Research eventually demonstrated that the acid had travelled long distances. Most of it came from coal burned in the Ohio Valley, emitted high into the air where the sulfur combined with oxygen to form the acid, then deposited in rain, snow, fog, or powder in the northern countryside where the soil lacked buffers to neutralize the acid. The Canadian Shield contains the oldest rock on the planet and also has the thinnest and most worn nutrient-lacking soil. When acid rain falls on better soil to the south, alkalies neutralize it so the damage is less. In Europe, sulfur from coal burned in England drifts north over Norway and Sweden, which also has thin soil. Fortunately, in the American west, acid rain causes little damage because the soil contains more alkalies. To compound the problem, during the 1960s coal burning plants built extra tall smokestacks to disperse their emissions. The effect gave the sulfur a headstart in reaching the high altitudes.

Based on better scientific information, the Canadian government demanded the United States control its pollution. In eastern Canada, fourteen thousand lakes were acidic. The two governments first agreed to monitor the air and coordinate their research, then as the cause became clearer, to limit emissions. In 1991, the two countries signed a treaty. However, the problem of acid rain is not confined to the extreme northeast and Canada. Nearly six hundred streams in the mid-Atlantic states are acidic. The worst area is the New Jersey Pine Barrens, where 90 percent of the streams are acidic. The acid in the air damages spruce trees in the Appalachian Mountains from Maine to Georgia. It cuts visibility in half and corrodes stone and paint on buildings and automotive finishes. The sulfates also contribute a quarter of the particulates people inhale.

GEORGE BUSH, THE ENVIRONMENTAL PRESIDENT

Clean air policy stayed on the back burner through the end of the Reagan administration. In 1988, George Bush declared during his campaign that he wanted to be "an environmental president." Once in office, Bush sent a draft bill to Congress to amend the Clean Air Act. As always, an "Administration Bill" is prepared by the agency responsible. Built on the framework of the 1970 and 1977 versions, the seven-hundred-page draft addressed ambient air quality, motor vehicles, toxic emissions, acid rain, and the hole in the ozone. The 1990 debate returned Congress to normalcy, leaving behind the extremes of the Reagan years.

In addressing air pollution control, the president and Congress discovered that acid rain presented the toughest problems. The sin of the Ohio Valley polluters is due to geography. The region, rich in coal, has little natural gas and vir- tually no oil, and the wind blows the regional industries' emissions to the east and north. Industry in the region, to caricaturize its argument, states: "Don't blame us for our fuel, the prevailing wind, and your weak soil. Other locations and auto exhaust cause acid, just not with such bad results." The region backed up this argument with eighty votes in the House of Representatives. The only way to get enough votes for the bill was to conciliate the Ohio Valley representatives. When finally passed, the law gave all factories and plants an annual allowance of the number of tons they could emit. Starting in 1995 with the first phase, one hun- dred ten plants in the midwest and east were required to reduce emissions. The second phase, beginning in the year 2000, will further reduce their emissions and will add smaller plants. Many companies are listed by name with their tonnage of emissions. Most of the industrial facilities are coal-fired generating plants; others are smelters, chemical plants, and factories.

The law directs the EPA each March to sell approximately one hundred fifty thousand additional "allowances" to emit a ton of sulfur dioxide. The Chicago Board of Trade conducts the sale on behalf of the government. This function fits the board since it runs exchanges for corn, wheat, fertilizer, and stock market futures (that is, a contract to buy some months or years in the future). In terms of economic theory, the advantage of allowances is that a company can buy or sell according to its individual costs of abating the pollution. If a company has a high cost to abate, it buys, and if a company has a low cost, it sells. This means the companies that can abate more efficiently, do so. For example, a seller might sim- ply close a decrepit plant and sell the allowances that go with it. Consumers ben- efit because rates are lower. Moreover, the law requires the total tonnage be reduced each time it is traded, which benefits the public more. The companies like having greater autonomy to decide themselves rather than waiting for a deci- sion from the EPA or a state agency. It is also possible for a dedicated (and wealthy) environmentalist to buy a ton of sulfur dioxide and retire it. By simply not using the allowance, one ton less goes into the air. School children in Glens Falls, New York, in the Adirondack Mountains raised $18,000 to purchase 292 allowances. The National Healthy Air License Exchange (INHALE) bought 454. An agreement between Arizona Public Service Company and Niagara Mohawk Power Corporation resulted in the donation of twenty-five thousand allowances to the Environmental Defense Fund, and Northeast Utilities of Connecticut donated ten thousand to the American Lung Association.

Unfortunately, the program has not worked too well. At the first sale in 1993, a ton of pollutant sold for about $300, and cost as much as $450. The next year the average price was lower: $132 a ton. The price has drifted downward each year to $67, then rose to $110 in 1997. At the beginning of the program, the Board of Trade hoped to start a futures market for the allowances where a com- pany, environmentalist, or investor could buy or sell at any time, not just once a year. The price collapse ended that proposal. The chief impediment appears to be the cost of transacting the deals. A typical electric utility company does not have its own expert to track the prices, search out other companies interested in a deal, and organize a sophisticated market strategy. Therefore, they have to pay big fees to brokers and hire consultants to advise them. A second reason is the particular auction the 1990 law requires, which is more cumbersome than other Board of Trade methods. A third reason may be that sulfur dioxide is only one of many pollutants a company has to put into its calculus. Giving flexibility for one factor may not be enough. More generally, the program demonstrates the differing bureaucratic and business cultures. The EPA staff cannot get rid of the reformer's impulse to improve and tinker. Business people cannot overcome their anxiety that the EPA will change its regulations, because it has so often in the past. Environmentalists (some even on the EPA staff) do not trust the electric companies and are not comfortable with the Board of Trade. They believe selling the rights to pollution is environmentally and morally wrong. Industry critics call this the "two faces of the EPA": the agency promises to be flexible, but then imposes rigid regulations.

The problem of smog in the large cities further demonstrates the difficulties when trying to change patterns of industry and auto transportation. The EPA learned the hard way in 1975 that trying to force Los Angeles to adopt tough limits to automobile travel was a form of bureaucratic suicide. Yet, the problem remained, while the plans in many large cities had failed to attain good air quality. The 1990 amendments established five levels of nonattainment. Those only marginally over the limit for ozone had to comply in three years, while Los Angeles, where the problem was severe, had twenty years. A different timetable governed non-attainment areas for carbon monoxide: 1995 for moderate excess and 2000 for serious excess. Once again, the greater offender got greater privileges. On the other hand, the impossibility of the dirtiest cities complying should not mean that other cities should not move forward. Just as nine years before, the two key Democrats were John Dingell, still chair of the Energy and Commerce Committee, and Henry Waxman, chair of the subcommittee on Health and Environment. By now, however, the adversaries found grounds for more cooperation. Dingell feared that not many Representatives outside the Detroit region would support the auto industry and Waxman feared that pushing for the strictest standards might cause backlash.

As the 1992 election neared, a bureaucratic reform came face-to-face with interest group politics. The reform was regulatory negotiation, referred to as "reg neg." Ever since its establishment, the EPA had contended with lengthy court battles as soon as the agency promulgated major regulations. Those dissatisfied, either industry or environmentalists, routinely sued and the court would issue a temporary injunction to suspend the regulations, while the court made its decision. Frequently, the lawsuit took years. Environmentalists and industry also made special appeals to members of Congress to pressure the EPA and occasionally amend the laws. The controversies took years to resolve, paralyzing the agency and leaving industry without definitive guidance. While industry did not like many of the rules the EPA approved, neither did it like the uncertainty, which prevented planning for new investment and technology. If the rules could be certain, at least the corporations could make the correct decisions. Reg neg was supposed to solve this problem by recognizing that interest groups would shape the decision and asking them for their views before proposing the regulations. The goal was to avoid the court battles and pressure from Congress for favors and exemptions.

In the year after Congress amended the Clean Air Act in 1990, the EPA convened thirty people from industry and environmental groups to negotiate on reformulating gasoline by adding ethanol, which is derived from corn. In the 1978 Energy Tax Act, Congress had lowered the tax on "gasohol" in order to reduce oil imports with grain alcohol. Farmers loved the generous subsidy because it expanded their market for corn. After six months of negotiation over the regulations, all thirty parties signed the agreement. The benefit to the air is that the reformulated fuel reduces emissions of carbon monoxide, but the disadvantage is that it also increases the emissions of hydrocarbon that lead to ozone, the first stage in smog. Therefore, the reformulated gasoline would not meet the standards for smoggy cities like Los Angeles, New York, and Denver, which amounted to a tenth of the market.

The ethanol industry negotiators had not realized its full economic loss until after signing the agreement. To sell in the smoggy cities it needed a waiver allowing more ozone. In the past the EPA had granted waivers, but the reg neg agreement did not. Ethanol interests pressured the EPA directly and through members of Congress. At their urging the Senate passed a non-binding resolution labeling the regulations as "illegal." To counter the pressure, the Natural Resources Defense Council and the Sierra Club joined their usual opponents, the American Petroleum Institute and the American Methanol Institute, to point out that the ethanol negotiators had signed the reg neg agreement. In response, the ethanol team claimed the regulations were not the same as the ones to which they had agreed. As the election neared, Bush worried about losing the votes of farmers, so he announced he would grant a waiver. Bill Clinton also wanted farmer votes; two days before the election he wrote to the National Corn Growers Association pledging his support for ethanol.

THE OZONE HOLE AND THE
GREENHOUSE EFFECT

In the early 1980s, scientists in the Antarctic made a startling discovery. The natural layer of ozone in the stratosphere, starting six miles above the earth and extending thirty miles higher, simply disappeared each spring. Each year the hole was larger, growing to be twice the size of Europe. In the northern hemisphere, the ozone layer is also shrinking, portending another hole like that at the South Pole; in fact, it is thinning out everywhere. The ozone molecule leads a double life. Close to the ground it is a health hazard because the sunlight cooks hydrocarbons from automobile exhaust causing smog. In the stratosphere it sustains life, because it blocks out dangerous ultraviolet rays that cause blindness and skin cancer. Unfortunately, the low-lying smog does not rise to replenish the stratosphere.

Scientists determined that the cause of the ozone hole was man-made choloroflorocarbons (CFC) released from junked refrigerators and air conditioners. The gas escapes, floats up six miles, and breaks apart the molecules. In 1987, one hundred fifty nations signed a treaty, the Montreal Protocol, to phase out the production of CFCs by the year 2000. The Ozone Action group, however, considers the treaty riddled with loopholes, pointing out that the DuPont corporation continues to manufacture CFCs under an exemption from the EPA. DuPont responds that the CFCs are manufactured at the request of the government for defense and that the corporation leads the industry in manufacturing alternatives.

The other global danger is that the earth will heat up like a greenhouse. However, the weight of scientific proof is not so strong here as it is in the case of the ozone hole. As the amount of carbon dioxide in the atmosphere increases, more of the natural radiation of the sun on the Earth is absorbed rather than reflected back into space. Water vapor (clouds) has the same effect. For millions of years since plant life evolved, the amount of carbon dioxide crept up in tiny increments. With the Industrial Revolution, however, the carbon dioxide levels increased dramatically. Digging up coal and pumping oil and natural gas to fuel furnaces and engines releases carbon that has been literally out of circulation for millions of years. The amount of carbon dioxide is 25 percent higher than one hundred fifty years ago and is rising half a percent a year. This increase in carbon dioxide levels will cause the average temperature to increase between one to six degrees Fahrenheit in the next century. Some climatologists even believe global warming has already caused more hurricanes and blizzards.

A few degrees can cause tremendous changes, which may be impossible to reverse. Ten thousand years ago the last ice age was only seven degrees Fahrenheit cooler than the present. Ice floating on the Arctic Ocean, which now reflects back into space most of the sun's radiation, is close to the melting point. If it melts, the blue water will absorb more heat and the ocean will be too warm to refreeze. Presumably, new ocean currents will flow into the north Atlantic and Pacific oceans. More ominously, a rise in temperature will melt the ice caps presently covering Greenland and the Antarctic. This added water will raise the sea level by six inches by the year 2030 and twenty inches by the end of the next century. In the United States, it will flood half of Florida, while creating more deserts. Overseas, the rising sea level will flood the Netherlands, the Bahama Islands, the Egyptian delta, and half of Bangladesh. Island nations like the Maldives will disappear beneath the waves. On the favorable side, it will make it possible to grow wheat in northern Canada and Russia.

From the political perspective, the uncertainties loom large. First of all, the danger is far from being scientifically proven. During the mid-twentieth century the average temperature dropped, not increased. In recent years it increased, with

Burning the tropical rain forest in Brazil destroys the habitat for many species and increases the carbon dioxide in the atmosphere, which leads to global warming.

1990 and 1995 tying for the hottest years since scientists began recording. For the past one hundred thousand years, the planet has experienced six ice ages, the most recent ending only ten thousand years ago. From 1100 to 1300 Europe suffered a "little ice age." Science cannot determine how the long term fluctuations fit. Assuming that the planet is heating up, the next question is what can be done. Although fossil fuels appear to be the culprit, motorists, consumers, and industry are not willing to stop refining them. However, reducing their burning slightly may be possible. One way would be to switch to nuclear power, but many people are concerned about the radioactive nuclear waste. Furthermore, the cause is truly global, so for the United States to restrict burning fossil fuels would not be enough.

A cool planet is a collective good. On one hand, every person on earth enjoys the benefits whether or not he or she uses fewer fossil fuels. On the other hand, the leading consuming nations are few in number; seven countries consume over half of the world's coal. While it is a collective goods problem, the

51

reality is that cooperation among a small group might resolve it. A lesson of collective goods problems is that they are often transformed by a few of the biggest members cooperating and all the others following along. For instance, if the United States and the European Community agreed to a plan, it would reduce the vast majority of greenhouse gas emissions. Even if the other countries supported the agreement only weakly, the total reduction might be enough. In 1992, under the auspices of the United Nations, 165 nations negotiated the Framework Convention on Climate Change, which, as its name implies, is not an agreement so much as a framework for future agreements. The parties set a goal of stabilizing the amount of greenhouse gases, primarily carbon dioxide. Unfortunately, the various countries do not shoulder the same burden, which falls most heavily on the rich countries that consume the most fossil fuel. Underdeveloped countries have been unwilling to forego economic growth. Eastern Europe and the former Soviet Union are allowed time to get their economies more competitive. These have been among the least efficient users of fossil fuel as well as the worst polluters. The world's largest coal consumer is China. As its economy develops, it will burn more coal. Presently, China is not willing to sacrifice its progress nor is it capable of moving quickly to nuclear power.

Destruction of rain forests causes global warming just as burning fossil fuels does, because three-hundred-foot-high trees, with vines, parasites, and fungi lockup huge amounts of carbon. When settlers burn or chop down the forest, the fields they plant in its place do not have nearly as much biomass. The excess carbon goes into the atmosphere adding to the greenhouse effect. Today, farmers in the Amazon Basin, Central Americas, and southeast Asia are destroying thousands of acres of rain forest a year. The Central American ranchers are raising cattle for the McDonald's and Arby's restaurant-chains.

Not all rain forests, however, are tropical. The forests of the Pacific northwest from Oregon to Alaska are just as densely packed with carbon as those in Brazil. Until recently, the U.S. Forest Service sold trees from the Tongass National Forest to Japan. The amount of biomass released will never be recouped. Although environmentalists have objected, the Forest Service maintained it was only carrying out the law. While the Forest Service usually decides how much timber is to be harvested based on general laws and its technical expertise, Senator Frank Murkowski of Alaska introduced a bill that guaranteed enough wood from the Tongass National Forest for the Ketchikan Pulp Company (in which the senator owns stock) to maintain twenty four hundred jobs. When deciding on the number of trees to harvest, jobs are just one factor along with the condition of the forest, the soil, the water supply, the market demand, wildlife, and recreation. Because of his party, Murkowski became chair of the Natural Resources Committee when the Republicans won the Senate in 1994. For a key staff position, he hired the chief lobbyist of the American Forest Products Association. Opponents are organized in the Southeast Alaska Conservation Council. Although the conflict concentrates on the trees themselves, its consequences lead to the greenhouse effect.

CONCLUSION

GASP, the Pittsburgh Group Against Smoke and Pollution, fits the mold of a grass roots movement. It began its life cycle spontaneously with ordinary citizens discontented by the poor quality of the air. A few met in Michelle Madoff's home, elected her chair, and began their campaign to clean the air. Their devotion and amateur talents and Madoff's entrepreneurship enabled them to arouse the public and convince the city government to enforce and strengthen the smoke ordinances. More generally, all across the country during the 1950s and 1960s citizens turned their vague discontent into political action when people became aware of their shared grievances. According to the social science theories, a movement begins for technical and economic reasons. People tolerated dirty air after the unemployment of the Great Depression and in order to defeat the Nazis. Following the war, the number of automobiles on the road grew tremendously after the end of World War II and industry continued its expansion. However, once victory came and prosperity returned, Americans realized they needed to cleanup their cities. On the other hand, the number of people involved was never truly massive. Only a handful of cities had citizen groups like GASP. Political and civic leaders became advocates of clean air with little prodding.

Interest groups have played a big role in air pollution policy, usually on the side of industry. Electric utilities, manufacturing companies, and the auto industry began lobbying vigorously in 1969 when Congress began a serious debate on the Clean Air bill. The disturbance, that harbinger of mobilization, was that the bill would regulate them at the national level. Many corporations set up Washington offices at the time. Not all were against the bill, for example, the Corning Glass company that stood to profit by making catalytic converters. This validates the benefits of pluralism of balancing one interest against another. Health groups supported the bill and continued to urge Congress and the EPA to strengthen protection, for instance, the American Lung Association and the Clean Air Coalition. The 1997 controversy over higher ambient air quality pitted the American Lung Association against the American Petroleum Institute, auto manufacturers, and electric utilities.

Partisanship appears to explain more of air pollution policy than the other two theories. The rivalry between Senator Muskie and President Nixon to strengthen the bill in 1970 grew out of their desire to garner votes in the 1972 presidential election. The 1970 Act fit the Democratic New Deal heritage of intervening in business, regulating directly, and centering power in Washington. At that seemingly distant time, the Republican party did not find this repugnant; Nixon carried a lot of the New Deal in him. In contrast, by the time of the 1990 Amendments to the Clean Air Act, the GOP was more strongly opposed to direct regulation. The 1990 law addresses the problem of acid rain with "allowances" that companies can buy and sell in the market. In the budget gridlock between the Republican-controlled Congress and President Clinton in 1995 and 1996 environmental programs were some of the most contentious. The House of Representatives refused to approve a budget for the EPA, thereby closing the agency for several furloughs, one lasting three weeks. Finally, in May the Republicans began to read the public opinion polls more carefully and realized that they were losing support; Americans wanted the EPA to protect the environment. For the past two decades policy on environmental protection has been one of the most important divisions between the two parties.

Government procedures shed light on many aspects of air pollution policy. For example, in the House, the fragmented committee responsibilities produced continual squabbling between Henry Waxman of Los Angeles and John Dingell of the Detroit area on auto exhaust. The Republican victory in 1994 shunted both Democrats aside, however. Legal procedures have given powerful tools to environmentalists. The Sierra Club obtained an injunction against the EPA for incorrectly interpreting Section 101. The court ordered the agency to promulgate regulations for the prevention of significant deterioration, an action it never would have undertaken.

Like all bureaucracies, the EPA is specialized, autonomous, and technical. Its staff consists of scientists, engineers, lawyers, and accountants who look at dirty air as a series of problems to be solved, not as a political issue to be debated and compromised. In 1975, the EPA declared that Los Angeles had to reduce auto traffic by as much as 90 percent to meet the requirements of the Clean Air Act and seemed surprised that commuters and politicians were furious. In 1997, its health experts decided that the .10 level for particulates was not low enough to protect health and proposed to lower it to .08. Again, the outcry of protest surprised the EPA. The specialists in the agency tend to favor direct regulations and clear standards for easy enforcement and technology. Regulations were extensive and detailed. The best solution for smokestack emissions was a machine to scrub them clean. On the other hand, some of the EPA staff promoted the idea of the bubble, offsets, and negotiable allowances—economic solutions that encountered resistance from the engineers and lawyers on the staff.

NOTES

1. EPA Office of Air and Radiation, "National Air Pollutant Emission Trends 1900–1994," EPA 454/R 95–011.
2. "Clean Air Regulations" *Washington Post* June 10, 1996; "EPA Report on Benefits of 1970 Act" *Wall Street Journal* June 11, 1996; and "EPA's True Cost" *Wall Street Journal* June 27, 1996.
3. Charles O. Jones, *Clean Air* (Pittsburgh, PA: University of Pittsburgh Press, 1975), 21.
4. Ibid., 23, 46.
5. Ibid., 150–152.
6. Wyn Grant, *Autos, Smog, and Pollution Control* (Aldershot, United Kingdom: Edward Elgar Co., 1995), 25, 31.
7. Matthew A. Crenson, *The Un-Politics of Air Pollution* (Baltimore, MD: Johns Hopkins University Press, 1971), 177–178.

8. By far the best explanation remains: Mancur Olson, *The Logic of Collective Action* (New York: Schocken, 1968).
9. Randall Ripley cited in Jones, 35.
10. Quoted in Jones, p. 37.
11. Jones.
12. Ibid., 176.
13. George Hoberg, *Pluralism by Design* (New York: Praeger, 1992), 6.
14. Shep Melnick, *Regulation and the Courts* (Washington, DC: Brookings, 1983), 41.
15. Anne [Gorsuch] Burford, *Are You Tough Enough?* (New York: McGraw Hill, 1986). After her marriage in 1983, Gorsuch used only her husband's name.

CHAPTER 3
WATER POLLUTION CONTROL

Nearly all the large rivers are polluted: the Mississippi, the Ohio, and the Missouri. In the east the Hudson, the Delaware, and the Potomac suffer. The bottom of the historic James River, site of the first English colony in 1607, holds kepone that causes sterility in men. Every year tons of garbage and medical waste washes up on Atlantic beaches.

Fifty percent of Americans live within fifty miles of the Atlantic Ocean, Pacific Ocean, Gulf of Mexico, or the Great Lakes. In the future, even more people will live nearer to these bodies of water, as people gravitate to the coasts. A concern that develops from this prediction is that the coastal zone is delicate, with shallow marshes easily contaminated. These marshes are home to clams and oysters and the brooding sites for ocean fish. In the past decade a deadly, one-celled pathogen has infected fish and people along the east coast. Originating in Pamlico River in North Carolina and spreading as far as the Chesapeake Bay, the *pfiesteria* epidemic afflicts its human victims causing muscle pain and memory loss. From New Hampshire to Florida narrow sandy islands form barriers to protect the mainland from Atlantic storms and hurricanes. For drinking water, Long Island and Florida depend on wells driven into fresh aquifers, but salt is intruding. Great Plains cities and farmers depend on the Oglala aquifer for drinking and irrigation that is drying up. Los Angeles drinks water from the Colorado River pumped in a two-hundred-mile canal from the Arizona border. It is not enough, however, so Los Angeles wants to build a canal four hundred miles from northern California. Amazingly, in spite of the sewage and chemicals dumped into rivers, water quality has improved since 1972. Since then, local and federal governments have spent nearly $200 billion on sewage treatment.

For millions of Americans who live in the west and on low coastal plains like Florida and Long Island, the good news about cleaner water is not enough. They worry whether or not enough will be available. Ironically, the areas with the greatest population growth are those with the least water. Southern California and the interior west are naturally arid. Although Florida and Long Island have enough rainfall, they lack rivers.

In contrast to air pollution, the health dangers of dirty water are not as great. Drinking water is not a collective good; pipes carry it separately for each house or business. For the most part, adding chlorine makes it safe to drink. Children who want to swim can go to a pool instead of the lake or river. People who fish can learn to only eat coho salmon ten times a year to avoid the pesticides and heavy metals in the meat.

BACKGROUND

The Constitution of 1787 owes a debt to what now would be called environmental politics. Since early colonial times, Virginia watermen went into the Mary-land portion of the Chesapeake Bay for oysters and fish. Even though the British Crown approved, the Marylanders resented the Virginians, and in 1785, after the United States had won its victory over England but was still governed by the Articles of Confederation, the Virginians were forbidden to fish in the Maryland portion of the bay. In retaliation, Virginia forbade Maryland ships to sail through the Virginia portion of the bay to the Atlantic Ocean, thereby paralyzing its foreign commerce. Cooler minds soon prevailed and the two states sent commissioners to Annapolis to negotiate a treaty, which was in operation until 1967. In the afterglow of their success, the commissioners lamented the inadequacies of the Articles and decided to revise them. They called for a convention of all thirteen states. Not enough representatives came to Annapolis the following year, but these commissioners renewed the call for Philadelphia in 1787, resulting in the Constitutional Convention.

The ancient Romans knew the importance of clean drinking water and of removing the waste in sewers. Their aqueducts, drains, and sewers displayed better engineering and health management than Europe experienced again until the nineteenth century. At that time, cities began to recognize the problems, if not the medical causes. For example, in 1854, London experienced a local epidemic of cholera on Broad Street and the city asked Dr. John Snow, a pioneer in public health, to investigate. The physician visited the houses, shops, and taverns along Broad Street to interview the survivors and the caretakers of the victims. When he plotted the locations on a map, all the cases were within a two-block radius of the street. He also learned that the victims had all drunk water from the same pump. Snow soon recognized that the well was contaminated with cholera. His remedy was swift: he broke the handle off the pump and the epidemic ended. Snow solved this medical puzzle using maps, interviews, and medical diagnosis, without knowledge of microorganisms, which would not be discovered until Louis Pasteur developed his "germ theory" forty years later.

With the technology of sanitary engineering improving by the end of the nineteenth century, cities began to build sewers and safeguard their drinking water. They established public health departments that employed physicians and nurses to control epidemics and quarantined people with infectious diseases. They purchased watersheds in the countryside to supply clean water and built reservoirs to store it. New York City began its aqueduct from the Croton River in 1842. They relaid old wooden mains with iron ones and began to construct sewers to take the waste out of the city, typically dumping it directly into a river or harbor with no treatment, a method they were to regret later.

The new sewers made the cities cleaner and safer, but polluted the waterways. By the 1910s, cities began to treat their waste water, with settling tanks and by adding chlorine to kill the bacteria. By the 1920s, sanitarians realized that a single sewer system was inefficient during a rainstorm because, in one to two hours, thousands of gallons of rain poured into the system and overwhelmed the capacity of the treatment plant. To have a separate system of storm sewers flowing that could bypass the plant into the river in an emergency was found to be a better design. The storm water was relatively clean since it did not contain human waste. When cities ran out of money during the Great Depression, the New Deal took up the slack. The WPA gave millions of dollars for municipal sewers and treatment plants. In five years, sewer service to the population increased by 73 percent. This proved to be a high point, for World War II suspended the improvement and the Chemical Revolution that occurred after 1945 strained city sewerage with tons of chemicals. Treatment was inadequate because it was designed only for organic waste.

Municipal sewers were not the only source of pollution. In the country, barnyards and feedlots drained manure into streams and creeks. When farmers joined the Chemical Age by using artificial fertilizers and pesticides, most of it washed off their fields into the streams. With cheap fertilizer and big tractors, farmers saw less need to save their topsoil by plowing with the contours and leaving the stubble over the winter. In the mountains, once miners depleted a coal mine, it filled with groundwater that leached the acid from the coal and eventually leaked out, making the streams too acidic to support plants or fish. Large factories and power plants commonly drained their effluent into the nearest river without treatment. Industrial waste was far more deadly than municipal waste. Lead and soot from automobile exhaust settled on the streets, where it washed into the storm sewers whenever it rained. Many of these drainage sewers did not have any treatment before flowing into a river.

WATER IN THE FEDERAL SYSTEM

Until the 1970s, the governmental level most concerned with water pollution was municipal. Cities supplied clean water and removed dirty water. Progressive municipalities owned watersheds in the countryside, built conduits and reservoirs, laid mains and sewers, and treated the effluent before discharging it. A second aspect centered at the national level. Since the War of 1812, the Army Corps of Engineers had dredged harbors, maintained river channels, and dug canals. The Army got this job for two reasons. First, it had to build fortifications, like Fort McHenry in Baltimore, to protect coastal cities against invasion, so improving the harbor was an obvious next step. Second, for many years West Point was the only engineering school in America, so the Army was the most qualified to build them. The national government's program of improving navigation and digging canals was the policy of "internal improvements" advocated by the Whig party from 1824 to 1852. Congress passed its first Rivers and Harbors Act in 1824, initiating the "pork barrel." The annual laws gave a canal to one congressional district, dredged the harbor in another, and so forth. Politicians joked that everyone feasted on the delicious meat.

The Army continues its responsibilities for "navigable water" in the present. While originally Army personnel did the actual work, in the twentieth century they have employed civilians for the planning and design and hired private contractors to do the dredging, pouring concrete, and other field work. In 1899, Congress passed the Refuse Act to assure that the Army could keep its channels clear. The act forbade dumping in "navigable waters" without a permit from the Corps of Engineers. In the 1960s, environmentalists rediscovered this law and used it to prevent dumping human and industrial waste.

Scientific and popular attention turned to water pollution in the 1950s and 1960s much as it had for air pollution. The industrial mobilization for World War II dumped waste into the rivers as much as it did into the air. Cities had time and money to rebuild sewers and treatment plants neglected since before the Great Depression, while new suburbs needed water mains and sewers. Citizens were no longer willing to tolerate the filth in their rivers. In Pittsburgh, citizens took water samples that showed bacteria from human waste was high. Volunteers paddled canoes on Monongahela River to gather samples of sediment on the bottom. Samples taken at the outfalls from the steel mills were so filled with metal that they could be collected with a magnet. A city that did a good job of treating its sewage found its effluent was cleaner than the water already in the river. In Washington, Congress could look at the Potomac knowing that it contained untreated sewage dumped by West Virginian cities.

As was the case for air pollution control, the U.S. Public Health Service was also in charge of water pollution control. In its first law on water pollution in 1948, Congress gave the Public Health Service the authority to advise the state health departments and to make loans to construct municipal sewage treatment plants. In 1956, the Federal Water Pollution Control Act changed the loans to grants and provided limited power for enforcement. The 1965 Water Quality Act required the states to develop water quality standards and spun off the Public Health Service division as the Water Pollution Control Administration. The following year the Johnson administration moved it to the Interior Department before becoming half of the new EPA in 1970.

A Cleveland fireboat sprays water to put out the fire when the Cuyahoga River caught fire in 1969. This was the third time oil and garbage floating on the river burned.

The Cuyahoga as it appears today, after extensive cleanup and implementation of pollution controls.

A series of environmental accidents in the 1960s stirred up concern. In the early 1960s, millions of fish died in the Mississippi below Memphis when a single plant accidently discharged a pesticide. In 1968, scientists discovered high levels of DDT and other pesticides in the fish of Lake Michigan. Long Island residents found their tap water foamed from phosphates that had seeped into their delicate aquifer. Phosphates dumped into Lake Erie created algae blooms that turned the water a sickly green and took oxygen away from fish, and before long, limnologists declared the lake was dead. In Cleveland, the scum of oil and trash on the Cuyahoga River ignited and the entire river burned on three occasions. An oil well just off shore from Santa Barbara, California, blew out creating an oil slick, killing birds, and fouling the beaches of this wealthy city.

Water pollution gained attention in Washington. In 1966, Johnson declared it was the nation's most urgent natural resource problem. Although he did not want to back this up with money, a generous Congress began to appropriate funds for construction grants for waste water treatment plants, which increased to $1 billion by 1970 and the EPA contribution for each facility increased from 30 percent to 55 percent with the 1972 Clean Water Act.

The establishment of the EPA in 1970 magnified pressure for a national role. Staff of the new agency felt frustrated because state agencies were slow to develop programs and lackadaisical in enforcing them. Although forty-five states had programs on paper, only fifteen to twenty were effective. The concept of measuring the water quality in the river instead of how much pollution came out the pipe seemed flawed, and pinpointing the offender was difficult. The EPA had supplemented its authority by using the 1899 Refuse Act to require discharges to get a permit, but a 1971 court decision prevented the Corps of Engineers from issuing the permits.[1] Quickly reacting, Ralph Nader publicized the problem nationally.

THE 1972 WATER ACT

Inspired by its success on the Clean Air Act of 1970, Congress began to overhaul the water program. As is common, it took the name of an existing law, the Federal Water Pollution Control Act of 1956, even though the new act was a complete rewriting. In general, Nixon favored the overhaul. It fit his view that environmental issues appealed to the middle-class voters at the core of the Republican party and his belief in good administration and delegation to state and local governments. In February 1971, he sent his proposed administration bill to the Hill.

Congress replayed the Clean Air Act scenario. Muskie still chaired the Public Works Subcommittee on Air and Water Pollution. His success two years prior gave his fellow Senators confidence in his ability to understand the technical and scientific aspects, and, until March 1972, he was the leading candidate in the Democratic presidential primaries. The bill Muskie led the subcommittee to adopt was stronger than Nixon's bill, again augmenting as in 1970. It gave the EPA full authority, while reducing state agencies to handmaidens. A critic considered this authority as "lip service federalism."[2] Command and control was in full bloom.

Scorecard for WATER POLLUTION CONTROL

LAWS

Clean Water Act 1972, 1977 and 1987 (originally called the Federal Water Pollution Control Act). Safe Drinking Water Act 1974, 1986. Coastal Zone Management Act. Omnibus Water Act 1992.

POLLUTANTS

Municipal sewage   Population served by secondary treatment up 84%

Toxics (from industry)   Down 75%

Fertilizer (manure and   Little progress
top soil from farms)

Wetland loss   Reduced from 460,000 to 80,000 acres per year

CONGRESS

House Committee on Transportation and Infrastructure, subcommittee on Water Resources and Environment

Committee on Science, subcommittee on Energy and the Environment

Senate Committee on Energy and Natural Resources (formerly Interior), subcommittee on Water and Power

Senate Committee on Environment and Public Works, subcommittee on Drinking Water, Fisheries, and Wildlife

Committee on Commerce, subcommittee on Oceans and Fisheries

AGENCIES

Environmental Protection Agency (EPA)   Municipal water departments
Army Corps of Engineers   Councils of Government
State environmental agencies

INTEREST GROUPS

American Public Health Assoc.   Izaak Walton League
American Rivers   National League of Cities
American Water Works Assoc.   National Water Resources Assoc.
Assoc. of California Water Agencies   New York Water Environment Assoc.
Ducks Unlimited   Water Environment Federation

Source: EPA *25th Anniversary Report* 1995.

The bill required effluent permits for every discharger and compelled comprehensive planning. For construction grants, Nixon originally proposed $3 billion over three years; by 1972, he doubled it to $6 billion. The Senate bill proposed $12 billion. The goal of zero discharge was speculative. The city of Muskegon, Michigan, provided a model, whereby its sewage plant did not discharge anything, but allowed the nearly clean water to evaporate or seep into the ground leaving behind any remaining pollution. Adopting the zero discharge technique demanded the government control the effluent instead of the receiving waters.

In March, the House passed its version which gave less authority but more money, $18 billion. The two bills went to conference until September when the conferees reported a compromise closer to the Senate bill for authority and the House bill for the grants. The election campaign affected the situation. Members of Congress sought to be on the side of the angels. The Senate passed it by a vote of 74–0 and the House, by 366–11. Nixon worried that the $18 billion would strain the federal budget and trigger inflation. The strong bill gratified the EPA. And fighting water pollution with adequate enforcement and funds was now possible. Ruckelshaus sent the president a thirty-three-page letter urging him not to veto it. The president and his administration, however, believed the bill went too far. Nixon immediately sent his veto message to the Senate. His entire objection was the expense. With the election only three weeks away however, the president did not want to oppose clean water. Nixon's administration made little effort to prevent Congress from overriding the veto, which it did the next day by overwhelming votes.[3]

Giving vent to its high hopes, Congress wrote Section 101, declaring the lofty goal of totally ending discharge of pollutants by 1985. The interim goal for 1983 was to protect fish, shellfish, and wildlife and to provide for recreation in and on the water, which was popularly referred to as "fishable and swimmable." Even in 1972 most people considered these goals as rhetorical fluff. Both the Nixon administration and Congress sought a delegated program where the states would implement the programs. They believed the bureaucracy in Washington was too big and that different states had particular needs for pollution control that were not uniform. This pattern of delegation to the states had been the technique of the Clean Air Act and, before that, of Great Society programs like Model Cites.

A small sewage treatment plant. The Clean Water Act gave cities and towns grants to build modern facilities.

Two ways in which the law differed from the Clean Air Act were its generous grants and requirements for permits to discharge. Congress greatly expanded the money going to municipalities. Local governments were responsible for the discharging of waste water, while private companies and automobiles were to blame for air pollution emissions. Members of Congress liked giving grants, and cities in their districts were grateful for receiving them so the grants increased congressional members' votes in the next election. Moreover, this was still an era of federal largesse; during the Great Society years, total grants to states and cities grew from $8 billion to $20 billion. Nixon tried to bring the spending under control, but the grant-giving mentality was hard to rein in. The water act provided that the national government would pay 75 percent of construction costs, up from 55 percent. When in 1972 the EPA surveyed the cities to ask how much money they needed to upgrade their sewers and plants, the total was $22 billion, a shockingly high number. However, once the EPA proposed to use the cities' estimates to determine their actual grants, other cities that had not given high figures realized they were at a disadvantage for their self restraint. They prevailed on their members of Congress, who ordered the EPA to again survey municipal needs. The wisecrack by the EPA staff was "now everybody can lie about their needs."

One of the best innovations in the law was to demand metropolitan areas coordinate their efforts. It did little good for one city to treat its effluent to the highest level if its neighbor up stream dumped raw sewage into the river. Moreover, if all the municipalities in an area combined their efforts, perhaps to build only a single treatment plant, the entire process would be more efficient. Section 208 called for areas to establish councils including elected officials. Soon labeled "208 councils," they coordinated plans; however, the EPA would not give a grant without the council's approval. The EPA had about $100 million each year to divide among the councils, so they did not lack money. A typical one, usually called a Council of Governments (COG), received $100,000 a year, making it better funded than many city planning agencies. Besides water planning, they dealt with air pollution, transportation, and attracting business. Although funding is scarce today, most still continue their work on a modest scale. As a logical extension, the law also required planning for entire river basins.

Like the Clean Air Act, the water law split its standards into discharges and the ambient water. Congress had been disappointed in trying to implement ambient standards, but recognized it was the ultimate goal. Congress also chose not to set specific levels for effluent; instead, it required municipal plants to use "the best practicable control technology reasonably available." Private facilities were to use "the best available technology economically achievable." Critics complained that the law "sounded like a bunch of amateurs wrote it," which was true in a sense. Unlike the air law, the water law considered economic efficiency.

The water act required a permit to discharge, a feature not in the Clean Air Act until 1990. The permit requirement was easier in the case of water because there were fewer facilities and they were easier to identify. The 1899 Refuse Act had already required a permit to dump in "navigable water." Section 404 rewrote the Corps of Engineers duties, assigning it specific instructions to protect municipal water supplies, shellfish, fish spawning marshes, wildlife areas, and recreation sites. Now navigable waters meant more than the harbor or channel in a river: "If you can put a canoe in it, it is navigable." This responsibility for wetlands turned the Corps' old orientation on its head. It shifted to protecting, when often before it had despoiled, the environment. The Corps did not feel comfortable with its new duties or the requirement for citizen hearings.

Almost immediately, the EPA recognized a serious gap in the law because it gave no authority over groundwater. For example, if the EPA determined that a factory generated certain chemicals that were too dangerous to discharge into a river, the factory could legally pump them down a well on their own property. Many towns, villages, and small cities depended on groundwater for drinking. Ironically, the law increased the danger to them. At the urging of the EPA and environmental groups, Congress passed the Safe Drinking Water Act in 1974. Under its provisions, the EPA set standards for chemicals and microbes. Perhaps more importantly, it closed the loophole for discharge permits. Congress strengthened the law in 1986, requiring the agency to set twenty-five standards a year. This quota reflected congressional frustration at the EPA's slow headway as well as putting the national government squarely into an area long left to municipal government and to state health departments.

In 1977, Congress amended the law to extend its deadlines. To the new portion it gave the name Clean Water Act, the title eventually, although incorrectly, applied to the whole law. For most of the twentieth century, congressional, executive, and judicial branches named laws after their sponsors in the Senate and House (The Taft Hartly Act or the Wagner Act, for instance). The 1970s were a high point for long, correct titles for laws. Federal Water Pollution Control Act Amendments was a mouthful, even for the EPA employees. FWPCA was not easy either. Eventually, the EPA administrator issued a press release announcing the name change to the Clean Water Act. Although this had no legal basis, everyone was relieved. More recently, Congress has taken once again to using the names of sponsors, now officially included in the laws themselves.

REAGAN APPOINTS ANNE GORSUCH

Ronald Reagan's assault on the EPA began even before his inauguration. The vanguard of the Reagan Revolution was his Transition Team. Newly elected presidents usually assemble a hundred advisors from their party, business, and interest groups to identify candidates for political appointments and new directions in policies. The 1980 team was bigger and more zealous than ever before. Several hundred conservative Republicans and sympathetic businessmen travelled to Washington in November and December. Anne Gorsuch herself flew in from Denver to help and in hope of a job like an EPA assistant administrator. To get the top position surprised her as much as anyone else. Conservative "think tanks" like the Heritage Foundation and the Mountain States Legal Foundation, which formed the hub of the Transition Team, believed the EPA epitomized the morass of regulations that crippled business and annoyed municipalities.

The first attack came from the president's Office of Management and Budget (OMB). Reagan nominated David Stockman, a Republican Congress-man, to direct it; by the time he assumed office in January, Stockman already had detailed plans for "regulatory reform." The new president froze for sixty days all rules in the process of promulgation. This defused an explosion of last minute rules the Carter administration hoped to push through. The OMB next disapproved a series of regulations already promulgated before Reagan's inauguration. In quashing new proposed regulations, the OMB's cynical modus operandi was "to leave no fingerprints," that is, its staff did not keep written files on their actions which pre-vented a court at a later date from subpoenaing documents and challenging the OMB procedures. At the same time, Reagan established the Task Force on Regulatory Relief chaired by Vice President George Bush. Environ-mentalists accused the Task Force of being merely a channel for big business to neutralize laws protecting consumers, workers, and the environment.

While the OMB conducted a frontal assault on behalf of industry, the new political appointees at the EPA assisted individual companies. The Dow Chemi-cal company learned of a report prepared in the EPA's Chicago regional office that identified its Midland plant as discharging dioxin, a deadly byproduct of pes-ticide manufacturing that scientists discovered in fish and gull eggs. It reported that Dow appeared to be the chief, and perhaps the only, source of all the dioxin in the Great Lakes. Dow complained to John Hernandez, the new EPA deputy administrator. Hernandez, in turn, pressured the Chicago office to tone down the report.[4]

WETLANDS

When Congress wrote Section 404 of the Clean Water Act, it yoked two agen-cies, the EPA and the Army Corps of Engineers, chiefly to coordinate the envi-ronmental side with the Corps' function of maintaining navigation on rivers. The law's authors recognized that the two functions conflicted. The environmental lawyers' creativity in seizing on the 1899 Refuse Act for its requirement that the Corps approve discharges had dragged the agency into water pollution responsi-bilities that made the Corps uncomfortable. In 1899, the law intended to prevent dumping dredged material, not pollutants. Now the Corps' responsibilities grew larger. Moreover, with each year regulations to implement Section 404 expanded its scope.

Until 1968, the Corps used only one criterion in permitting dumping: its effect on navigation. But when the federal government became more concerned about the environment, it revised its regulations to cover pollution, fish, wildlife, ecology, esthetics, and conservation. Originally, Section 404 gave the EPA responsibility for reviewing and approving the permits for those factors. Almost at once this responsibility became one of the most controversial environmental

The 1997 Grand Forks, North Dakota, flooding, in which 70 percent of the city's inhabitants were evacuated, testifies to the need for more realistic floodplain control policies.

programs. The original Section 404 does not actually use the terminology "wetlands," but the EPA regulations in 1975 did. It encompasses "swamps, marshes, bogs, and similar areas." Besides coordination with the EPA, the Corps must coordinate with the Fish and Wildlife Service for refuges, the National Marine Fisheries Service for salt water, and the Department of Agriculture for "swamp-busting." This colorful word refers to the provision of the 1985 Farm Act which discourages destroying wetlands for dry crops.

Over the years government programs themselves have encouraged destruction of wetlands. Coastal Louisiana includes 2.5 million acres of marshes and six-hundred thousand acres of forested wetlands, comprising 40 percent of the total wetlands for the lower forty-eight states. Since 1879, the government has constructed four-hundred-fifty miles of levees within the Atchafalaya Basin Floodway. The goal has been to prevent the Mississippi River from cutting a new channel to the Gulf of Mexico that would bypass New Orleans.[5] This artificial manipulation speeds the flow of the "Father of Waters" to the Gulf without depositing its silt where it could create valuable new land. Instead, it deposits the silt in deep water. Other federal programs cut drainage canals to assist oil and gas drilling, consequently letting salt water intrude and damage the marshes.

Upstream, the Corps' levees for flood control extended as far north as Minnesota and North Dakota. Levees prevent high water on the Mississippi and Missouri Rivers from spreading out onto their historic flood plains. The effect is to put the rivers in a straight jacket. Without flooding small areas upstream, the torrent has to continue down the channel faster and faster until it finds a weak spot in a levee and spills out uncontrollably. Rain in 1993 was up to twice the average. The floodwater breached or overtopped a thousand levees stretching nearly six-thousand miles. Property damage was $12 billion; fifty-six-thousand homes suffered damage.[6] In 1997, the disaster came again to Minnesota and North Dakota; this time the Red River overflowed, causing over $5 billion in damage.

Ironically, only a year earlier the National Research Council and an Inter-agency Task Force had both recommended moving away from building levees to managing the floodplain—after all, the river is just reclaiming its natural terrain. Returning areas to wetlands will provide habitat for birds and animals, improve soil conditions, and enhance groundwater availability and quality. One technique is to permit high water to flood low-lying agricultural land. Farmers can build dikes around their barns and houses, and the government can insure against the loss of their crops in flood years. Providing the flood space to expand rather than channeling the water downstream to breach a dike would benefit those who live along the river as well as the river itself. Another technique is for cities to discourage building on low ground and turn those areas into parks that, when necessary, could be flooded for a few weeks during high water. The money saved would be tremendous. Again, ironically, the Federal Emergency Management Agency's program for flood insurance put the incentives the wrong way. By insuring buildings in flood plains, it encouraged people to construct houses, factories, and businesses there. Private insurance companies, however, consider those areas too risky to insure.[7]

At the upper reaches of the Missouri and Mississippi Rivers from Minnesota to Montana and far into Canada potholes dot the prairies. These small, shallow depressions make perfect sites for ducks and geese. Farmers get no financial benefit from keeping the potholes, so they drain them. To discourage conversion, the EPA and the Corps joined the state agency and the private Ducks Unlimited to educate people about the need to obtain a Section 404 permit and to identify wetlands so permission is not given prematurely.

Central Valley of California once had four million acres of wetlands, but now it contains less than a tenth as much. Over the years, the Corps of Engineers and the Bureau of Reclamation have drained marshes and brought irrigation to make the valley one of the premier farming areas in the United States. The irrigation water, however, brings naturally occurring salts and heavy metals that enter the soil, but cannot wash out completely because the total flow of water is too small. The water that does drain out contains excess fertilizer that contaminates the remaining wetlands. High levels of selenium and boron forced closing of the Kesterson Wildlife Refuge. The Bureau of Reclamation is now required to

69

remove and safely bury all of the contaminated soil and vegetation from the refuge.

The Bush administration advocated "no net loss of wetlands," but controversy soon surrounded the definition used in the Corps of Engineers' technical manual (proving that anything can be the subject of political debate). Officially, the *Wetlands Delineation Manual* was strictly internal, not subject to the Administrative Procedure Act requirements for public comment. Moreover, the Corps kept calling it a "draft," making it even harder for outsiders to influence its content as each new version expanded the definition of wetland. Later, the EPA began its own "draft" manual similarly expanding the definition. If the EPA and Corps officials hoped to capitalize on secrecy to avoid the anti-environmental doctrine hanging on from the Reagan administration, the strategy fell short. The manual came under scrutiny by the White House Council on Competitive-ness. Chaired by Vice President Dan Quayle, the council's purpose was to assure that American industry could compete in exports. For the most part this amounted to easing the regulatory burden. The council pressured the EPA and the Corps to reconsider.

With the inauguration of Bush, the EPA and the Corps, along with the Fish and Wildlife Service and the Soil Conservation Service, issued the manual. The final version gave the EPA and the Corps jurisdiction under Section 404 so extensive that it included land that had been under water for as little as five to ten years out of a hundred. Once the EPA and the Corps permitted public comment, farmers, business people, and members of Congress expressed their outrage. Farmers and real estate developers claimed that the EPA greatly expanded its jurisdiction by overly generous delineation of a wetland. They believed the agencies had claimed too much. Both organizations recognized they had to backtrack, but instead of opening the process to the public, they retreated behind closed doors, issuing a revised manual in 1991, which, in the opinion of environmental groups, was even worse. Congress reacted with the 1992 Water Appropriations Act by forbidding the Corps to use the 1991 criteria.

The 1996 Farm Act embodies a compromise. The Swampbuster program will continue, but with a lighter hand from the regulators. For example, regulations under the 1985 Act declared that crop land not cultivated for several years was "abandoned," and had to revert to wetlands. The 1996 Act is less harsh. As the bill moved through Congress, pressure came from two directions. The main thrust was to get the farmers off "welfare," that is, endless and expensive subsidy payments. Countering this free market theme, the Swampbuster and wetlands programs perpetuated regulation.

Section 404 confronts government with hard issues of defining the concept, of regulation versus private property rights, of balancing benefits to farmers, industry, and the public at large, and of possible exploitation for improving water quality. A scientific definition is impossible because the physical characteristics of one level merge into another. In 1972, Congress did not fully anticipate the impact on private land because it thought in terms of the 1899 law on dumping refuse into a river. The Corps accretion to the definition in its draft manuals struck Congress and the public as facile and unwarranted. Farmers and business people feared losing money when the Corps designated their property as wetlands, because Section 404 makes no provision for its financial consequences.

Many scientists would reverse the conclusion from the Kesterson Wildlife Refuge. To them it demonstrates the effectiveness for cleaning polluted water. While granting this is not the purpose of a refuge, diverting polluted water through a swamp can purify it. As the water filters through, a process that may take weeks, the sediment settles to the bottom, bacteria break down pesticides, and plants transform the sediment into nutrients. Yet, purification will not work if spring rain washes the dangerous pollutants into a nearby creek. Although scientists are optimistic about using a marsh or swamp as a natural filter to purify polluted water, the long term aspects are unknown. On Sandusky Bay in Ohio, the Winous Point Shooting Club has maintained detailed records dating back to its founding in 1854. This duck hunting club, the oldest in the United States, has gone from ink drawings, to photographs, to satellite images. Today, scientists are correlating core samples of the bottom to the 140 years of maps and pictures.

WATER FOR ELECTRICITY AND IRRIGATION

Whether water will be available is a political issue at least as complex as its quality. Its politics, however, are nearly separate from the pollution question. Geographically, water resources are a western concern. East of the 100th meridian, which runs through the middle of the Dakotas, Nebraska, Kansas, Oklahoma, and Texas, rainfall is adequate for farming. Rivers and streams supply city reservoirs. West of this line, water becomes more scarce.

In regions acquired from Mexico, the law came from Spain, itself an arid country. Spanish law gave highest priority to municipalities. Its colonial Pueblo de los Angeles had the right to use the water from the Los Angeles River, which it exploited ruthlessly to force annexation of the suburbs until the river ran completely dry around 1930. Extending the colonial rights took fancy legal footwork; in 1910, the city argued successfully that water from two hundred fifty miles north in the Owens Valley would replenish the Los Angeles River, hence it still could force annexation. Once it needed water from the Colorado River on the border with Arizona, however, its legal power terminated and it could no longer expand its city boundary. Some blame the hodgepodge of municipalities in the basin on the termination of the Spanish water grant after one hundred fifty years.[8]

In the rest of the west, the role of the national government came naturally from homesteading, sponsoring the railroads, and Army exploration. The land needed irrigation to be productive. The Bureau of Reclamation, established in 1902, fit the Progressive politics of the era. Men like Theodore Roosevelt, who had operated a ranch in Dakota Territory in 1888, believed government should take an active role in helping citizens. He knew personally that the west was too big, too dry, and too cold to handle alone. People needed to help each other. The bureau's goal was to "reclaim" arid land for crops, although in fact it never had supported that much natural vegetation. As an added benefit, hydropower from the dams could supply electricity.

Paralleling its role in forestry, the federal government began irrigation of western land. In the Salt River of Arizona, archeological excavations show prehistoric Indian irrigation systems. Pioneers had constructed small irrigation projects, but the systems needed to be much bigger to be efficient. Three years after Congress passed the Reclamation Act, the Bureau of Reclamation supplied water to three million acres. The dams also generated electricity. Yet, private companies could not establish dams and irrigation because of the great expense, the large number of customers, and the need for local government to cooperate. The law's author, Senator Francis Newlands, lost his entire fortune of $500,000 constructing an irrigation project in Nevada.

Dams became larger and more ambitious. As early as 1902 the Bureau of Reclamation was making preliminary plans for the Colorado River basin, the only dependable source of water in the arid southwest. Unfortunately, its flow is only seven million acre feet, not really enough for all the cities and farms it is supposed to supply. Today, the river's water leaves its basin to supply Denver on the east and Los Angeles and San Diego on the west. Irrigating the warm and fertile Imperial Valley was an early accomplishment, although developing the Colorado Basin has also exacted an environmental price. Reservoirs have flooded ancient canyons and caused excessive evaporation (i.e., water is being taken out of the river). To provide hydroelectric power, the dams store the spring floods and release it throughout the year, encouraging trees to grow along the banks in an unnatural manner and causing evaporation and eliminating the natural cycle that scours the beaches. Conflict between the states about withdrawing the water blocked any agreement among the seven states in the basin until 1922. A key ingredient of the 1922 Compact was that the upper basin states—Wyoming, Colorado and Utah—would guarantee seven and a half million acre feet of water per year at Glen Canyon, the half way point. According to critics, this artificial counting was the sole purpose for building the Glen Canyon Dam on the Colorado River in northern Arizona, which unnecessarily destroyed the canyon, flooded ancient Anasazi ruins, damaged the Grand Canyon, and caused excessive evaporation. They assert, moreover, that the original hydrologic estimates for the compact were too high; the river rarely has that much flow.

Dam building appealed to easterners as well. Cheap electricity was its foremost advantage. While governor of New York from 1929 to 1933, Franklin Roosevelt began the damming of the Massena Rapids of the St. Lawrence River. South Carolina dammed the Santee and Cooper Rivers. The most ambitious project was the Tennessee Valley Authority. During World War I, the government constructed a dam and gunpowder plant at Muscle Shoals, Alabama. After the armistice, it no longer needed the gunpowder but it still had the generators and factory. The progressive Republican senator from Nebraska, Frank Norris, pro-

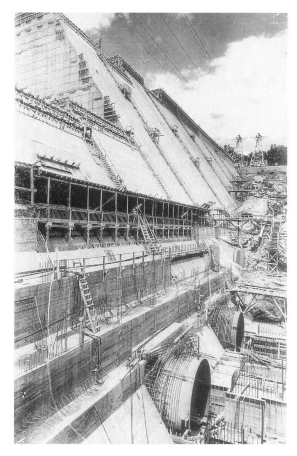

The New Deal presaged aspects of the environmental movement. TVA projects such as Norris Dam, shown here in 1935 when it was two-thirds completed, generated electricity and helped control flooding. Today, environmentalists tend to oppose dams.

posed the dam manufacture fertilizer, generate electricity, and improve navigation. He suggested building several other dams. Although his fellow Republicans in Congress and the White House gave little support, once Franklin Roosevelt won the presidency in 1932, Norris found an ally. Within ten years the TVA had six dams, the fertilizer plant, and a social program of adult education and organizing. Each dam eventually flooded a mountain valley and changed the quality of the water, and the reservoirs themselves will slowly fill up with silt.

The New Deal worked to control flooding. Even though states and cities along the river had been building levees for eighty years, record floods along the Mississippi River in 1927 broke through the levees and spread across twenty thousand square miles, displacing seven hundred thousand people and killing hundreds more. The Roosevelt administration extended the effort. It also built dams upstream to control flooding like the massive one on the Missouri at Fort Peck, Montana.[9]

Water projects exemplified American politics from the New Deal through the Great Society. The New Deal was the birth of big government. The 1929 stock market crash and the Great Depression exposed the failure of old fashioned business. The Roosevelt administration and victory in World War II showed the vitality of a nation mobilized under Washington's direction, and planning was a tool of big government. The TVA managed electricity generation, farm assistance, and flood control over a seven state region. On the Missouri River, the Agriculture Department, the Interior Department, and the Corps of Engineers coordinated their efforts. The national agencies brought in state government planners as well. The form was an interagency commission like the National Resources Committee established in 1935 or, later, the Federal Inter-Agency River Basin Committee.

Executive branch pressure for centralization came up against congressional pressure favoring fragmentation. Individual Representatives and Senators remained eager to get pork barreling for their districts, and central planning threatened to diminish their goals. The Corps of Engineers maintained close relations with members of key committees on the Public Works Committees. The annual Rivers and Harbors bill remained a "Christmas tree" on which every representative wanted to "hang an ornament": a dam, a canal, an irrigation aqueduct, or a ship channel. This subgovernment, as it came to be known, took the form of a triangle of the Corps, the Public Works Committees, and local interest groups who wanted irrigation, cheap electricity, or flood control. It rarely gained the attention of the president, the rest of Congress, or the general public. This fragmentation gave latitude to the three-part core to make their deals in a nearly private arena. The agencies and Congress tried to serve their constituencies much like a business serves its clients.

The water subgovernment was not the only one in Washington. Highways, petroleum, and cotton farming were others. At a later date, the form gained the clever label of "iron triangle." This closed pattern dominated until the 1970s when citizen groups like the Sierra Club and Ralph Nader's Public Citizen group and Citizen Action opened up the political process. Many consider this the acme of interest groups. Local interest groups got their dams or irrigation. Congressional representatives got the votes from grateful constituents. The executive branch agencies found niches where they could act autonomously. Agencies preferred to reach accommodation with their rivals, hence, on the Mississippi River the Corps took charge of the downstream portion and the Bureau of Reclamation took the upstream portion. Both united against a proposal in 1937 to establish an independent agency similar to the TVA.

The fragmentation of the 1930s through the 1970s did not wipe out central planning, but only crimped it. The two tendencies moved on parallel tracks. The 1936 Flood Control Act introduced cost-benefit analysis to the planning. The Corps and the Department of Agriculture were to build a project only "if the benefits to whomsoever they may accrue are in excess of the estimated costs. . . ."[10] Soon, all water planning agencies began to calculate the costs of a project then compare them to the economic benefits and eventually the technique spread government wide. While, today, cost-benefit analysis is seen as a means of reining in government spending, the Roosevelt administration sought to stimulate the sluggish economy. The White House exhorted agencies to incorporate "social benefits" and "intangible benefits."

Jimmy Carter made one of the first blunders of his term only a month after his inauguration when he reduced funding for nineteen water projects in his first budget. They included the $1.4 billion central Arizona project and the $562 million Garrison diversion in North Dakota. The new president announced his purpose was to save money by cutting those that appeared to be financially or environmentally unsound. When outraged Senators from these states complained, Carter told them they should not be surprised because he had campaigned against unnecessary spending for water projects. However, he soon reversed his budget cutting when faced with pressure from Congress.

OTHER WATER LAWS AND PROGRAMS

Development along the coasts presented a more complex problem. Since colonial times, draining swamps and filling in marshes has been a routine way to enlarge farms and give cities room for future growth. Eventually, however, people began to see the disadvantages. Wetlands spawned fish and fed wildlife, and houses built on sand would not stand. Cities like Atlantic City and Miami Beach were foolishly constructed on barrier islands that naturally shifted and faced continual pounding from wind and waves. Government spent millions of dollars constructing jetties and breakwaters, building dikes, and strengthening bridges. Hurricanes, such as Hugo in 1989 and Andrew in 1992, wrecked them. The national government paid nearly all the expenses for Corps of Engineer jetties and disaster relief, while the states contributed only small amounts.

Although Congress recognized the irrationality of fighting nature, it had to tread lightly. The first difficulty was that cities and resorts along the coast found many advantages having the government save their beaches and insure them against disasters. The second difficulty was that the national government had limited jurisdiction over city and states. Even states had little authority. Municipalities and counties controlled development through zoning. The fact that Washington paid much of the cost was not enough. Congress found a solution by giving grants for planning, a technique begun during the New Deal years. Because local governments always liked to receive federal money, the subtle tactic was that once they developed a plan, they would logically implement it. Moreover, the planning would play into the hand of local advocates of limiting development. The other hook was that the national government could decline to make other grants when a locality did not have a plan. It was legislative jujitsu.

THE REAGAN YEARS AFTER GORSUCH

Congress in 1986 amended the law on privately owned dams on navigable streams. Previously, a company such as an electric generator could look forward to automatic renewal. Now, they had to consider the environmental consequences. Dams blocked salmon from migrating upstream to spawn; reservoirs released water without regard for vegetation, waterfowl, or recreation. Moreover, cleaning up these rivers under the 1972 law made it worth the effort of improving their flow and access for fish. Until the water was "fishable and swimmable," the dams were merely one of many problems. In Maine, environmentalists intervened on the Edwards Dam on the Kennebec River that blocks the migration of the Atlantic salmon, as well as smelt, sturgeon, shad, and bass. At a later date, the New England Power Company agreed to environmentally sound management on its nine dams on the Deerfield River in Vermont and Massachusetts. The interveners opposing the license renewal were the Appalachian Mountain Club, the Conservation Law Foundation, and American Rivers. New England Power agreed to increase the habitat for trout and salmon, build roads for public access, and release enough water thirty-two times a year for "adrenaline-rush" kayaking.

The same logic applied to government-owned dams. To the surprise of many, the Department of the Interior supported the idea, at least with words. The secretary of the interior, Donald Hodel, who came to the position after a career of politics and government that included five years heading the Bonneville Power Administration in the Pacific northwest, proposed to scale back the Bureau of Reclamation. He pointed out that all the good sites were dammed and proposed that the agency move its headquarters to Denver and reorient itself to the environment and recreation. To further shock those used to the federal government's endless catering to industry and farmers, Hodel suggested the National Park Service tear down the dam that turned the Hetch Hetchy Valley into an ugly reservoir.

The Glines Canyon Dam in the Olympic National Park in Washington state came under suspicion. The 210-foot-high dam blocks the spawning runs of the giant chinook salmon. Built in 1924 before the park was established and before fish ladders were required, the dam supplies electricity to a pulp mill now owned by a Japanese corporation. A seven-year study by the Fish and Wildlife Service recommended tearing down the dam as the only way to restore the salmon run. Revitalizing the river would yield income of $500,000 a year for fishing and tourism for the Olympic peninsula.

A thousand miles to the south, the Glen Canyon Dam on the Colorado River has altered the river's course through the Grand Canyon. During each afternoon and evening, water swirls through the turbines to generate electricity for the peak demand; at night, little electricity is generated. The water volume can fluctuate from three to thirty thousand cubic feet per second in a single day. The effect is an artificial tide downstream that erodes beaches. The Interior Department finds itself on both sides of the issue: its Park Service wants to protect the Grand Canyon National Park, while the Bureau of Reclamation wants to supply electricity. Eventually, the Bureau of Reclamation reversed its policy and released surges of water to mimic natural floods in order to scour the river banks. Kayakers and rafters loved it.

SINCE THE REAGAN YEARS

In his 1988 campaign, George Bush sought to recapture middle-class support for the environment that Nixon had tapped twenty years earlier. Since that time, and especially in the Reagan years, the environmental vote had gone largely to the Democrats. In his speech accepting the Republican nomination, Bush declared that he intended to be "an environmental president." He attacked his opponent, Michael Dukakis, in his home territory by taking a boat around Boston Harbor, pointing out its foul pollution and noting that as governor of Massachusetts, Dukakis could have cleaned it. The state had not bothered to apply for the EPA grants. To head the EPA Bush appointed William Reilly, who had directed the World Wildlife Fund.

In 1989, one of the largest oil tankers in the world, the *Exxon Valdez*, strayed off course through the Prince William Sound in Alaska. The giant ship had just

When the *Exxon Valdez* ran aground in Prince William Sound in Alaska, it spilled a quarter of a million barrels of crude oil, making it the worst spill in U.S. history. Here a smaller ship attempts to off-load the remaining oil from the *Valdez*.

77

left the port of Valdez where it had loaded crude from the pipeline that pumped the oil eight hundred miles from the North Slope. The *Exxon Valdez*'s captain had been drinking and its first mate was unqualified to steer it. Riding fifty-feet deep in the water, the tanker scraped bottom on a reef forty-feet below, spilling two hundred and fifty thousand barrels. The oil seeped out and formed an enormous slick that washed up first on nearby Bligh Island, then on the shore of the Sound. The oil blackened the beaches, fouled the feathers of the birds, contaminated the seals, and poisoned the fish and other sea life. Waves splashed the crude oil on the rocks and rolled it into little tar balls. Eventually, the spill contaminated eight hundred miles of shoreline.

A newly recognized water pollution problem is herbicides in drinking water. Since the late 1950s, farmers have been spreading millions of pounds of chemical weed killer on their crops during April and May. Most of the herbicide washes off into creeks and rivers or filters into the underground aquifers. A 1995 survey of the drinking water in twenty-nine midwestern towns and cities discovered herbicides in all of them. Levels in Illinois were thirty-four times the safe standard. A glass of Fort Wayne water contained nine different kinds of herbicides. New Orleans, which gets its midwestern pesticides second hand from the Mississippi River, also had large concentrations.[11]

The sources for lead, one of the most dangerous pollutants in drinking water, is not agriculture, but pipes. The EPA estimates that more than 10 percent of municipal drinking water contains too much lead. Charleston and Columbia in South Carolina, Utica, New York, and suburban Boston are the worst. The lead typically enters the water in the house from lead pipes or copper pipes with lead solder. Newer plumbing is the worst because plumbing older than ten years has usually leached out the material. Soldering with a lead alloy has been illegal since 1986, but not all plumbing work since then has conformed.

Old-fashioned bacteria have not disappeared from drinking water, as Milwaukee residents discovered in April 1993, when cryptosporidiosis infected four hundred thousand of them. This dangerous protozoa, which causes severe nausea and diarrhea, was in the city's water supply. Scientists determined the sources of the bacteria were manure from animal feedlots, illegal dumpings by a slaughter house, and a sewage treatment plant less than two miles from the intake for Milwaukee's water. The city filtration plant was old, the monitoring equipment was broken, and the staff did not act quickly. Critics of the Safe Drinking Water Act program assert the problem is too much regulation. They argue the EPA was paying too much attention to lead, which should have been a low priority, so it missed the cryptosporidiosis threat. To reduce lead, the plant was experimenting with different chemicals, which confused them when the parasite appeared. The EPA rebutted that low funding during the Reagan administration put them behind schedule.

After more than two decades of the Clean Water Act, many cities and industries still discharge raw sewage into rivers. The main problem occurs during rainstorms that overwhelm treatment plants. Ohio leads the dishonor roll with 1,593 sewer overflows, followed by Pennsylvania with 1,260, New York with 1,200, and Illinois with 1,015. On the successful side of the ledger, Boston has finally built the sewage treatment plant Bush accused Dukakis of neglecting during the 1988 campaign. The city has reopened beaches closed for years, and seals have returned to the harbor.

CONCLUSION

Clean water was a rallying cry for Earth Day 1970; as a general goal, it attracted wide support. But how to get clean water was largely an engineering problem. Cities needed to purify their sewage; factories had to do the same. Political leaders were quick to join the crusade so citizens groups did not have a long battle.

The most important way to clean the water was to build and improve municipal sewage treatment plants. The 1972 Clean Water Act had a generous grant program; a multibillion dollar pork barrel for local government. Cities were engaged in lobbying as much as businesses do routinely. Industry could ease into the pork by discharging into a municipal sewer. While they did have to pay, it was cheaper than building their own systems. Like the case of air pollution, the disturbance to industry was the passage of the law. All dischargers now have to have a permit.

Again, like the Clean Air Act, political partisanship helps explain the Clean Water Act. Democrats were more favorable to the environmental side. They were more prone to intervene in business, to regulate directly, and to concentrate power in Washington. All of these characteristics were anathema to the Reagan administration. The 1988 presidential campaign produced a rhetorical reversal when George Bush accused Michael Dukakis of not cleaning up Boston Harbor. Although dams and irrigation projects are not so central to water pollution, they display strong partisan characteristics. Damming rivers was a center piece of the New Deal that built the TVA, Fort Peck, and Bonneville. Republicans considered this close to socialism. On the other hand, the Republicans' strength in the arid west brings pressure for dams and irrigation. Because Congress can log-roll to accommodate local projects for many members, each year produced its crop of projects without divisive conflict.

Government procedures and structure offer insight into water pollution policy, which fits well with the bureaucratic bent for expertise, autonomy, and technology. As a whole, water pollution has offered a series of problems for engineers, scientists, and lawyers. The EPA determined the standards, then the municipalities designed treatment plants and applied to the federal government for money. The grant system was expensive and suffered from rigidity and goal distortion. The program paid for construction costs, but not for operating costs; therefore, municipalities would design plants that might be expensive to build (with the EPA money) but cheap to operate (with their own money). Water planning fit well with bureaucracy. The most successful has been the regional councils of governments that continue to prosper all over the country, even after the EPA grants dried up.

NOTES

1. Harvey Liebermann, *Federalism and Clean Waters* (Lexington, MA: DC Health, 1975).
2. Ibid., 196.
3. Ibid., 83.
4. Jonathan Lash, *A Season of Spoils* (New York: Pantheon, 1984), 33–35.
5. John McPhee, *The Control of Nature* (New York: Farrar, Straus, and Giroux, 1989).
6. Mary Fran Myers and Gilbert F. White, "The Mississippi Flood" *Environment* 8 (December 1993): 7–9, 25–34.
7. Federal Interagency Floodplain Management Task Force, *Floodplain Management in the United States* (Federal Emergency Management Agency, 1992) and National Research Council report.
8. Vincent Ostrom, *Water and Politics* (Los Angeles: Haynes Foundation, 1953).
9. Peter Rogers, *America's Water* (Cambridge, MA: Massachusetts Institute of Technology Press, 1993); Beatrice Holmes, *A History of Federal Water Resources Programs*, 1800–1960 (Washington, DC: U.S. Department of Agriculture, Economic Research Service, 1972); and *A History of Federal Water Resources Programs and Policies, 1961–70* (Washington, DC: U.S. Department of Agriculture, Economics, Statistics, and Cooperative Service, 1979).
10. Holmes, *History 1800–1960*.
11. *New York Times* August 17, 1995.

CHAPTER 4
SOLID, HAZARDOUS, AND
TOXIC WASTE CONTROL

Every day Americans generate over two hundred million tons of solid waste: paper, cardboard, grass clippings, food garbage, cans, concrete and lumber from construction sites, and waste from industry. The amount averages four pounds of waste per day per person. Of the total of 207 million tons, forty-five million tons is recycled directly or is burned for energy, while the rest goes to landfills. Big cities like New York and Cleveland have literally run out of space. New York loads thousands of tons a day onto trains bound for Ohio. Once the waste lies buried under the dirt at the landfill, it does not decay as it did in the past, but simply remains as is for a century or more. A portion of that solid waste, less than 1 percent, is hazardous. This means that it may ignite, corrode, react with other chemicals, or be toxic or poisonous. Whereas the bulk of solid waste comes from households, most hazardous waste comes from industry. Chemical manufacturing accounts for half; most of the rest comes from the metal, petroleum, paper, food, and mining industries. Motorists discard hazardous waste such as old car batteries and used oil and tires. Pesticides and herbicides from farms wash into streams, seep into the ground, or blow away, spreading their poison.

The danger to human health is high. Pesticides can kill directly, and lead damages the brain. Chemical byproducts cause cancer. In 1977, epidemiologists mapped New Jersey counties that had high levels of cancer. They discovered that these counties lay in a band stretching from Philadelphia to New York. Dotted with oil refineries, chemical manufacturers, and pharmaceutical factories, the band quickly earned the title of "cancer alley." Within a few years epidemiolo-

This landfill on Staten Island in New York City is the largest in the world. By night time, all the garbage will be covered by eight inches of dirt. Gulls, which are natural recyclers, flock to landfills.

gists identified regions in other states that had similar industries and high rates of cancer.

BACKGROUND

Solid waste is as old as civilization; indeed, since the word "civilization" is a derivative of the Latin term for city, solid waste is an inevitable product of civilization. Half of the profession of archeology seems to consist of digging through ancient garbage dumps for discarded flint, pottery, and shells. Yet, until a hundred years ago, the volume of trash discarded was much smaller. Food was not wrapped in paper and plastic. Cardboard had not been developed. Books and newspapers were rare. People used their tools, utensils, and toys for generations. Besides being less in volume, the garbage of yesteryear could rot or, to use the present term, biodegrade.

By the mid-nineteenth century, city governments began to cart away garbage in order to improve public health as well as to prevent foul smells. The old dump gave way to the modern landfill only in the past fifty years. Covering the waste with dirt at the end of each day controls disease and odor. Lining the pit with impermeable clay or plastic and keeping off rain water that would leach out chemicals is quite recent. Prior to the Chemical Age, however, leachate was not so dangerous.

The volume of municipal solid waste more than doubled from 1960 to the present. In part, this increase was due to the rise in population, but the amount per person increased too, from 3.3 to 4.4 pounds per person. Most goes to landfills, 61 percent; 23 percent is recycled or composted, and 16 percent is burned, producing energy. While in 1960 incinerators burned 30 percent, they did not produce any energy and, worse, their smoke polluted the air.

Before the Chemical Age, the amount of waste that presented a hazard was small. For example, lead from pipes appears to have plagued the ancient Romans. More specifically, the aristocracy liked the taste of lead, which they mixed into their toppings that were spread on their food as a condiment. The emperor's family suffered the most since they lived in the most luxury. A large number of the children raised in the imperial palaces suffered brain damage. Even so, the real danger of lead poisoning multiplied fifty years ago.

Dichloro-diphenyl-trichloro-ethane (DDT) was invented in Germany and first produced by a Swiss company in the 1930s to kill insects. Contemporaneously, the Nazi war machine experimented with nerve gas, which has a chemical formula nearly identical. When war broke out, the Nazis tested its secret new nerve gas as a weapon. In World War I, both the Germans and the Allies had used gas, causing death and blindness for thousands of soldiers. Legend tells how at the beginning of World War II the German scientists demonstrated the gas to the army by releasing it in a field filled with tethered sheep. The sheep died instantly. Then, to their horror, soldiers guarding the far side of the field fell dead; next, farm hands even farther away fell dead. The Germans knew they had a powerful weapon, but never used it because they reasoned that if the Americans had DDT (the Swiss company had also sent samples to the United States just before the war), they also had nerve gas. In fact, the Nazis were wrong; Americans did not discover nerve gas until after the war.

The U.S. Army sprayed DDT extensively during World War II to kill typhus-carrying lice and malaria-carrying mosquitos. After the war, millions of veterans were familiar with the pesticide so they began to use it to protect crops and to control disease, calling it the "atomic bomb of insecticides." Heavily used, its long-term dangers remained hidden for over a decade. A tiny amount sprayed on a bush or a pond is safe; the dose is insignificant to an animal larger than an insect. The peril of DDT, however, is its permanence—an animal cannot get it out of its body. Thus, when a bird eats a contaminated insect or seed, the DDT remains in its body. If a fish eats a contaminated mosquito larva, it remains in the fish. The more it eats, the more DDT it has, permanently. Bigger fish further concentrate the DDT when they eat the small fish. Eagles are highly vulnerable because they are at the top of the food chain, eating fish, mammals, and birds that can all be contaminated with DDT.

One woman recognized the danger, turned the tide against DDT, and did much to spark the environmental movement. Rachel Carson was a biologist employed by the Department of the Interior in the Biological Survey now named the Fish and Wildlife Service who wrote books popularizing science in her spare time. In *Silent Spring*, Carson argued that pesticides were reducing the bird population so much that in the future no song birds would live. Spring would be silent. The risk for eagles was the greatest because DDT prevented the females from laying eggs with strong shells. The weight of the mother broke the eggs while she brooded. The pesticide also deformed the chicks' beaks so they could not eat.[1] Prior to publication as a book in 1962, the *New Yorker* ran it as a serial where it gained wide attention from the magazine's elite audience. One captivated reader was President John F. Kennedy, who immediately directed his science advisor to assess the problem.

RESOURCE CONSERVATION AND RECOVERY ACT (RCRA)

Worries about hazardous waste had taken a backseat to air and water pollution during the early 1970s. But, by 1974, Congress was ready to take up the matter. An EPA study identified thirty-two to fifty thousand sites with hazardous waste and declared twelve hundred to two thousand of them extremely dangerous. Congressman Paul Rogers, chair of the Commerce Subcommittee on Public Health and the Environment, began hearings. The Nixon administration lacked enthusiasm, however. The president believed the cleanup for hazardous waste was too expensive and preferred state and local government to handle the problem. But a few months later he was gone, having resigned in the Watergate scandal. Because of Watergate, Democrats won many additional seats in Congress the following fall. When Congress convened, President Gerald R. Ford instructed the EPA not to cooperate in drafting a bill. Thus on two counts, Democrats in Congress felt they had a freer hand. By the time Congress finally approved the Resource Conservation and Recovery Act (RCRA) in mid-October 1976, Ford was only two weeks from the election day in which he hoped to win the presidency on his own. Because he did not want to alienate pro-environmental voters, he signed the bill into law.

With an inspiring title, the RCRA sets the framework. Like other modern laws, it begins by defining its terminology. It classifies a material as hazardous in two ways. First, the chemical may ignite, corrode, react with other chemicals, or be toxic or poisonous, and second, the law may list it specifically. Other laws cover chemicals that are pesticides or toxics. The RCRA covers hazardous waste from the cradle to the grave. The company that generates the material must register each amount and track it until its ultimate disposal. For example, a chemical company manufactures a thousand gallons of arsenic, ships it to a metal finishing company for cleaning the sheet metal, the second company uses it and

Scorecard for SOLID, HAZARDOUS and TOXIC WASTE CONTROL

LAWS

Resource Conservation and Recovery Act (RCRA) 1976, 1984. Solid Waste Disposal Act 1978, 1980. Used Oil Recycling Act 1980. Federal Insecticide, Fungicide, and Rodenticide Act (FIFRA). Toxic Substances Control Act 1976. Comprehensive Environmental Response, Compensation, and Liability Act (Superfund) 1980, Superfund Amendments and Reauthorization Act (SARA) 1986. Community Right to Know Act 1986.

POLLUTANTS

Garbage   Increased from 3.3 to 4.4 pounds per person per day

                        Industry disposes of 258 million tons of hazardous waste and 7 billion tons of regular waste each year.

Industrial toxics   Decreased by 43%

Superfund sites   Approximately 1,300; cleanup completed on 349.

CONGRESS

House Committee on Commerce, subcommittee on Finance and Hazardous Materials
Senate Committee on Environment and Public Works, subcommittee on Superfund

AGENCIES

Environmental Protection Agency (EPA)
State environmental agencies
Municipal trash collection departments

INTEREST GROUPS

All industries   American Farm Bureau Federation
Chemical Manufacturers' Association   Pesticide manufacturers
Chemical companies like Dow and Du Pont   Love Canal Homeowners Association
Farmers   NIMBY groups

Source: EPA 25th Anniversary Report 1995.

recovers nine hundred gallons of waste into steel drums, which a disposal company picks up and takes to a disposal site. At the dump, the disposal company buries the drums in a pit lined with impermeable clay and a tough plastic liner. After burying the drums with dirt, it covers the whole pit to keep out rain, pumps out any leachate, and monitors the site indefinitely.

With the RCRA, Congress ventured into the wasteland of garbage traditionally left to the cities. Before, it was not considered an issue for the national level. Two perspectives may explain its expansion. At the macro level, this was still the period of big government when citizens and politicians believed that Washington could do a better job than cities and states. The "Feds" had expertise and the tax dollars had rolled in during the 1960s. The Clean Air and Water Acts were models, and the EPA under William Ruckelshaus and Russell Train appeared to fit the bill. Municipal efforts seemed inadequate. Crime had tainted cities like Elizabeth, New Jersey, where the Mafia controlled garbage collection.[2] Having completed its labors on the Clean Air and Water acts, Congress had time to turn to less severe pollution. The Safe Drinking Water Act of 1974 gave the EPA authority over groundwater, but contamination remained a danger. Disposal companies transported hazardous waste across state lines, but where it actually went was sometimes mysterious. Highway patrol officers occasionally found hazardous waste illegally dumped along rural roads, and sometimes it went to landfills where it leaked out.

LOVE CANAL AND THE SUPERFUND

Lois Gibbs, a housewife in Niagara Falls, New York, wondered why her son had epilepsy, why women in her neighborhood had so many miscarriages, and why foul chemicals oozed out of the ground. She soon discovered that she lived near an abandoned chemical dump. Starting in 1942, the Hooker Chemical company buried twenty thousand tons of its waste in an abandoned canal on its property. In 1953, it filled in Love Canal (named for William Love who dug it in 1892). At that time, no laws required a company to guard against future danger by lining the pit and keeping out water that would leach the waste. Later, the city board of educa-

Lois Gibbs trims a Christmas tree in the Love Canal Homeowners Association office with ornaments naming some of the chemicals found in Love Canal at Niagara Falls. The sign at the top reading "Hooker is no angel" refers to the Hooker Chemical Company, which used the site as a chemical dump for ten years. On the wall are posters warning of dioxin, another highly toxic substance found at the dump.

In Her Own Words: Lois Gibbs
Founder of the Love Canal Homeowners Association

When we moved into our house on 101st Street in 1972, I didn't even know Love Canal was there. It was a lovely neighborhood in a quiet residential area, with lots of trees and lots of children outside playing. It seemed just the place for our family. . . . There was a school within walking distance. I liked the idea of my children being able to walk to the 99th Street School. The school's playground was part of a big, open field with houses all around. . . .

It is really something, if you stop and think of it, that underneath that field were poisons and on top of it was a grade school and a playground. We later found out that the Niagara Falls School Board knew the filled-in canal was a toxic dump site. . . .[1]

The Love Canal Homeowners Association will go on in some form. We have been successful. We fought "City Hall," and we won! The association brought a new awareness to the world of what can happen if toxic, hazardous wastes are buried in the earth—our earth, not industry's earth. We are searching for alternative methods for toxic waste disposal. There is new legislation to handle "Love Canal," the Superfund.[2]

1. Lois Marie Gibbs, *Love Canal: My Story* (Albany: State University of New York Press, 1982), 9.
2. Ibid., 172.

---

tion asked the company to donate the site for an elementary school. At first the Hooker company refused, pointing out that the site was contaminated, but after pressure, sold the land for $1 on the condition it could not be liable for future danger. Eventually, the board built the 99th Street Elementary School on the site. Over the years the dangerous chemicals leaked out to poison the neighborhood. Homeowners complained of blisters when they dug in their gardens, of black sludge seeping into their basements, and of sickening vapors.[3]

When Gibbs recognized the problem she was twenty-six years old, had only a high school education, and was timid about speaking to strangers. Her first information came from a June 1978 article in the Niagara Falls' *Gazette*. In fact, the *Gazette* had published articles on the problem before, but no one, citizen or governmental, had taken action. Gibbs became the entrepreneur who mobilized the movement. After reading old articles in the newspaper morgue, she sought the advice of her brother-in-law who taught high school biology. Alarmed, Gibbs asked the school superintendent to transfer her six-year-old son to a different school in September. After he refused, she decided to circulate a petition among parents. When she knocked on the first door, anxiety overcame her and she quit. The next day she tried again, going to the father of her son's best friend, who signed. Her courage grew after other friends signed and she began to approach neighbors whom she did not know. In a few weeks, she recruited another mother who was willing to circulate the petition.[4]

Gibbs had few resources other than her time and her brother-in-law's advice about biology. In spite of her naivete, her natural talent for leadership soon emerged. When neighbors heard the Health Commissioner had rebuffed Gibbs at a meeting in Albany, four hundred people spontaneously gathered at the canal to welcome her home. Other mothers began to identify the cause as their own. They agreed that the Hooker Company was their antagonist and found a name to label the situation: "Love Canal." Their feelings were emotional and intense. With tears streaming down, a neighbor told the Niagara County legislature that "my little Julie is dead"—her baby girl was stillborn.[5]

By August 1978, the group organized itself as the Love Canal Homeowners Association. The association identified block captains, recruited members, and rented an office. When Gibbs's first captain said she did not know what to say when she knocked on a door, Gibbs wrote down a script, setting the grievance into a litany. The association raised the residents' consciousness about the contamination. It promoted its cause with conventional techniques of petitioning, writing letters, meeting with government officials, voting, and holding demonstrations. Eventually, it used unconventional techniques of taking hostages and sit-ins. When two EPA officials visited from headquarters, a crowd of five hundred surrounded the building and would not let them leave until the FBI rescued them.[6] Once at a public meeting, Gibbs would not leave the podium when the chairman ordered her to; after the police removed her from the room, she sneaked back twice—once, by pretending she was on a television crew and the other time through an unguarded door.

The Love Canal protesters communicated with the neighbors face-to-face in meetings and rallies. They soon learned the advantage of television and newspapers, which began coverage as soon as demonstrations started and frequently attended meetings and hearings with politicians. Even a local talk show invited Gibbs and her brother-in-law to talk about the association. When she appeared on the Phil Donahue show, she got a national audience, but showed her inexperience by using technical terminology and deferring too much to a scientist on the program.[7] Donahue invited her back two years later, along with forty neighbors. This time the show went well and boosted the movement. Later, Gibbs appeared on ABC's "Good Morning America." She and other mothers went to Washington to testify before Congressman Al Gore's subcommittee. During the 1980 Democratic Convention, association members went by bus to New York City to demonstrate outside Madison Square Garden.

Love Canal struck a chord throughout the country. Members of Congress began to champion the movement. The EPA and the state of New York negotiated an agreement to evacuate residents and clean the site. To capitalize on this for the election only six weeks away, Carter came to Buffalo to sign the agreement with the governor. Gibbs took the opportunity of being introduced to the stage to lecture Carter for twenty minutes on the residents's needs. In the years to follow, Gibbs rose in prominence, eventually heading the Citizens Clearinghouse for Hazardous Waste in Washington. Her spontaneous act of asking for signatures on a petition for her son's school led to Congress passing the Superfund law.

Although the Love Canal movement was extremely successful, numerous other organizations are born in the same manner. Like many environmental groups, the goal of the residents was quite specific. The mothers wanted to clean up their neighborhood, literally, their back yards. All across the United States, citizens want to clean up their neighborhoods, preserve a nearby river, block a factory near their homes, and so on. The term for this is NIMBY: Not In My Back Yard. The disturbance is literally close to home. The neighbors organize to prevent it and maintain the old situation. The new group does not particularly object to the facility being located far away. After all, they need electricity from new generating plants and consumer products from new factories. Hence, NIMBY is a subset of interest group behavior. NIMBY frustrates industry, even companies that want to be environmentally good citizens. An electric utility, for example, needs to build a new generating plant because its customers demand more electricity, but every time it finds a good location, nearby citizens object. They picket the site, intervene before the public utilities commission, and sue in court. Politicians usually back up the citizens because they want their votes.

While Love Canal was a tragedy, the potential cost to the chemical industry to detoxify old disposal sites was astronomical. A few barrels of poison that leak from a dump into the water table can cost millions to clean up. Unlike Hooker's Love Canal, most sites were not owned by a single company. The typical owner was a disposal company, many of which got into the business long before the industry recognized the risks or knew how to control them. Moreover, many dumped their chemicals in a municipal landfill so a city government (typically short of money) now bears the burden.

Based on Love Canal, Carter and many members of Congress believed only the national government could stand up to the power of the chemical industry. Furthermore, they did not want the government to pick up the whole expense, so industry was to help pay. Therefore, the Carter administration proposed a $600 million trust fund with contributions from both government and industry, but Congress augmented it to twice that amount: $1.2 billion. At one stage the subcommittee proposed the fund be $4.1 billion. Because the costs were so great, people began to call it the Superfund.

The Chemical Manufacturers Association lobbied hard against these proposals. The big companies feared the wide net the Superfund cast for liability, which was to be "joint and several." This definition meant that for a site which many companies had used over many years, any one of them could be forced to pay for the entire cleanup even if its own share of disposing had been slight. For example, if General Motors had used a dump, along with many other companies over the past fifty years, many of which were no longer in business, GM (along with the companies still in operation) would have to cover the entire cost to detoxify the dump. Obviously large companies were against the idea. The Chemical Association's lobbying was not very successful, however, especially since members of Congress wanted to protect their constituents. Two of the biggest association members, Du Pont and Union Carbide, broke ranks, fearing that since it seemed inevitable Congress would pass some kind of law, for them to be reasonable and obtain a compromise made more sense. The eventual law had a fund of $1.6 billion and eliminated "joint and several liability."

The Superfund law, officially the Comprehensive Emergency Response, Compensation, and Liability Act (CERCLA), was supposed to respond to the emergency in Love Canal and a thousand other dumps. The motto was "shovels first and lawyers later." The EPA was to assess the damage, find one or more companies that could pay to clean it up, and later have that company collect from other companies that had used the site. If private money was not available immediately, the $1.6 billion revolving fund would ensure money to begin work immediately. Later, the EPA would identify the responsible parties. The goal was to remove leaking barrels, drain holding ponds, and dig up contaminated soil.

In fact, little happened. The EPA identified thousands of dangerous sites and determined several hundred that were first priority. It even began cleanup on some sites. But at most locations the agency was stymied. The potential costs to a company were so high that it found the costs to be much cheaper to fight the EPA in court than to detoxify the dump. Moreover, the law was uncertain about its objective, whether it was to contain the damage, to make dumping sites as clean as other industrial land, or to make them 100 percent clean. Worse still, the contaminated waste and soil often merely went to another dump where it could again leak out. CERCLA also allowed the EPA to consider the cost, which exacerbated this shell game.

The Superfund became Anne Gorsuch's downfall; her angel of death was Rita LaVelle. Like Gorsuch, LaVelle came to Washington at the beginning of the Reagan administration to look for a political job. Her chief qualification was an influential friend, Ed Meese, one of Reagan's top three aides in the White House. At age twenty-two she had been Meese's secretary back in California. Most recently, she had worked on the public relations staff of the Aerojet General Corporation in California, but her education was minimal and her reputation for intelligence was not high. Meese asked the White House personnel office to put LaVelle on a list of job candidates sent to the EPA. As the EPA administrator, Gorsuch interviewed LaVelle and declined to hire her, but later she accepted her to head the Superfund program due to White House pressure and the absence of other candidates. Gorsuch rationalized her choice on the basis that the division had two talented career civil servants as managers.

LaVelle's vague connection with the White House is far from unique in Washington. Every new administration faces the need to fill about six hundred vacancies at that level or higher throughout the bureaucracy. A paramount concern is loyalty to the new president and his team. Too often a new administration has discovered to its regret that it has given jobs to those who do not advance its policies. The most common problem is officials who keep working on the policies of the previous administration. Meese, who had devoted most of his career to state government, did not share the common belief of the Reagan administration that government was an embarrassment. On the other hand, the Reagan

White House was vulnerable to an ambitious man or woman exploiting a vague connection. The president himself probably was already suffering the early stages of Alzheimer's disease, an affliction that takes decades to develop. Also, the White House staff during the first term did not have a chief of staff, but three co-equals, which prevented clear lines of authority.

Almost immediately upon beginning her job, LaVelle displayed a pattern of disregard for the EPA mission and abuse of her authority. She quarreled with other divisions of the EPA. She pressured the Enforcement Division to be lenient toward polluters; the regional offices believed she was keeping money to which they were entitled at headquarters. Gorsuch soon heard that LaVelle telephoned the White House several time a week, but did not know to whom she talked. If the calls were for Ed Meese, Gorsuch would have reason to be nervous; perhaps, Meese was giving LaVelle secret orders. When Gorsuch wanted to work on Superfund matters, she bypassed LaVelle and went directly to the civil service managers. As a whole, LaVelle seemed to have abused her powers and contradicted the EPA's mission. For example, LaVelle wrote a letter claiming that toxic waste was no more dangerous to children than eating a candy bar. Congressman Dingell received a copy (presumably passed on by an EPA employee), and hauled her before his committee to justify it. Her testimony was confused and unconvincing. On a visit to Milwaukee, she arrogantly demanded a private jet and a police escort. She lied to Gorsuch and put two employees to work on puffing up her personal image. LaVelle took an active interest in cleaning up the Superfund site at Stringfellow in California where her former employer, Aerojet, had dumped hazardous wastes. In her EPA position, she could save Aerojet millions of dollars. When this came to the attention of Dingell, she testified under oath that she had "rescued" herself (that is, not participated) in decisions about Stringfellow. More generally, LaVelle had a bias in favor of private companies to the detriment of the environment.

The last straw for Gorsuch was when LaVelle wrote and leaked to the *New York Times* a letter criticizing her rival, the head of the Enforcement Division. The Enforcement Division had been negotiating with a company over penalties for a violation and had reached an impasse. LaVelle intervened to talk with the violator herself, thereby sabotaging the Enforcement Division. On Friday, February 4, Gorsuch told LaVelle she was fired. Unfortunately, Gorsuch was not following the correct personnel procedures; because LaVelle was a presidential appointee, Gorsuch had to get White House approval. On Monday, Meese agreed and had the president sign her official dismissal. However, Gorsuch had forgotten to get LaVelle's office key on Friday, so LaVelle came in over the weekend to remove official documents.

In a rare proceeding, LaVelle was indicted in a criminal action. She was charged with making false statements to the EPA administrator Gorsuch, obstructing a congressional committee, perjuring herself twice before the Senate Committee on Public Works and the Environment, and perjuring herself before the House Committee on Public Works and Transportation. LaVelle was tried and convicted in December 1983 and sentenced to six months in jail, a $10,000 fine, and five years probation.

In fall of 1982, Gorsuch found LaVelle was only one of her troubles. Her critics blamed her for poor management of the EPA, ousting dedicated scientists and administrators because they did not toe the Reagan line, misplacing $53 million of Superfund, being too cozy with industry lobbyists, favoring friends in industry, and excessive secrecy. Gorsuch herself attributes much of the unraveling to becoming a guinea pig for White House and Justice Department lawyers eager for a Supreme Court case to promote executive privilege, the legal doctrine that the president can withhold information from Congress. Nixon had asserted this privilege when trying to defend himself during the Watergate scandal.[8]

In early 1982, these lawyers intended to use James Watt, the secretary of the interior, but Watt would not cooperate. Needing a new guinea pig, they recruited Gorsuch, saying Reagan wanted her to do it. According to her account, the episode was contrived to enhance the authority of the president, and behind that, to enhance the reputation of the lawyer—the case had nothing to do with environmental policy. The chief conflict centered on information Dingell requested for his committee. Soon thereafter, Congressman Levitas requested information too. Gorsuch directed the EPA to give Dingell's committee "several drawers" of paperwork, minus twenty-three pages that would indicate specific investigations. The EPA also withheld several dozen pages from Levitas's subcommittee. Once the EPA refused to turn over the material voluntarily, the subcommittee issued a subpoena, which the EPA refused to honor. In December, the subcommittee voted to recommend to the full House of Representatives to hold Gorsuch in contempt of Congress, a rare procedure. The House passed the contempt citation by 259 to 105. Dingell's committee moved in parallel with its own subpoena and, finally, contempt citation.[9]

At this point, when the Reagan administration and the Democratic Congress had joined the issue for grand combat before the Supreme Court, the White House had second thoughts. It began negotiations with Levitas about a compromise. Then in response to a question at a press conference, Reagan replied "I can no longer insist on executive privilege if there is a suspicion in the minds of the American people that it is being used to cover up wrong-doing." Reagan's press officer promptly issued a press release "correcting" the president, stating that he really did not mean what he said.[10]

By March, Gorsuch's situation became hopeless. The White House and the Justice Department gave up on pushing the president's right of executive privilege, even though the congressional contempt citations were against her, not them. Their negotiation with the congressional committees barely touched on the EPA. Finally, the Justice Department said it would no longer act as her lawyer when she testified before Dingell's committee, and it even hinted of a criminal investigation against her. Television reporters staked out Gorsuch's house every morning to ask questions before she drove to work and met her at the EPA headquarters when she arrived. If she were to go before Dingell's committee as scheduled in a few days, she feared she would be arrested and jailed for contempt. At last she hired an attorney to represent her personally and holed up in his office for two days. Resignation was the only way out. The White House wanted the problem to disappear and if she were not head of the EPA, she would no longer be in contempt. A small concession Gorsuch extracted from the White House was an exit interview with the president. There, she laid out her complaints for ten minutes, to which an ill-at-ease Reagan mumbled a vague reply and quickly terminated the conversation.[11]

RISK

In 1986, Congress amended the Toxic Substances Control Act to deal with the perceived problem of asbestos. This program, which took asbestos out of buildings, was expensive, and, in fact, created more danger than if the asbestos had simply been left in place and sealed. The blundering in handling the asbestos policy illustrates the problems government faces in dealing with risk and uncertainty. Managing risk is hard enough; uncertainty is worse. The distinction is that risk is a probability that is known, not an uncertain probability. For example, the risk over fifty years of dying in an auto accident is 2 percent, whereas the risk of dying from a nuclear meltdown is unknown. Statisticians do not have enough information to calculate the danger. This uncertainty was the dilemma for asbestos. In the early 1980s, the risk seemed high. Moreover, people tend to exaggerate the risk of rare events and underestimate the risk of common ones. Most believe that they are better than average drivers, more likely than average to live past the age of eighty, and less likely than average to contract cancer. On the other hand, people overestimate rare risks like being struck by lightning. As news about asbestos circulated in the early 1980s, people overestimated the risk.

A further problem government faces in dealing with risk is balancing it against the cost. Many toxic substances are extremely rare, but the EPA insists on controlling them regardless of the expense. The most extreme standard is to completely ban the chemical. For instance, the Delaney Clause of Food Drug and Cosmetic Act (named after the Congressman who proposed it) directs that the public should not be exposed to any carcinogen. This law forces the Food and Drug Administration to feed mice gallons of diet drinks before banning the products that cause tumors to grow. In fact, some low levels might be acceptable.

Environmental laws are not as rigid as this, but many do not permit the EPA to consider the costs. This leads to some astronomical expenses for every life saved. If the Superfund law were to be fully implemented, the outlay will be hundreds of billions of dollars. Strict controls on benzene emissions by tire manufacturers will cost $340 million for each life saved. Cleaning up waste uranium near mines will cost $190 million for each life saved. On the other hand, removing lead from gasoline has no net cost and protecting against radiation from X ray machines will be only $400,000 per life saved.

An alternative perspective is to compare the benefits of cleaning up a Superfund site to a different environmental danger such as old lead paint, radon, air pollution, and so on. The actual danger from chemical dumps is small. Would

93

it be better to spend $1 billion on a different pollutant? This risk-risk analysis compares one danger to another, then recommends spending money where it will do the most good. One economist argues that to spend more than $10 million to save a life is perverse, because there are many other risks that can be reduced for that amount. Others would put the figure lower.

Most generally, one may ask whether cleaning up pollution is better than increasing prosperity. The health benefits of wealth are clear: people with higher incomes live longer and are healthier. Reducing people's income by taxes or higher prices for products defies logic if a higher income would keep them healthier. The dollar amount for this trade off, however, remains unknown. A further twist is that people with more money enjoy the environment more. They own boats and summer cottages, travel to national parks, and have leisure time for hiking and canoeing.

The class and income bias of a clean environment means that people who are poor live in central cities and are non-white are at a disadvantage. Dumps are more likely to be in poor neighborhoods. A 1992 study of the Superfund found penalties under hazardous waste laws were five times as high in white areas as in non-white areas.[12] The Michigan Department of Natural Resources studied sport fishermen in order to determine acceptable levels of toxic discharges into the water. It found that racial minorities and those who had less income ate more fish.[13] Besides sportsmen, poor people fish for food. The consequence of this income and racial bias may be, however, not to clean up toxics but to increase prosperity. If a poor black man gets a good paying job, he may not have to fish for his dinner in the Detroit River.

The EPA frequently regulates according to technological standards. It requires a factory or sewage plant to use the best available technology or the best practicable technology reasonably economically available. The latter implies a trade-off with cost. Balancing the costs against the benefits of regulation forms an undercurrent. Environmental laws rarely endorse it, but the principle has a logic that is hard to ignore. Difficulties come in implementing technical standards. Determining the costs is relatively easy—a company must use different chemicals in manufacturing or remove certain toxins, and the EPA and state agencies must spend money for monitoring and regulating. Determining the benefits is where the difficulties begin to develop. If the manufacturer removes a toxin or particulates, how much cancer or asthma does it prevent? Knowing the numbers is nearly impossible.

Moreover, the government cannot agree on how to calculate the value of a human life. Is a person priceless? Is the value equal to future earnings minus living expenses and adjusted for the interest rate? This is the method courts use for accidents and murders. Typical amounts range from $100,000 to several million dollars for a working adult. Another avenue is to see how much premium pay workers demand for danger. A coal miner may earn an extra $5,000 per year for working underground where he faces one chance in a hundred of death. In effect, the miner places a $10 million value on his life. A third avenue is to base the calculation on how much people spend on safety equipment. Assuming a home smoke detector costs $20 and saves one life in ten thousand, the value a person places on his or her life is $200,000. Overall, economists estimate average middle-class Americans act as if their lives were worth $3 to $5 million.

A way to avoid the problem of placing a dollar amount on a human life is to compare the cost effectiveness of alternative means of accomplishing identical goals. For example, what is the best way to prevent ten thousand cases of cancer? One option is to clean up the environment, another is for the National Cancer Institute to conduct basic medical research, a third is clinical research, a fourth is screening people for early detection, a fifth is to educate the public, and so forth. For the past one hundred fifty years, basic research has given the biggest bang for the buck, but by its very nature, predicting its success is impossible.

The problem with removing asbestos is the danger to the workers doing the job. The initial objective was to protect the public, especially children in schools. But to remove it caused its dust to scatter into the air where the workers might breathe it in a concentrated form. This balancing was not one to one. Workers wore protective clothes and masks and received training for safety. Moreover, they knew the risks and could decline the job. After removal came the problem of transportation and disposal. Finally, the EPA realized leaving the asbestos in place and sealing it so none could escape was a better option. This was safer and much cheaper.

THE SUPERFUND AMENDMENTS AND THE REAUTHORIZATION ACT (SARA)

By 1985, the Superfund problems were obvious. Rita LaVelle's escapades had dramatized the dangers of corruption and incompetence. Anne Gorsuch's policy of not spending the fund all at once had failed to clean up more than a handful of sites. Moreover, Congress kept score by the number of sites identified rather than the number cleaned and Congress pressured the EPA to clean the worst dumps first, regardless of whether they presented the most danger to health. Many sites pose comparatively little risk because the amount of contamination is small, their location is remote, or rainfall is low. The EPA could not decide how clean was clean; should it be suitable for residential houses, a factory, or just enough to eliminate the chemicals seeping into the water table?

Congress was unhappy that a large portion of the expenditures, especially in the early days, were for attorney fees. This spending was because of the requirement to find the guilty parties and punish them. The law was retroactive, because in years past, most of the dumping was legal. Companies accused of being responsible feared not only high costs for their old chemicals, but because of the joint and several liability provision, they stood the chance of having to pay for other companies that were no longer in business. While lawyers were expensive, they were far cheaper than the actual removal of hazardous waste. Lawyers were not the only professionals to earn high fees, however. Environmental engineers, hydrologists, and chemists had to analyze the site to estimate its extent, drainage, and contaminants.

With the advice of William Ruckelshaus, whom Reagan had enticed back to direct the EPA after Gorsuch resigned, the president proposed reauthorizing the Superfund in his state of the union address in January 1984. He declined to send a draft bill, however. (Skeptics concluded it was election year posturing to avoid further tarnishing his image.) In fact, no bill passed and the authority expired in 1985. Congress studied and debated the issue another year until the election put pressure on Republicans in Congress and on Reagan. The inefficiency and manipulation at the EPA was a black mark to overcome. Besides, Reagan feared that Congress might make the fund even larger, perhaps to $20 billion. In October, Congress passed and Reagan signed the Superfund Amendments and Reauthorization Act (SARA). The election was less than three weeks away.

Although sites were located in nearly every congressional district, the Superfund did not fit the standard model of pork barrel. Having a site was an embarrassment likely to scare new business away from the region. Many communities tried to keep their toxic dumps off the list. In the first few years, the money was for analyzing the contamination and determining who was legally responsible, which meant the money went to engineers and lawyers, not local businesses. When the operation actually got underway, the work was so technical and risky that the contractors were big firms, and almost always from out of town.

The SARA increased the trust fund to $8.5 billion dollars, at least $3 billion more than the Reagan administration wanted. The money came from a petroleum tax of $2.75 billion, tax on chemical corporations of $2.5 billion, a tax on chemical feedstocks of $1.4 billion, a contribution from treasure general revenues of $1.25 billion, and $600 million recovered from industries that had used the sites. It directed the EPA to clean up 275 sites in three years and a total of 650 in five years. With a separate fund of $500 million, the SARA extended coverage to leaking underground storage tanks (LUST) such as those in old gasoline service stations, which soon put many small firms out of business. (The acronym of LUST proved too titillating so it was changed to UST.)

Motivated by the example of Lois Gibbs's problem that industry and government agencies kept secret information about what chemicals were dumped and what the dangers were, Congress included Title III, the Community Right to Know. In addition to requiring industry to inform the public about which chemicals they disposed of, it established a program of small grants for citizens like the Love Canal Homeowners Association. The money might be used, for example, to perform tests to identify and measure the contaminants.

Vacant buildings and abandoned industrial sites contaminated by chemicals lay a curse on older cities. Called brownfields (in contrast to greenfields outside the city), they scare away investors and bankers. CERCLA makes a new owner responsible for cleaning up the site in spite of the fact that the new factory will make the site safer than it was before. For instance, workers in a new factory or warehouse face little danger once the concrete is poured and the parking lot is covered with asphalt. Unfortunately, for both investors and cities, CERCLA leaves little flexibility. Furthermore, the new owner will be responsible for all costs to completely restore the land. The investor or bank does not know the future expenses or whether the site can ever be cleaned completely to satisfy the EPA. Even if the EPA is satisfied, local citizens who unreasonably fear cancer or toxics beyond scientific standards have many opportunities to intervene, causing delay or possibly deny permission.

Faced with such technical and legal uncertainty, most investors shun brownfields. The city is then left with the contaminated land and the unemployment. CERCLA even discourages the reuse of uncontaminated land, because no one can be sure if the land is unpolluted until it is tested, which can cost tens of thousands of dollars. An additional fear of investors and bankers is the EPA's reputation of changing its regulations. CERCLA retroactively imposed liability for dumping that was not illegal at the time. As a way to resolve this dilemma, a number of state environmental agencies began to evaluate brownfields case by case and, when the new use was industrial, for example, negotiate an agreement not to demand additional cleanup in the future. While the EPA recognized the benefits of this compromise, it was reluctant to make agreements of its own. As pressure built, however, it began to issue "letters of comfort," which were much the same except more cagy by not actually agreeing not to sue in the future. These were a lawyer's, rather than an engineer's, solutions.

Many cities are short of landfills. Ohio handled the problem by passing a law that requires all counties to establish a Solid Waste District or to join one with its neighbors. This district is to coordinate solid waste disposal, largely by controlling the dumps. Objections to the law are that it puts an unnecessary burden on cities that have planned for the future and have adequate landfills. Their costs increase without giving any benefit. An objection in terms of democratic procedures is that formerly the responsibility of a municipality or county lay with an elected mayor, council members, or commissioners whom the citizens could hold responsible. The board of directors which manages the district is appointed and hard to be held accountable. Districts combining several counties are less accountable still.

From the perspective of economic theory, solid waste should not be conflated with other forms of pollution like air or water, which are collective goods where all citizens or at least many citizens share in the benefits or costs and to deny the benefits to those who do not contribute is difficult. If the air is to be clean for one person, it has to be clean for everyone, at least everyone in the region. The benefits of clean water are not quite as collective. For solid waste removal, however, the benefit is not collective, but individual. Picking up garbage from one house does not benefit a neighbor who has his or her own garbage removal problems. (Of course if it rots, it becomes collective problem of air pollution.)

Traditionally, municipalities have picked up garbage free of charge and rural townships or counties have not. Rural residents either dispose of their own or pay a private company to collect it. In fact, cities are not as generous as they may seem. Typically they only pick up from single family houses and duplexes. Apartment houses of four or more units are required to make their own arrangements with a private company. Thus, the tenants pay a higher rent while those in houses receive the service at no cost. Today, however, municipalities are reexamining free collection that is paid for by taxes. A common source is a property tax, which has the hidden assumption that more expensive houses produce more garbage—an assumption not based on the facts, at least not proportionately to their taxes. Some cities use municipal income taxes, which has the hidden assumption that richer people produce more garbage—an assumption that is also inaccurate or at least exaggerated. Many of these cities tax commuters who work downtown, but live in a suburb, hence these tax payers receive no benefit at all.

Many municipalities see the advantage of changing to a more rational system where those who benefit will pay the cost. Having households pay a fee is logical and would release tax funds for more important priorities. Under the label of Reinventing Government and pressure from the recent fiscal squeeze, municipalities have begun to charge for collection. The next question becomes how to structure the fee. The same amount for all households gives no incentive to minimize the waste or to recycle. Charging $1 per can is more logical. Seattle bills this way, which leads to the "Seattle Stomp" in which once a week otherwise normal people stand in their garbage cans and stomp it down to make more room. Stomping does no good for the city as a whole because the trucks compact it anyway. On the other hand, charging according to weight requires the citizen to have faith in the garbage collector's eye or in the crew to actually and accurately weigh each can.

REDUCE, REUSE, AND RECYCLE

Recycling has gained popularity. Environmentalists idolize it and children beg their parents to do it. Many cities pick up aluminum cans, plastic bottles, and old newspapers at curbside or at centers near grocery stores. Curbside pickup is more expensive for the city due to extra labor and trucks, but the service increases the volume. Unfortunately, recycling often wastes money. Aluminum is about the only profitable material; a can is worth about a penny. States like Michigan and Vermont that charge a deposit of 5 or 10 cents may prevent litter, but at a high price. No material other than aluminum gives a net profit.

This does not preclude recycling, however, because even at a loss, it may defray the expense. For example, a ton of news print may be worth only $20, but the cost to dump it in a landfill would be $50. Recycling lowers the cost by $30. Old newsprint hovers at the border of profitability. In 1980, the price was high enough to cause a number of cities to collect it. But, ten years later, so many cities were recycling newspapers that the buyers could not use more. Regrettably, the ink, if not washed out, discolors the new paper, which increases the expense. Moreover, some inks are toxic and require special care. Corrugated cardboard is another prod-

Curbside recycling sorted into glass, plastic, newspapers, and cardboard. Although recycling rarely makes a profit, it defrays the cost of disposal.

uct close to profitability, being worth $80 per ton. Because retail stores receive and use so much cardboard, recycling can be concentrated, hence cheaper.

Plastics are a tough case. The four different types must be sorted. In the past, cities did this by hand, which was costly. Ottawa Hills, Ohio, used mentally handicapped workers. When a city uses curbside collection, it finds ordinary citizens are not very reliable in sorting. Buyers insist quality be controlled because having the wrong type will contaminate the rest of a batch. Now, machinery is improving, but only a few cities find recycling plastics worth the effort. In fact, Philadelphia stopped collecting plastic in order to save $400,000.

A suggested solution to the cost is to force manufacturers to incorporate it into the price they charge the consumer. Senator Max Baucus proposed this in 1993. His rationale was that old cans, plastic bottles, and yesterday's newspapers are a form of pollution like soot or sewage. Those who "emit" it should clean it up or pay a penalty. A technique might be for the EPA to analyze the extra cost for each type of bottle, can or wrapping a manufacturer produces, then charge a fee on the volume. As it is, municipalities or individuals pay. The flaw with this scheme, however, is that charging the manufacturer does not offer any incentive for the consumer. The idea did not find much support then, and the Republican victory in 1994 moved into eclipse. In the age of Reinventing Government, even Democrats do not want to establish a garbage police.

Despite being a symbol of environmentalism, recycling is the least desirable of the three methods. The best is to reduce the amount. The government bureaucracy itself has a great appetite for paper from reports that may not be read and for extra photocopies. The U.S. Postal Service urges business customers to be more efficient in bulk mailing by keeping accurate, up-to-date mailing lists. Constructing a new house generates seven tons of waste lumber, concrete, plastic and steel. Better planning and cutting can reduce this; so can using scraps on the job and recycling plastic and metal. Many corporations are redesigning their products. Bottles and cans are containing less glass or steel. Twenty years ago a bottle holding sixteen ounces of soda or beer weighed twelve ounces; today it weighs eight ounces, one third less. All this not only reduces the volume going to a landfill, but saves the manufacturer and distributor money.

Grass clippings and fallen leaves make up a quarter of the waste sent to landfills. Because most cities collect garbage free of charge, people have no reason to change. The regulations are supposed to encourage people to simply leave the clippings on the lawn or to compost the grass and leaves, both of which fertilize the yard. Modern lawnmowers can chop grass and leaves to a fine mulch. Nevertheless, voters prefer to have garbage trucks pick it up. The sanitation workers prefer it too because they fear less waste will lead to fewer jobs. In Toledo, where labor unions are powerful, the Teamsters' Union persuaded the mayor and council to rescind its plan to end collecting yard waste.

The Ohio solid waste law establishes centralized composting stations, perhaps one for every hundred thousand residents. Municipal trucks will take grass there and, a year later, will sell the compost. Many cities that collect leaves in bulk off the streets already take them to farms to put on the fields. The Ohio system of centralized composting strikes its critics as illogical because it seems to echo the big government methods of a former age. Buying every household a fancy compost bin to let them do it themselves would be cheaper.

The notion of reusing bottles amounts to recycling an old method. Fifty years ago the milkman delivered several quarts along with butter and eggs to the door each morning before breakfast. The family drank the milk, rinsed the thick bottles and the next morning the milkman collected them. While the good old days are gone, some residents of Minnesota can buy milk in reusable plastic bottles at their local 7-Eleven store. The price is lower than for disposable cartons.

Congress addressed the benefits of reduction, reuse, and recycling in the Pollution Prevention Act of 1990. Although passed along with the Clear Air Act Amendments, the law stands alone and applies to all forms of pollution and waste.

LYNN WHITE ON "OUR ECOLOGICAL CRISIS"

Hazardous and toxic waste epitomize the worst pollution modern industrial society faces. It is ubiquitous, found in every city and much of the countryside. It is inevitable for virtually no manufactured product is free of some dangerous byproduct. It is insulting, demonstrating that the best technology and government regulations cannot prevent it completely. On the other hand, sulfur dioxide emitted from smokestacks, phosphates discharged into a river, and garbage dumped in a landfill are ubiquitous, inevitable, and insulting, also.

In an article that has been debated for over three decades, Lynn White addresses the historical roots of the ecological crisis. He begins with the observation that both science and technology are Occidental. Unlike the traditional Orient, the Western world believes in the idea of progress. White holds that science and technology will not develop in a culture that believes things will not change or that they are cyclical, always coming back to the past. To believe in progress means that time is linear, not cyclical. White traces the origin of progress, that is the idea of time going forward in a line instead of circling back, to the religion of the ancient Hebrews and as amplified in Christianity. Jews believe God created the world and revealed himself to his Chosen People through Abraham, Moses, and the prophets. God created the earth, putting Adam and Eve in the Garden of Eden, where the purpose of nature was to serve humans. Judaism is a historical religion; it depends on knowing the past. Christianity extended this belief.[14]

White argues that the Judeo-Christian religion points humanity in the wrong direction by making time linear rather than circular. The sinister consequence is the idea of progress, which means more technology, more smoke, and more hazardous waste. In saving contrast, White tells how Greek paganism believed that time was cyclical and that trees, streams, and animals had guardian spirits. The Greek word for that spirit was *anima*. When a carpenter needed to chop down a tree, he prayed to the tree's *anima* to explain how he needed lumber to build a house and offered a small sacrifice. In this fashion, the Greeks respected nature. White maintains that, in contrast, Christianity puts nature in second place, where nature serves the purpose of humans. As further evidence, he points out that Christian saints do not live in trees or streams, but in heaven, as remote from nature as possible. White does identify one happy exception: Francis of Assisi. Francis rejected his father's wealth and the materialism of the thirteenth-century city of Assisi to live as a hermit in the hills where he prayed and sang. He lived in harmony with the sun and the moon and the birds and the beasts. Eventually, his holiness inspired followers to praise God through nature and to serve the poor and sick.[15]

In this popular critique, White takes aim at Judeo-Christianity both indirectly for fostering the assumption of time as linear and directly for not respecting nature. While many may agree with his insight about linear versus cyclical concepts of time, he does not consider other causes. Ancient civilizations other than the Hebrews advanced their technologies and organization, or in other words, made progress. Indeed, the Hebrews were not as advanced as the Egyptians, the Babylonians, or the Greeks. The invention of writing in Sumer appears to be more important than religion. Writing on clay tablets or on papyrus gave the capacity to store much more information than human memory. The topics on the very oldest tablets recorded business and taxes such as receipts for cattle and grain paid to the king. Written stories and religion came later.

Although White points to the Greeks as a positive example, by the Golden Age of Plato and Aristotle, they had deforested all their mountains and allowed the soil to erode on their once fertile coastal plains. Moreover, Greek life was cyclical, at least in part, because of their constant wars. Good government and skilled diplomacy might have helped the environment more than prayers to a wood nymph. White neglects the contemporaneous Persian and Roman empires. Ancient Persian laws regulated cutting trees and building irrigation systems. The Roman Empire, which remained pagan until A.D. 313, had environmental regulations and aqueducts for clean water. With respect to the timing of the damage progress inflicted on the environment, the crucial year is not in the ancient era but more like 1400 when the population of Europe began to grow upward with no stopping. Although historians do not agree on a cause for population and wealth increasing at this time, Christian theology seems unlikely.

White finds much company in criticizing Judeo-Christianity for anti-environmental beliefs. In the first of the two creation stories in Genesis, chapter 1, God creates the heavens and the earth for man's enjoyment, creates Adam in his own image (unlike the animals), and gives man dominion over the earth. In the alternative creation story in chapter 2, "The Lord God took the man and placed him in the garden of Eden to till it and tend it." God directs Adam to name the animals. White and others castigate this as commanding man to dominate nature, not to live as one being among others.

Theologians, on the other hand, interpret the creation stories as commandments to be a good steward of the natural environment. The Jesuit, Albert Fritsch, considers Adam's failure in Eden to be just the first of many sins against the earth which calls for a journey of redemption. Protecting the environment fits with protecting the poor, the hungry, and the sick. He concludes that ". . . because we have damaged the seamless web of life, we need to restore it."[16] Most Protestant and Jews agree; the old divisions are not echoed in regard to the environment. In his encyclical message, "The Ecological Crisis," Pope John Paul II writes that "the ecological crisis is a moral issue." The American Baptist Churches call for its members to be stewards of the earth at a time of "explosive growth of population, the depletion of nonrenewable resources, tropical deforestation, the pollution of air, land, and water, waste of precious materials, and the general assault on God's creation . . ."[17]

More recently, evangelical Protestant churches have revived the issue of humanity's place in nature. These churches, enjoying a surge of membership and energy, have allied with conservative Republicans to increase their political influence. Ardent evangelicals believe the end of the world is near. The logical consequence is to diminish the importance of the environment. If the whole earth is about to be destroyed, why bother with preserving forests or endangered species? Reagan's secretary of the interior, James Watt, gave voice to this only two weeks into the new administration when he told a congressional committee: "I do not know how many future generations we can count on before the Lord returns."[18] While Watt's sincere prophesy about the end of the world alarmed environmentalists, the movement itself often prophesizes its own apocalypse due to toxic chemicals and greenhouse gases.

The issue of hazardous waste seems to attract more than its share of heat and emotion. Lois Gibbs first exhibited this, then capitalized on it at Love Canal. The EPA's disintegration with Rita LaVelle's shenanigans with the Stringfellow site in California might have passed unnoticed if it were just one more factory polluting the air. The Delany Clause absolutely forbidding a food shown (often under farfetched assumptions) to cause cancer causes alarm because of the extreme fear of the disease. Cost benefit often flies out the window in the face of emotion. Congress passes laws that cost $500 million for every life saved, while ignoring cheap ways like prenatal care of mothers or ending subsidies for tobacco farmers. The only other environmental danger viewed in these extreme terms is radioactivity.

CONCLUSION

Lois Gibbs and her neighbors who sounded the alarm about Love Canal is a dramatic case of the life cycle of a mass movement. With chemicals oozing out of the ground, the grass roots protest started with a grievance, and grew eventually to national proportions prompting Congress to establish the Superfund. Only two and a half years elapsed from the time Gibbs learned of the danger at the 99th Street Elementary School until Congress passed CERCLA. Her personal skills at organizing and persuading were outstanding. She had a flair for publicity that advanced her crusade. On the other hand, when she began she was shy and inexperienced. She began with few resources other than her brother-in-law's knowledge as a biology teacher. The localized nature of hazardous waste lends itself to grass roots protest. In many less dramatic cases, neighbors have banded together to say "not in my backyard." Unlike air pollution, the disturbance is local and usually can be blamed on a single company or dump.

Gibbs's own organization evolved into a Washington interest group: the Citizens Clearinghouse for Hazardous Wastes. While this and other citizen groups exist, the better-financed interest groups are on the industry side such as the Chemical Manufacturers Association. The industry side enjoys the resources of money, expertise, and full-time lobbying. Its advantages compared to citizen groups are huge, which calls into question the argument of the pluralists that one group can balance another.

The Republican party's bias toward business lay at the root of its problems at the EPA while Rita LaVelle managed the Superfund. Her favoritism of her former employer, Aerojet, seemed to be the most outrageous. Although Anne Gorsuch was first unaware of, and later opposed to LaVelle's misbehavior, Gorsuch's response was too little too late. Moreover, Gorsuch tried to spend as little of the Superfund as she could, which delayed cleaning up dangerous sites. After about two years of these and other problems, the White House realized that the mess at the EPA and the Reagan administration's pro-industry bias had gone too far. Opposition came from Congress, even from Republican members, which threatened Reagan's popularity with the voters.

In principle, risk analysis ought to suit the bureaucracy well. It consists of identifying a "problem" and proceeding to solve it, supposedly what its experts thrive on. Engineers, scientists, and statisticians should excel. In fact, the EPA has taken the opposite tact, clinging to traditional definitions that are absolute, pointing out that the laws Congress passed do not permit the EPA to make decisions based on risk analysis. It must adhere to existing procedures. An alternative way to address the difficulties is to note that while some bureaucratic experts might thrive on risk analysis, a whole legion of others already have defined their environmental problems in a way that excludes the techniques of risk analysis. Lawyers and enforcement specialists are at the top of this list.

NOTES

1. Rachel Carson, *Silent Spring* (Boston: Houghton Mifflin, 1962).
2. Alan A. Block and Frank Scarpitti, *Poisoning for Profit* (New York: William Morrow, 1985).
3. Lois Gibbs, *Love Canal: My Story* (Albany, NY: State University of New York Press, 1982).
4. Ibid.
5. Ibid.
6. Ibid., 147–149.
7. Ibid., 76.
8. Anne M. [Gorsuch] Burford, *Are You Tough Enough?* (New York: McGraw Hill, 1986), 163.
9. Ibid.
10. Ibid., 173
11. Ibid., 225.
12. Marianne LaVelle and Marcia Coyle, "Unequal Protection: The Racial Divide in Environmental Law" *The National Law Journal* 15 (1992): S1–S12.
13. Patrick West et al., "Minorities and Toxic Fish Consumption" in Bunyan Bryant, ed., *Environmental Justice* (Washington, DC: Island Press, 1995), 131.
14. Lynn White, "The Historical Roots of our Ecologic Crisis" *Science* 155 (1967): 1203–1207.
15. Ibid.
16. Albert J. Fritsch, SJ, "A Catholic Approach" in John E. Carroll, Paul Brockelman, and Mary Westfall, eds., *The Greening of Faith* (Hanover: University Press of New England, 1997), 130.
17. American Baptist Churches, USA, "Creation and the Covenant of Caring" in Roger Gottlieb, ed., *This Sacred Earth* (New York: Routledge, 1996), 238.
18. Robert Booth Fowler, *The Greening of Protestant Thought* (Chapel Hill: University of North Carolina Press, 1995), 47.

CHAPTER 5
RADIATION CONTROL

In comparison to the widespread pollution of the air and water, or even hazardous waste, the problem of radiation is small. The physicists and engineers who built the atomic bomb and invented a reactor to generate electricity were aware of the dangers. The civilian nuclear industry has been regulated since its beginning, and the incidents of contamination have been few. Virtually no deaths can be attributed to power plants and only a few to mining. Nevertheless, public anxiety is high, higher than for much more dangerous pollutants. Protesters have picketed, chained themselves to fences, and gone to jail. Citizens routinely intervene before the Department of Energy and state public utility commissions to block new plants, and they often prevail. Environmentalists successfully pressured the utilities to shut down the Shoreham plant on Long Island and the Seabrook plant in New Hampshire.

Even though the American record for safety is excellent, popular fears have some justification, at least for the potential of danger. Radioactivity can kill and has in other countries. The explosion of the Chernobyl nuclear plant in Ukraine in 1986 killed 270 directly and thousands of others will contract cancer and die young. Within a few days of the accident, the radioactive cloud spread across central and northern Europe. While the United States has been both more careful and luckier, it has had several near disasters. In 1966, the Fermi I plant, south of Detroit, melted down. Had the gases escaped, a chain reaction explosion might have destroyed Detroit.[1] In 1978, the reactor at the Three Mile Island power plant, south of Harrisburg, melted partially, and actually cracked its concrete safety dome releasing a small amount of radioactive gas. A dozen other accidents have come close to these perils.

Certainly, thermonuclear war, which is capable of destroying civilization, is the ultimate cosmic pollution, but nuclear weapons are dangerous even when they do not explode. The plutonium at the heart of the bombs is the deadliest substance known to science. Moreover, it has a half-life of twelve thousand years. That is, after twelve millennia it is still half as radioactive as originally. Workers in factories manufacturing bombs and missiles have died; others have suffered illness and died relatively young. While the safeguards of the American military have been acceptable, those of the former Soviet Union have not been. The Soviets have had numerous misfortunes. The worst accident prior to Chernobyl was in 1958 when an explosion in the Ural Mountains killed hundreds and sickened thousands of people. The contamination extended over hundreds of square miles, and, even today, the region is off limits to civilians. Russian secrecy hides the exact nature of the accident; scientists in the West were not aware of the tragedy until 1976.[2] The political collapse of the USSR in 1989 (to a degree, triggered by Chernobyl) created more problems. Nuclear missiles were located in member republics, outside Russia proper, that declared independence. Although most behaved responsibly, not all of the missiles can be accounted for. Apparently a few renegade soldiers sold the warheads to terrorist groups.

BACKGROUND

Radioactivity was unknown until 1898 when Pierre and Marie Curie discovered, slightly by accident, that a certain mineral would develop film. After Monsieur Curie's unexpected death from being run over by a team of horses in a Paris street, Madame Curie continued their research, winning the Nobel Prize in 1911. The Curies found a whole new category of elements that were unstable, emitting gamma rays as they decayed. Physicists began to realize that the atoms of these metals threw off alpha and beta particles until the atom eventually became a different, yet stable, element; for example, physicists now know that uranium decays to radium and then to lead, which is non-radioactive. Because the decay is gradual and may be extremely slow or fast, scientists measure how long it takes for the element to lose half its radioactivity, calling it a half-life. The half-life for radium is 1,620 years and for radon, four days.

The Curie mineral, named radium because it emitted rays, soon found practical applications. Wilhelm Roentgen discovered rays penetrated flesh but not bone, leading to the X ray. Watch and clock makers applied radium to timepieces so they glowed in the dark. In a practical, but completely erroneous application, patent medicine manufacturers sold radium as a cure-all. Between 1925 and 1930, the Bailey Laboratories in New Jersey sold four hundred thousand bottles of Radithor.[3] Scientists did learn of the dangers of radioactivity, albeit belatedly. Madame Curie herself died of leukemia, while many other pioneer scientists suffered from cancer. More gruesomely, their skin would die and their fingers would fall off. By the 1930s, physicians diagnosed lung damage among radium miners in Czechoslovakia and discovered good ventilation underground prevented the illness. Scientists later pinpointed the cause to radon.

Research during the 1930s in Europe and America suggested the possibility of using radioactive elements to build a bomb. Because it would unleash the power of the atom's nucleus instead of merely its electrons, its power would be tremendous. The specter of Naziism and fascism under Hitler and Mussolini alarmed the physicists who understood the process. Great scientists like Albert Einstein and Enrico Fermi, who had fled fascism, knew the danger. Germany had physicists, engineers, and laboratories capable of building an atom bomb. Just weeks before Hitler invaded Poland, Einstein wrote President Roosevelt to warn of the possibility of a bomb and the peril if Germany were to build one first.

Within a few months, the U.S. Army, aided by British and Canadian scientists, began the top secret Manhattan Project. At the University of Chicago, Fermi turned theory into actuality by creating a chain reaction. At Oak Ridge, Tennessee, the Army began the diffusion separator, while the Air Corps flew uranium ore from the Belgian Congo in Africa, at that time the only supply in the world. Eventually, mining began in Colorado. At Los Alamos in the remote New Mexican desert, Robert Oppenheimer led a team that actually built the bomb.

The Manhattan Project leaders knew that uranium was dangerous, but were not fully aware of how dangerous. Mine tailings piled up next to the processing plant in Colorado; scientists suffered exposure at Los Alamos. The project was so secret that only Roosevelt and four members of Congress knew about it and approved the budget. Vice President Harry Truman only learned of it after he became president. Necessary as it was in wartime, the secrecy meant lack of responsibility for safety. Moreover, the Army culture of obedience to orders and operating on a massive (and often inefficient) scale overrode details like what happened to the waste uranium. Lastly, the urgency of winning the war justified sacrificing health and even life. Soldiers, pilots, and sailors were killed every day; the atomic bomb would prevent their deaths. Roosevelt and the Manhattan Project leaders knew that Nazi Germany had the capability to build a bomb and believed they were in a race. In fact, Hitler had considered it, but decided he would conquer all of Europe sooner than he could build the bomb.

The Air Force dropped an atomic bomb on Hiroshima on August 6, 1945, and, when the Japanese failed to answer the American demand to negotiate surrender, dropped a second one on Nagasaki three days later. The bombs killed over one hundred thousand people immediately and thousands more got radiation sickness. Horrible as the devastation was, it served as a natural laboratory for the effects of the atom. The Manhattan Project scientists were amazed that so many people died and were sickened from the radiation. They had predicted the destructive force of the blast itself, but had believed only a few would suffer from the radiation. As soon as the Japanese surrendered, the Army sent experts to the two cities to study the bomb's effects. The monitoring and evaluating continues to the present day. Since 1945, the two cities have symbolized the horror of nuclear weapons.

Within a few years the Cold War began between the Soviet Union and the West. Until 1948, the United States had a monopoly on the atomic bomb, then the USSR exploded its own. The forty-year arms race was underway. In 1952, the United States successfully tested a hydrogen bomb, hundreds of times more powerful than the atomic bomb, but only a year later, so did the Soviets. Eventually, the United States and the Soviets each had over ten thousand nuclear weapons, enough to blow up the earth a dozen times. Other countries built atomic bombs, as well. Americans helped the British in return for the contributions of their scientists in Los Alamos and their research on radar. Nuclear weapons proliferated. The French built a bomb in 1960. Communist China built one in 1964, and later India exploded a bomb, which it disingenuously claimed was "for agricultural purposes." Its traditional rival, Pakistan, built one, although not acknowledging it until much later. Although its government never admitted it officially, by the latter 1960s it seemed apparent that Israel had the weapon. In 1981, the Israeli air force attacked and destroyed a secret nuclear research facility in Iraq, which was developing a bomb. For hundreds of years, these Middle Eastern and Asian regions have been unstable; wars have been frequent there. Although any nuclear weapons present a risk, Western and communist leaders knew the dangers of rash action and both NATO and Soviet military managed their weaponry with strict discipline.

After World War II, the Manhattan Project was transformed into the Atomic Energy Commission (AEC). The 1946 Atomic Energy Act established the AEC and subjected it to direct congressional supervision by the Joint Committee on Atomic Energy, the only really powerful joint committee in history. Congress and Truman wanted to be sure civilians were in charge and that the new agency would develop non-military uses. Although the AEC floundered in developing a reactor to generate electricity, the Navy developed a small one to power a submarine. Prophetically, one officer assigned to the submarine project was Lieutenant Jimmy Carter. During this time an experimental reactor in Chalk River, Canada, melted down. With cavalier disregard for their safety, the Navy sent Carter and other officers to the reactor to disassemble the damaged core by hand, each allowed to work only ninety seconds due to the dangerous radiation.[4]

In 1954, private electric utility companies lobbied Congress to open up the AEC secrets so they could build their own reactors, resulting in extensive amendments to the Atomic Energy Act. The potential benefits appeared magnificent. The price to consumers would be so low it would not be worth installing meters. No smoke would pollute the air, and less coal mining would safeguard the landscape. Plants could be located near customers, making distribution cheaper.

Electric companies had incentives imposed by government to favor nuclear power. Electricity is a natural monopoly, that is, competition is inefficient because of the cost of stringing wires and the need for massive plants. To protect consumers in the absence of competition, government regulates the price. A state

public utility commission calculates a company's profit according to total investment, then applies a rate of return set by law or the commission. For example, an
electric company with $100 million invested in its plants, transmission lines, and
local wires, and having a rate set at 10 percent is entitled to charge enough to
make a profit of $10 million a year after paying for fuel, repairs, employees,
depreciation and so forth.

If the AEC were to build and operate the generating plants as the 1946 law
envisioned, the utility companies would have no investment on which to calculate a return. This seemed a strong possibility in that era of big government. The
TVA was exactly the sort of government giant they feared. Truman proposed to
duplicate the TVA on the Missouri River. In the Pacific northwest, the Bonneville
Power Administration of the Department of the Interior was nearly as intrusive
as the TVA. Nuclear generating plants seemed ideal for capital investment. They
were expensive, required much concrete and machinery, used little fuel (which
the AEC was supplying free at the time) and required few employees. Utilities
anticipated they could build them and just watch the money roll in. Big corporations like Westinghouse and General Electric anticipated parallel benefits. They
could sell the equipment and construct the plants for customers (the utilities) that
really did not care what the price was because the public utility commissions
would let them recover it. The more expensive the facility, the more money they
would get according to the fixed rate of return. The Duquesne Electric company
opened the first commercial nuclear plant in 1958 at Shippingport near
Pittsburgh. Other early ones were Oyster Creek in New Jersey, Calvert Cliffs on
the Chesapeake Bay, and Cayuga Lake in upstate New York.

The act assigned the AEC a dual role. One was to promote nuclear power and
the other was to regulate its safety. In practice, the commission virtually always
favored promotion. It gave the utilities the benefit of its technology and paid a
cash subsidy. It provided the enriched uranium for fuel at no charge. Safety was
secondary; environmental protection was barely taken into consideration.

Although under civilian control, the AEC continued much of the secrecy of
the Manhattan Project. When uranium miners began reporting difficulty breath-
ing and cancer of the lungs, the commission hushed up the problem, belittling it
as "lung damage." It denied a Colorado health inspector access to a uranium mill
because he did not have the supersecret Q clearance. The AEC justified its
secrecy because of the Cold War—nuclear information must be kept from the
communists. In actuality, the cause of the cancer was radon poisoning, which
European miners had learned to prevent twenty years before.

About this time, research on Hiroshima survivors demonstrated how a variety of cancers developed years after irradiation. Bomb tests in the Nevada desert
in the 1940s and 1950s exposed troops and civilians to excessive radiation. To
see if soldiers could fight under atomic conditions, the Army put them in trenches
within a mile of Ground Zero, immediately ordering them, after the detonation,
to maneuver through the blast site. While the solders could fight right after the
explosion, five, ten, or twenty years later many developed cancer. The AEC used

to invite civilians and school children from Las Vegas to witness the explosions, giving them only sunglasses for protection.

PUBLIC QUESTIONS ABOUT THE ATOM

Thermal pollution was the first environmental problem to gain attention. To generate electricity, the nuclear reactor heats water into steam, then the steam turns a turbine that generates the electricity, in a process almost identical to a fossil fuel plant. Coal is 60 to 70 percent efficient, meaning that 60 to 70 percent of its energy value becomes electricity; the rest of the energy, in the form of heat, goes up the smokestack with a small amount needing to be cooled with water from a river or bay that is pumped through the facility. In the arid west, coal plants have special cooling towers where a small quantity of water evaporates to release the heat. Nuclear energy is only about 30 percent efficient, and none of the waste heat is released up a smokestack. Hence much more heat needs to be carried away by water or cooling towers. The waste heat warms the river or bay unnaturally, which changes the biological habitat. In its first winter, the Oyster Creek plant in New Jersey warmed the bay so much that blue fish did not migrate south but remained there. In the early spring, when the plant shut down for annual maintenance, the bay cooled and thousands of blue fish died. The engineering solution has been to build more cooling towers, giving nuclear plants their distinctive landmarks of a cylindrical tower five hundred-feet high emitting clouds of steam.

Public anxiety turned to the more serious risk of the radiation itself. In 1957, the Windscale Plant in England suffered a meltdown. During a routine shutdown for maintenance, the reactor did not cool properly but began to heat up uncontrollably. The built-in safety features failed, then the heat started a chemical fire that destroyed the emergency equipment. The nuclear "fire" raged for three days. Radioactive gas escaped, amounting to a volume as great as a tenth of the radiation at Hiroshima. It spread over England, France, Belgium, the Netherlands, Germany, and Denmark. For two hundred miles downwind, radioactive iodine contaminated the land. Cows grazing on the grass concentrated the iodine in their milk, which the government had to purchase and destroy.

Popular concern with environmental damage and with the potential tragedy of thermonuclear war reinforced each other. Indeed within months of Hiroshima, the Manhattan Project scientists had organized an anti-war group which began to publish the *Bulletin of the Atomic Scientists*. With brilliant propaganda, the upper left corner of every issue since 1947 displayed the Doomsday Clock. The clock showed the time as 11:53 P.M., indicating the world had seven minutes until the midnight doom of destruction. When the Cold War worsened, the minute hand moved closer to midnight twice (11:58 P.M. in 1953, and 11:57 in 1983). When international relations improved, the hand moved back (11:48 in 1972, and 11:43 in 1991).

The first public demonstration against atomic power occurred in 1958 in Scotland at an American naval base, where Scots and Britons demonstrated against submarines carrying nuclear missiles. Linus Pauling, who won a Nobel Prize in 1954 for chemistry, capitalized on his fame to protest against nuclear weapons. His scientific reputation, fiery rhetoric, and shock of white hair inspired crowds and intimidated government officials. In 1962, he won a second Nobel Prize, this time for peace.

Hope occasionally broke through the Cold War gloom. President Kennedy and Soviet Chairman Khrushchev signed a treaty banning nuclear tests in the atmosphere. Underground testing was permitted because it would not cause fall-out. The Cuban missile crisis stimulated the heads of the two superpowers to rein in their atomic weapons. In October 1963, the Soviets stationed missiles in Cuba to support Fidel Castro. With a range of a thousand miles, they could attack Washington and every city south of it. After eleven nerve-racking days of secret negotiation, Khrushchev withdrew the missiles. Both he and Kennedy realized that they had come too close to war.

A proposed nuclear plant at Meshoppen in northeastern Pennsylvania stirred opposition from Quakers and other pacifists. Their first objection was that to construct a civilian nuclear facility encourages weaponry. Next, the opponents examined local dangers. Professor Ernest Sternglass of the University of Pittsburgh concluded that the radiation would cause more cancer. The AEC assigned a staff member to refute Sternglass's accusation. John Gofman, who was both a chemist and physician, reviewed Sternglass's research. While he quibbled with some of the statistical analysis, he agreed with most of Sternglass's findings and further concluded that the plant would increase infant mortality.[5]

A 1966 melt down at Detroit Edison's Enrico Fermi plant came close to catastrophe. Named in honor of the Italian physicist and refugee from Mussolini's regime, the reactor was the first to use sodium to cool the reactor. Less than a year after the reactor began operation, the flow of sodium was blocked by a broken piece of sheet metal. The reactor began to heat uncontrollably, much like the Windscale accident in England. Fortunately, the emergency equipment worked and cooled the uranium core. Had it failed, the explosion could have imperiled two million people in Detroit and its suburbs. The reactor was ruined and the massive radioactivity it generated prevented repair, so after several years of indecision, the company simply buried it under tons of concrete. Detroit Edison and the AEC hushed up the incident. Eventually, it built a conventional reactor, Fermi II, nearby.

Four years later the public did become aware of the risks at the Calvert Cliffs plant on the Chesapeake Bay. The first alarm was over thermal pollution. A citizens group, the Chesapeake Environmental Protection Association, demanded that the AEC comply with the National Environmental Policy Act (NEPA) provision that it prepare an Environmental Impact Statement (EIS). The commission resisted, claiming that an operating permit did not require an EIS, but the Circuit of Appeals ruled that an EIS was required. The hearing was formal and legalistic, and witnesses swore to tell the truth and could be cross examined. The NEPA heralded a major shift in bureaucratic procedures. Experts in government lost their monopoly of decision making, chiefly because they had to respond to outside information and justify their conclusions. The law opened up agency operations and procedures. On the technical side, AEC scientists and engineers ignored environmental issues. Contemporaneously, Congress was opening up its decision-making by holding public sessions to mark up bills and increasing the authority of its subcommittees.

In two more years, the Long Island Lighting Company (LILCO) proposal to construct a reactor in Shoreham sparked a similar firestorm by well-educated, wealthy neighbors. When LILCO requested permission to use the site, government officials and civic leaders lauded the plan. One called it "a perfect type of industry for the area." Another declared his support, saying he would oppose a coal-fired plant. The Bookhaven Town Board voted unanimously in favor. Coincidentally, the town was home to a large AEC laboratory; its scientists supported LILCO. Less than two years later, LILCO proposed a second nuclear plant at Lloyd Harbor nearby. This time the citizens were not enthusiastic. Lloyd Harbor, which served as a home to wealthy businesspeople and professionals, was more familiar with the controversies percolating up and valued the natural environment. Residents included leaders in the Nature Conservancy, the Audubon Society, and the Conservation Council. These upper-crust residents established the Lloyd Harbor Study Group.

An amendment to the Atomic Energy Act in 1957 had given local citizens the right to present their views in public hearings before the AEC staff when a utility applied for permission to begin construction or to begin operation. Until this point, few citizens took advantage of this right to intervene. The hearing on the construction permit began in September 1970. The president of LILCO spoke of the rapid growth in demand. A group of scientists from the Brookhaven National Laboratory declared their support, while claiming they were acting as citizens, not AEC employees.

The Lloyd Harbor Study Group opposed issuing the permit and grandly countered that its goal was to set an example for the whole world, not just one plant. The group demanded seventeen "minimum requirements," including the total elimination of any radiation emissions, no thermal pollution, and a building strong enough to withstand the crash of a large airplane or a missile attack by the Soviet Union. One witness for the Lloyd Harbor Study Group was James Watson, a local resident who had won a Nobel Prize for discovering the double helix of DNA. In fact, Watson's impressive scientific accomplishments had nothing to do with nuclear energy; his testimony was a philosophical denunciation of the AEC and the industry. Arthur Tamplin, an employee of the AEC Lawrence Livermore Laboratory in California, testified that the commission ought to lower the safe amount of radiation by 90 percent. Ernest Sternglass testified that it should be lowered by 99 percent.

Two other events strengthened the environmental side. Commission experiments at its Idaho laboratory showed that a meltdown would be more severe than previously estimated, the U.S. Appeals Court ruling in *Calvert Cliffs* made perfectly clear the necessity of an EIS. In spite of this, the AEC hearing board ruled in 1973 to permit construction to begin. The Lloyd Harbor Study Group had the satisfaction of discovering many flaws in the AEC, and industry technology and standards, and in delaying construction for two years.

Richard Nixon, in making two successive appointments for chair of the Atomic Energy Commission, pushed it in an environmental direction. In 1972, he nominated James Schlesinger, whose career started as an economics professor, who then worked for a think tank evaluating the dangers of nuclear weapons proliferation, and finally moved to the Office of Management and Budget to monitor the Defense Department spending. At the OMB he added the responsibility for environmental budgeting. Besides his professional expertise, Schlesinger was an avid bird watcher. Once appointed, he announced the AEC would adhere strictly to NEPA and would change its role from promoting the nuclear industry to being a referee balancing the pros and cons. Eighteen months later, Nixon shuffled his cabinet to fight off the Watergate scandal and appointed him as director of the Central Intelligence Agency and, five months after that, to become secretary of defense. Gerald Ford dismissed him from the cabinet, because, in the president's words, "I want my guys." In the 1976 campaign, the disgruntled ex-secretary crossed party lines to advise Jimmy Carter on defense and energy policy. Schlesinger's hope was to return as secretary of defense, but Carter recognized that that would be seen as an insult to Ford. He placed Schlesinger in charge of formulating energy policy and establishing the Department of Energy, both major planks in Carter's platform. Once the new department was organized, Carter appointed him to be its first secretary.

When Schlesinger left the AEC, Nixon appointed Dixy Lee Ray as chairman. Ray was a marine zoologist specializing in shrimp, crabs, and lobsters. She had directed the Pacific Science Center in Seattle, which popularized science for children and adults. Ray became both the first biologist and the first woman to serve on the commission. Despite her career in ecology, she championed the nuclear industry. Indeed, toward the end of her life, she co-authored two books criticizing "environmental overkill," to use her terminology. Ray's sharp tongue and unorthodox lifestyle kept her in the news. She lived in a trailer in the country and took her dogs to her office. At the end of the Ford administration, Ray returned to Washington state, where the voters elected her governor.

The oil crisis of 1973 gave hope to nuclear advocates. The fuel was not subject to boycotts by the Arabs or price gouging by the Organization of Petroleum Exporting Countries (OPEC). France announced a goal of generating half its electricity by the atom (presently, it generates 70 percent). The figure for the United States then was 4 percent with plans of eventually rising to 23 percent. The crisis focused attention on the AEC flaws. The commission moved slowly, overused secrecy, and stifled innovation. The result of its dual role of promoting and regulating the industry was a bias that favored promotion and neglected safety and environmental damage. Nixon, always the advocate of efficient management, proposed to reorganize it. Thus, two months after Nixon resigned,

Congress amended the Atomic Energy Act to form two agencies: the smaller Nuclear Regulatory Commission (NRC) and the larger Energy Research and Development Administration (ERDA). The NRC was to assure safety independent of any duty to promote. The ERDA, perhaps unfortunately, was the same old AEC with a few additional responsibilities for petroleum, coal, and solar energy. Eight-five percent of its personnel and funds came from the terminated commission.

In his presidential campaign in 1976, Jimmy Carter said the Ford administration was not doing enough about energy. He promised that he would establish a Department of Energy at the cabinet level where it would have visibility, power, and new leadership. In spite of his Republican background, Carter appointed Schlesinger to be his "Energy Czar," a man who was to supposed to have complete charge. Capitalizing on his technical knowledge, many friends, and smooth manner, Schlesinger piloted the president's Department of Energy Organizational Act through Congress. A Senate aide observed that "Schlesinger had most of these guys eating out of his hand."[6] To ERDA, the law added oil regulation and the Federal Power Commission, changing its name to the Federal Energy Regulatory Commission.

Protest and Response

Opponents of reactors sparked a non-violent "nuclear war" on a New England beach. The Public Service Company of New Hampshire was preparing a site at Seabrook for two reactors, each capable of generating 1150 megawatts of electricity. Local residents worried about the eight hundred thousand gallons of sea water the plant would circulate every minute for cooling. Virtually all the electricity was surplus and destined for sale out of the state. Originally, the plant was projected to cost less than $1 billion, but rose to $1.6 billion and appeared to be headed toward $2.5 billion. The New Hampshire customers would have to pay for the extra investment in their monthly bills.

The first protest was solo. A local farm hand climbed 175 feet to the top of a company weather tower in January 1976, where he camped out at the top for thirty-six hours before the frigid cold drove him down. In April, three hundred people demonstrated against constructing the power facility. In August, six hundred protesters from all over New England rallied and eighteen of them trespassed on the site where they planted tree saplings to "beautify" it. The protesters adopted the name Clamshell Alliance in honor of the clams living in the nearby marshes.

Their technique was non-violent civil disobedience. Martin Luther King, Jr., had employed and refined this form of protest in the Civil Rights Movement starting with his bus boycott in Montgomery, Alabama. King had copied it from the Hindu leader, Mahatma Gandhi, during the movement for India's independence from British colonial rule. In turn, Gandhi had adopted civil disobedience from Henry David Thoreau, who wrote of his protest at Walden Pond, lying only forty-five miles to the south in Massachusetts. Non-violent protest had come full circle over twenty thousand miles and 140 years. The tenets of civil disobedience are that citizens do not have a duty to obey an unjust law, but that they must not use violence to oppose it. Protesters must accept the consequences of their disobedience even if it means imprisonment or death.

The non-violent civil disobedience traces a spiritual connection back to Jesus's Sermon on the Mount. In England and America, Quakers have advanced it. They believe killing and violence are morally wrong. Quakers do not withdraw from the world, but relish politics. They believe that violence is wrong even when lawful, such as executing a convicted murderer or fighting a war. Gandhi affiliated his movement with Hindu beliefs of the sanctity of life. King anchored the Civil Rights Movement in his own Baptist denomination. Opposition to the war in Vietnam centered on resistance to the draft. Dating back before the Revolutionary War, Quakers have often been conscientious objectors, and federal law provides exemptions for this. In the face of Vietnam, conscientious objection gained in popularity among many denominations.

The two leading boosters of the nuclear plant in New Hampshire were arch-conservatives. Governor Meldrin Thomson was infamous throughout the country for his far-right views. His chief backer was William Loeb, who published the *Manchester Union Leader*, the only statewide newspaper. During the 1972 Democratic presidential primary, Loeb personally attacked Senator Edmund Muskie and his wife. Many believed he had driven Muskie out of the race.

The following April the Clamshell Alliance rallied two thousand people to demonstrate at the construction site. Loeb spent the week leading up to the day denouncing the nuclear opponents as "communists," "perverts," and agents of "terrorism." The crowd marched onto the company property, sang songs, cheered the speakers, and pitched tents for their occupation. At a park across the marsh, another three thousand protesters lent moral support. The following afternoon, Governor Thomson and the state police commander demanded that the two thousand leave the reactor site. Upon their refusal, the police placed the protesters under arrest and spent the next twelve hours loading them on school buses and National Guard troop carriers to go to the four Guard Armories around the state. The governor required a $1,500 bail for each protester.

Nearly all of the prisoners refused to post bond or could not afford it. Four days later most demonstrators were still confined; they lacked beds, sanitary facilities, and access to attorneys. Judges went to the armories to conduct the trials, sentencing most to fifteen days in jail. The following week over five hundred were still confined in the armories waiting trial. The cost to the New Hampshire taxpayers was $50,000 a day, big money in the Granite State. On the thirteenth day, the alliance and the governor signed an agreement to release the last 541 detainees on their own recognizance. The occupation and arrests had captured attention around the world. During the days while New Hampshire detained hundreds in the armories, thousands of sympathizers rallied at ten other nuclear plants in nine states. Other groups adopted the Seabrook terminology to form the Abalone Alliance in California and the Oyster Shell Alliance in Louisiana. Others call themselves Armadillo, Catfish, Crabshell, Palmetto, and Redwood alliances.

Across the continent on the Pacific Ocean, the Diablo Canyon nuclear power plant was under construction. Although the initial geological evaluations claimed it was safe from the danger of an earthquake, later measurement discovered it was two miles from a major fault line. At that distance, a quake could register over seven on the Richter scale, ten times the reactor's safe level. Problems increased. Many pipes were defective and had to be replaced. Documents leaked to the press showed the Nuclear Regulatory Commission wanted the plant on line even if it was not as safe as planned. The original estimate of $350 million rose to $1.4 billion. In multiple occupations, police have arrested five hundred members of the Abalone Alliance.

Although citizens have often opposed nuclear power plants, until 1978 the dangers had only been potential. That changed when the Metropolitan Edison Company erected a nuclear plant on Three Mile Island south of Harrisburg, Pennsylvania. Critics say Met Ed began full scale operation prematurely in order to meet a financial (not technical) deadline by the state public utility commission. On March 28, a cooling system pump failed, as did the relief valve. Next, a relief valve inside the reactor failed as well. Dangerously heating to over three thousand degrees, the core began to melt. When the operators pumped in water for cooling, the water turned to steam, threatening to explode a crack in the concrete safety dome. This dilemma forced the operators to release some of the radioactive gas and steam into the atmosphere. The Pennsylvania Department of Environmental Resources measured high radioactivity, the mayor of the town across the river began to organize an evacuation, and the governor declared an emergency. The NRC staff that arrived from Washington detected radioactivity sixteen miles downwind. An NRC official announced it was "one of the most serious nuclear accidents to occur in the United States." Meanwhile, the Met Ed president claimed it was minor. President Carter arrived by helicopter to inspect the damage with a scientific eye, as did the Democratic chairman and ranking Republican of the Senate subcommittee that oversaw nuclear energy. (Members of Congress often visit disaster locations to educate themselves about problems and, incidentally, to get on television.)

In the end, the amount of radioactivity released turned out to be small. The financial consequences, however, were not. Met Ed had to spend millions of dollars to rebuild. Lawmakers and citizens realized that even if the Three Mile Island accident caused minor damage to the environment, a more serious one could easily happen. The whole nuclear industry felt the sting. The NRC tightened its regulations. State public utility commissions became reluctant to allow electric companies to put nuclear plants into their rate base. The electric companies held off plans for future plants; worse yet, they canceled some already ordered. At the time of the oil crisis in 1973, nuclear power seemed ready for a golden age. Instead, it began its present decline.

THE NUCLEAR INDUSTRY IN ECLIPSE

When Ronald Reagan won the Republican nomination in 1980, he seemed an ideal friend to the nuclear industry. From 1954 to 1962, the General Electric corporation had employed the movie star to host *GE Theatre* on television and to be a goodwill ambassador. GE sold 30 percent of the nuclear reactors on the market, only slightly behind Westinghouse's 35 percent. During his eighteen years with GE, Reagan shifted his political beliefs from liberal Democratic to conservative Republican. And, throughout his presidential campaign, Reagan promised to revitalize the nuclear power industry and build more nuclear missles to counter the Soviet military threat.

Reagan's choice for secretary of energy, James Edwards, surprised many people because Edwards lacked background in both nuclear energy and business. Previously, Edward was a dentist who served as the Republican governor of South Carolina from 1974 to 1978. Although he was a booster for nuclear power, his acquaintance came because as governor he tried to capitalize on the AEC-ERDA facility at Barnwell as a means of economic development. He liked to brag that South Carolina was "the world's nuclear energy capital." Reagan's appointment came after he had selected most other Cabinet officers and needed to find a southerner to repay the region for its electoral victories in those states. Even from the Reagan perspective, Edwards quickly became a nuclear disaster. His technical ignorance was obvious. Although popular in his home state, his public relations skills did not transfer to Washington. He told news reporters that opponents of nuclear power were under the influence of "subversive elements"[7] and were playing into the hands of the Soviets. He telegraphed congratulations to the Saudi Arabian oil minister for OPEC's increase of the price of oil because he believed it would encourage the demand for nuclear power.

President Reagan's Strategic Defense Initiative to defend the United States against Soviet thermonuclear missiles alarmed those opposed to nuclear power. Known to its detractors as Star Wars after the movie, the idea was to launch thousands of U.S. missiles into space where they would shoot down the Soviet missiles. At first, the Department of Defense's secrecy hid the plan's technical impossibility. Star Wars demanded thousands of warheads. Because the Atomic Energy Act placed weapons production under civilian control in 1946, the Department of Energy manufactures all weapons. To get large amounts of plutonium, the Department of Energy proposed to reprocess plutonium from spent fuel from civilian plants. However, since the Eisenhower administration, American policy has been that civilian fuel would never cross the line to the military. In addition to betraying the promise of peaceful uses for the atom, Star Wars would generate large quantities of radioactive waste from the new weapons.

Fortunately for the Reagan team, Edwards resigned a year later to become president of the Medical College of South Carolina. He was one of the first to leave as the Reagan administration moderated its most extreme anti-environmental policies. Judging from his background, his replacement did not seem much better, but Donald Hodel, who had been James Watt's deputy at the Department of the Interior, knew not to use civilian fuel for weapons and not to infer that opponents were "subversives" allied with the Soviets. Although the Reagan administration never officially ended Star Wars, the program faded away.

In keeping with George Bush's announced goal of being an environmental president, his secretary of energy announced that the DOE facilities themselves were major sources of contamination. The worst offender was at Barnwell where the department shut down reactors producing plutonium and tritium for warheads because its radioactive waste was fouling the soil and seeping into the Savannah River. The Natural Resources Defense Council and Greenpeace went to court to demand that the DOE file an Environmental Impact Statement before restarting them. At the Rocky Flats facility near Denver, waste was stored in barrels and tanks above ground because no dump was available. The secretary, James Watkins, was a retired Navy admiral who knew how to charge ahead at full speed. Bush, however, was somewhat uncomfortable with his zeal.

Increased safety drove up the costs of nuclear plants. In the early 1970s, an electric utility company could build a plant for about $170 million, whereas ten years later the same plant would cost $1.7 billion. The amount of steel increased 41 percent, the tons of concrete increased 27 percent, and the length of electric cable increased 36 percent. The industry blamed the increase in building material on "regulatory ratcheting," meaning that safety requirements always went up and never went down. Delay was a big factor because a partially finished facility could not earn any money. During this period, the time to complete a plant went from five years to twelve years. Anti-nuclear interveners sometimes acknowledged using the financial burden as a means of eliminating a facility. A number of utilities abandoned plants under construction, and no plant ordered after 1974 was completed. Safety was not the sole reason the industry floundered. Planning greatly overestimated future demands, high interest rates confounded cash flow calculations, and public utility commissions. The 1992 Energy Policy Act deregulated prices, which meant inefficient nuclear plants had to be closed. Previously, companies had to keep them operating to add to their rate base.

Chernobyl

On April 27, 1986, news sped around the world of a gigantic nuclear accident. For the first day, its location was unknown. Routine monitoring in Sweden detected high radioactivity in the atmosphere. At first, the Swedes thought it was one of their own reactors. Then, German stations picked it up and soon the site was traced to the Soviet Union, and eventually to Chernobyl near Kiev in the Ukraine. For ten days the Soviet government in Moscow denied everything (in its old Communist manner). The USSR had barely begun it *glasnost*, an opening up of the repressive totalitarian government with the goals of modernization, efficiency, and freedom. The Communist reformer, Mikhail Gorbachev, had been in office for only a year. Soon, Moscow could no longer deny the enormity of the

An aerial view of the Chernobyl nuclear power plant shows the damage from the explosions and fire that occurred in April 1986, when the plant sent large amounts of radioactive material into the atmosphere.

disaster as further monitoring and American spy satellites pieced together the basic facts. The Communists admitted its nuclear power plant suffered a melt down and exploded.

After midnight, Reactor 4 was shutting down for routine maintenance. The technicians wanted to test how late in the process they could restart the turbine without using the auxiliary diesel generators. The experiment, poorly conceived from the beginning, was never approved by the plant director, but the test crew went ahead anyway. First, power fell too quickly, then the crew tried to raise it. The water for cooling turned to steam, which expanded uncontrollably. Power bolted to one hundred times the safe level. Fuel pellets began to shatter. Two giant explosions occurred, one of steam and the other of the fuel vapor, which blasted off the pile cap, allowing air to enter. Within the reactor, the oxygen reacted with the graphite, a type of carbon much like coal. This enormous fire emitted the radioactivity into the atmosphere as a fine soot, the most dangerous form possible.[8]

The explosion ejected at least eight tons of uranium and plutonium from the core into the air. The fire released more radioactive material, including cesium and iodine. The amount was a hundred times as much as Hiroshima. With unusual weather that day, the poisonous cloud drifted northwest over eastern Europe, still under Communist domination so Poland, Czechoslovakia, and East Germany kept the secret, then over Sweden and West Germany. In a few days, the prevailing westerly winds blew the radioactivity back over all of the Soviet Union, Japan, across the Pacific, over the United States, and to Europe again. Immediate casualties were thirty dead and 238 sick from radiation. Severely contaminated victims vomited, collapsed, and died. Those less contaminated suffered burns and ulcers. Those who recovered faced cancer. Hospitals in Kiev and Moscow established emergency wards, and asked American and European physicians for help. Many of the people who put out the fire succumbed. While estimates vary, perhaps five thousand have died as a direct effect, twenty million have been exposed, and three hundred thousand may have shorter life spans.

The Chernobyl explosion was the final blow to the old Communist system. When Soviet citizens learned of the disaster, first from shortwave radio broadcasts from the West, then from their own newspapers and television, the magnitude of the governmental recklessness discredited the old ways and enhanced *glasnost*. Millions of Soviets learned of this massive blunder. Gorbachev exploited the disaster to discredit the totalitarian secrecy and oppression. For the USSR, he sought a middle way between state and socialism and a free market. As for the eastern European satellites it had dominated since 1945, Gorbachev recognized the futility of maintaining Soviet control. At home, events overtook his moderation. On New Years Day of 1991 the USSR peacefully dismantled itself, while its people stumbled toward a free market. No other pollution episode has had such dramatic political consequences.

Disposal and Decommissioning

When the uranium in the fuel rods of a reactor decays to the point that the rods are no longer efficient, the operator removes them (using robots due to the danger) and replaces them with new ones. Typically, a plant replaces all rods over a three year period. Some of the old ones are reprocessed. Most old rods, however, need to be disposed of permanently. Here lies the biggest stumbling block for the industry, because there is nowhere for them to go. The United States does not have a permanent disposal facility. In fact, it never had one. All the nuclear waste material since the Manhattan Project is in temporary storage. The AEC complex in Hanford, Washington, begun during World War II, put some in steel barrels underground, which have since leaked into the groundwater. Electric utility companies are forced to keep their spent rods. They simply put them in pools of water, which should only be used for the short term.

Government efforts have not been successful so far. The AEC and DOE have searched for sites in granite tunnels, abandoned salt mines, and basalt caves, but none seem satisfactory. The solution, unfortunately, is not just a matter of building fences and hiring security guards. Due to the long time to decay, the disposal facility must be safe for thousands of years. The longest half life is for plutonium: twelve thousand years. Whenever the DOE tentatively has identified a possible site, citizens from miles around arise in protest. People do not want a nuclear dump in their backyard. A current plan is for a single disposal facility at Yucca Mountain near Las Vegas. The mountain is extremely dry so water will not leach the plutonium and uranium. Its geology is stable. No one lives nearby, no cattle can graze, and no valuable mineral resources will be lost. DOE proposed to drill 115 miles of tunnels at a cost of $15 billion. Then a potential problem arose. Although the mountain is dry, evidence appeared that in the geological past, water trickled through the rock, and may do so in the future. With the permanent facility delayed, Congress considered a temporary storage site near Yucca Mountain. Opponents have worried that this short-term answer will be expensive, delay a better permanent solution, and expose the public all over the country to danger as the waste is transported by rail and truck to Nevada.

Disposing of military nuclear waste presents a danger just as great, perhaps even greater, but the tradition of military secrecy has allowed DOE to proceed with fewer obstacles. Its Waste Isolation Pilot Plant (WIPP) near Carlsbad, New Mexico, plans to dispose of plutonium and other transuranic materials from military facilities including dismantled weapons. The waste will be buried two thousand feet underground in rock salt, which will melt from the radioactive heat, then solidify to form a seal. However, legislation forbids WIPP from receiving any waste from civilian nuclear power plants.

The end of the Cold War brought a happy problem. As the United States and Russia began to dismantle their nuclear bombs and rockets, the plutonium of the warheads needed disposal. After three years of analyzing the situation, an expert committee of the National Academy of Sciences recommended a dual approach. Pursuing two tracks together would give practical experience, then if one proved unsatisfactory, it still had the second option. After gaining experience, the Energy Department would drop the less satisfactory one. The first option was to encase the plutonium in glass (vitrification) and place it into permanent storage. The second was to dilute the plutonium with uranium fuel and burn it in civilian electric plants, a process expected to take ten years to use up the plutonium fuels. Immediately on hearing the news, a few anti-nuclear protesters announced their opposition to the contamination of civilian facilities with military plutonium.

An uncertainty about civilian facilities is that, to date, no one in the United States or abroad knows what to do when nuclear plants wear out. Recalling the naval submarine origins of the industry, the term is decommissioning as for a ship. After use for thirty to fifty years, a reactor is highly irradiated—its steel and concrete is as deadly as the spent fuel. The solution used for Fermi I, burying the reactor in concrete, probably would not win approval, nor would it meet with the greater environmental consciousness and stricter regulations now in effect. When the first plant at Shippingport wore out in 1982, Duquesne Light Company had no plan for decommissioning. After letting it sit for five years, it disassembled the plant. The reactor itself was small, only 770 tons, so cranes loaded it on a barge, floated it down the Ohio and Mississippi Rivers, through the Panama Canal to the Columbia River and upstream three hundred miles to the DOE (previously the AEC), facility at Hanford. This process will not work for other reactors that are much larger.

Low-Level Waste

Low-level waste refers, a bit arbitrarily, to nuclear waste that does not come from reactor fuel rods or weapons. In fact, a great deal of it is dangerously radioactive. Much of it is the paraphernalia of power plants: protective gloves and clothing, broken pipes, and tools. Other comes from hospitals, laboratories, and universities. Cancer patients receive rays to kill a tumor; a surgeon may insert little capsules near the lesion. Another example is a nuclear stress test to diagnose heart disease. A tragic accident in Gioania, Brazil, highlighted the danger. A medical clinic scrapped a worn out machine that treated cancer with cesium-137. At the city dump, scavengers pried it open and played with the green powder they found inside. They took it home, showed it to their families and discovered that it glowed in the dark. Within a few days forty-one people were hospitalized with radiation poisoning. In all, 240 were contaminated and four died. Many face the early onset of cancer.

When Congress addressed the low-level problem, it chose a different tactic than for other environmental legislation. Sensitive that it had overloaded the national government with all the laws of the Environmental Decade, it gave primary jurisdiction to state governments. Nevertheless, Congress structured the program. The Low-Level Waste Policy Act of 1980 provides that states shall assume responsibility individually (e.g., New York, Illinois, and Texas chose to run their own programs), while other states are to join interstate compacts. Within each group, the state that produces the most waste is responsible for building a repository to last twenty years, then, responsibility shifts to the next biggest producer, and so on.

In the midwest, states from Minnesota to Ohio joined a compact. Their assumption was that Illinois would join and be first in line, but the Land of Lincoln withdrew. Michigan was next in line because it generated more than the other states. Michigan conducted an elaborate three-year search for a site, which many people considered phony. It began with a law ruling out 97 percent of the state. It then rejected several possible locations in granite in the remote Upper Peninsula as unsuitable and finally selected Riga Township near Detroit, Ann Arbor, and Toledo. The site was poorly drained and the water flowed into the Ottawa River. Citizens in the region said they did not want it in their backyard so Michigan gave up, which meant that Ohio was next in line.[9]

Ohio went through the same types of delay and evasion until, in 1997, the compact dissolved itself, leaving each state with its own waste. The procedures of the Low-Level law gave an incentive for state political leaders to delay by throwing up barriers and by encouraging citizens to claim NIMBY. As long as the search officially continued, the state did not have to build its own dump or accept waste from outside the state. Michigan continued to receive money from other states in the compact for its search. A more candid and prompt refusal would have triggered penalties. The Michigan governor encouraged the state's congressional delegation to propose amendments to the law.[10]

Ever since the New Deal, Congress has been extremely cautious of pushing authority over to the states, when giving up its power. This push was the first instance of the national government mandating states to form interstate compacts. While providing a framework in the Low-Level law may portend other compacts in the future, Congress has not used the technique since then. Critics, most of whom are at the state level, argue that Congress just wanted to dump a tough problem on them. On the other hand, state governments have been taking the lead in protecting the environment for both high- and low-level waste. California, often in the vanguard, declared a moratorium on the new construction of power plants until the utilities could find adequate storage and disposal sites. Illinois restricted transportation of nuclear waste by truck or rail. Because public utility commissions regulate the electric industry, they are typically the agency responsible.

RADON

In 1984, during a routine check at the new Limerick nuclear plant of the Philadelphia Electric Company, safety inspectors identified an employee with an unsafe reading on the radiation badge he wore. This indicated that the worker had been receiving too high of a dose, so they searched the plant for the source of contamination, but found none. The next day, he again had an excessive amount, so they redoubled their search. Ultimately, they realized the employee was not being contaminated at the plant but at home. The safety team went to his house, which they discovered was filled with radon.

This colorless, odorless gas is a byproduct of the decay of uranium. Found scattered throughout the world, it is especially prevalent in mountains and foothills. Eastern Pennsylvania turned out to be a hotspot. The radon seeps out of the rocks and into basements. In a well ventilated building or outside, the wind blows it away and it decays harmlessly. Inside a basement, however, it builds up to dangerous levels. Each year it causes fourteen thousand deaths and is the leading cause of lung cancer for non-smokers. For toddlers, infants, and fetuses, radon damages their genes. They are particularly vulnerable because they are young and because they play and crawl on the floor. Radium and uranium miners had known of the danger for seventy years, but its presence in houses came as a surprise. Its location depends on the underlying rocks and is not easy to predict, while its prevalence is based on the underlying rocks, the porousness of the soil, and moisture. Although radon gas can travel swiftly through cracks in the rocks and soil, wet soil slows it.

```
┌────────────────────────────────────────────────────────────────┐
│ ████████ Scorecard for RADIATION CONTROL ████████               │
│                                                                  │
│  LAWS                                                            │
│  Atomic Energy Act 1946, 1954, 1974. Low-level Radioactive Waste │
│  Policy Act 1980. Nuclear Waste Policy Act 1982, 1987. Uranium   │
│  Mill Tailings Reclamation Act. National Environmental Policy    │
│  Act.                                                            │
│                                                                  │
│  SOURCES                                                         │
│  High-level uranium fuel from reactors                           │
│  Low-level waste from electric-generating facilities             │
│  Radioactive medical waste                                       │
│                                                                  │
│  CONGRESS                                                        │
│  House Committee on Science, subcommittee on Energy and the      │
│  Environment                                                     │
│  Committee on Commerce, subcommittee on Energy and Power         │
│  Senate Committee on Energy and Natural Resources, subcommittee  │
│  on Energy                                                       │
│                                                                  │
│  AGENCIES                                                        │
│  Nuclear Regulatory Commission                                   │
│  Department of Energy                                            │
│  State public utility commissions                                │
│                                                                  │
│  INTEREST GROUPS                                                 │
│  Electric companies              Critical Mass                   │
│  Edison Electric Institute       Clamshell Alliance              │
│  Nuclear Energy Institute        NIMBY groups                    │
└────────────────────────────────────────────────────────────────┘
```

New England, the Appalachian Mountains and foothills, the midwest, the northern great plains, and the northern Rocky Mountains have high potential for radon. Glaciers covered these regions, grinding up the bedrock and soil. Ironically, the U.S. Geological Survey, which does most of the research on the problem, has its headquarters in Fairfax County, Virginia, on one of the hotspots.

The first impact was on the real estate market. Home buyers began to demand that the seller prove the house was free of radon. A simple test consisted of placing small cakes of charcoal that would absorb small amounts of radon in the basement over a period of two to three days, then mailing them to a commercial laboratory, which counted the radiation. The sales contract typically gave the buyer the right to cancel if radon was present. Unfortunately, the three-day tests were unreliable, while the more accurate tests typically required several months to complete. For those houses with radon, the problem has been solved by ventilating the basement or, if more serious, boring several four inch ducts under the house and attaching a fan. Except in extreme cases, the costs to make a house radon-free have varied from a few hundred to a few thousand dollars.

Unlike other environmental problems, radon is quite individual, rather than collective like air pollution. Hence, the market solution of adding a condition to a purchase contract worked well, while private laboratories sprang up to meet the demand for a cheap test. The argument for a government role has been that the private market of real estate and private laboratories needs the government to research the problem and to set standards. At first, even the engineers and geologists were baffled. The U.S. Geological Survey discovered the problem and its extent. The EPA published information on levels that were safe and techniques to correct the contamination. Some people have viewed radon as an issue of public health, believing that the government should not ignore a risk to millions of people. Still, when an event like this occurs, irrespective of collective goods theories, many people whose houses lose value turn to government. This happened in Love Canal. Determining the proper role for government and for the free market is a question of philosophy as well as cost-benefit.

LOVING OR HATING THE ATOM

Nuclear pollution poses a paradox for environmentalists. Its benefits are great and its damage is low. Widespread nuclear electricity offers the only alternative to burning fossil fuel without reducing economic growth. Coal especially, but also oil, natural gas, and wood, all add carbon to the atmosphere which results in the greenhouse effect. Global warming will melt the icecaps, flood coastlines, and create deserts. The atom does not produce any carbon dioxide at all. Moreover, fossil fuels, especially coal, pollute the air with soot and sulfur. Millions suffer from asthma, emphysema, and lung cancer due to electric generating plants. While the atom cannot power automobiles directly, in a utopian nuclear future, electrified railroads and subways could increase their share.

The second benefit of nuclear power is its excellent safety record compared to fossil fuels. Coal mining for years has been the most dangerous occupation and, even now with strip mining, still ranks third behind farming and construction. Petroleum drilling and pipelines, though safer, are still much more dangerous than working in a nuclear facility. Even solar energy panel installation has a high accident and death rate as workers cut themselves on sheet metal and fall off roofs.

Yet, in spite of all these benefits, the atom continues to have a bad reputation. This stems largely from fear, some justified and some exaggerated. The greatest legitimate fear is weaponry. Countries like Israel and Pakistan both have bombs and feel threatened by their neighbors. China also has nuclear weapons. Rogue governments like Iraq and North Korea nearly built bombs and have a history of invading their neighbors. North Korea was nearly into production in 1978 when the United States mobilized the International Atomic Energy Agency (IAEA) to intervene. North Korea has a communist regime that fought against South Korea and the United States for three years, has routinely rejected negotiations, and has assassinated southern leaders. With the break up of the Soviet Union, a number of nuclear missiles disappeared, presumably sold illegally to outlaw governments or stolen by organized crime syndicates. The United States and Russia have signed a treaty to destroy many of their weapons and the United

States has offered to buy uranium and plutonium, with the latter posing a threat in the hands of terrorists.

In 1963, the United States and the USSR signed a treaty to end testing above ground. Cesium-137, an "artificially" produced radio-isotope, is still floating about the atmosphere from bombs detonated between 1945 to 1963. In 1968, these two atomic nations, along with Britain, signed the Non-Proliferation Treaty. Most countries in the world signed it, with the significant exceptions of those who were developing weapons: France, China, India, Israel, and Pakistan.

France continued testing bombs in the atmosphere until recently when worldwide complaints caused it to announce the end of testing. A citizen organization deserves most of the credit for condemning France. In 1972, Canadians from Vancouver, British Columbia, choosing the name Greenpeace, protested an American underground nuclear test in the Aleutian Islands off Alaska, sending a small ship into the forbidden zone. After the United States cancelled its tests, Greenpeace shifted its protests to the French nuclear tests, conducted in its colonies in the south Pacific. It, again, sent its ship into the forbidden zone and continued to intimidate the French every year they conducted tests. The French navy warned the ship away and even rammed it once. In 1985, when the Greenpeace ship was in port in New Zealand, French naval frogmen secretly boarded it one night and planted an explosive charge. The explosive blew a hole in the ship, sinking it and killing a man on board.

A second fear, real but exaggerated, is an accident at a nuclear power plant. Chernobyl is the worst example. In the United States, Fermi I and Three Mile Island flirted with disaster. The departments of Energy and Defense take great care in manufacturing, transporting, and storing bombs, but no system is perfect. The IAEA, with headquarters in Vienna, Austria, inspects nuclear plants everywhere in the world. Every year, especially since Chernobyl, equipment and safety procedures improve, operators get more training, and the IAEA inspects more throughly.

Fear of the atom is great, not so much because of the likelihood of an accident, but of the gruesome and exotic effects. Given a choice of death, cancer is probably the worst. It takes months or years, eats away at the body tissues, causes mental depression, is expensive, and forces cruel decisions about surgery and chemotherapy. Cancer afflicts the young and middle-aged more than do heart attacks and strokes. The actual probabilities of a nuclear accident, and the number of and severity of future accidents are all unknown. In a perverse fashion, the risk is uncertain because accidents are so rare. Accidents in coal mines and oil rigs are common enough that statistics are available. Even with better safety recently, mining accidents continue to kill. In America, the number of fatalities for uranium mining and reactor operation is essentially zero, but a single meltdown could kill dozens, perhaps hundreds or thousands.

A third reason for the fear is the invisibility of the danger. Radiation is not painful; it does not come from a hot red flame. Damage does not appear until hours later in the worst case or until years later for milder doses. Moreover, it varies by the individual—one person can be more sensitive than another.

The government does not deal with radioactivity in the same way it deals with other pollutants. The EPA role is minor. The Atomic Energy Commission kept most information secret, and the Department of Energy continues to keep weapon manufacturing secret. In fact, the AEC subordinated its safety responsibility to its mission of promoting the industry. When Congress established the AEC after World War II, it created the powerful Joint Committee for its own purposes. State governments had little role in the late 1960s, and the secrecy combined with technical complexity to put the topic beyond the realm of public debate until that time as well. Much has changed in the past two decades, however. Public-minded scientists have entered the debate. The National Environmental Policy Act allowed citizens a mechanism for probing government information. Public utility commissions began to assert themselves when the companies applied for permits to build and operate plants. Congress abolished its Joint Committee and split off the AEC's responsibility for safety to the Nuclear Regulatory Commission. The Low-Level Waste Act turned the federal system upside down.

Today, opponents of nuclear power and weapons seem to hold the upper hand. In general, they tend to be well educated, politically experienced, and comparatively wealthy. Indeed, they may own waterfront property that would be less valuable if a plant were built nearby. Besides scientists, many lay people have developed expertise in the technology. The opponents have multiple opportunities to intervene when the electric company wants permits for planning, constructing, and operating its plant. Opponents have an ally in the high costs of nuclear generation. With regard to the dangers of nuclear weapons, for years friends of the atom held up the specter of communism to justify building and testing weapons. The present danger from accidents, criminals, and outlaw nations is far less as is the need to test weapons.

CONCLUSION

Concern about the dangers of radiation has spawned dozens of grass roots organizations. People from New Hampshire to California have spontaneously organized to protest against nuclear reactors. The farm hand who impulsively climbed the tower at Seabrook gave a dramatic start to the protest. Later, the hundreds of dedicated protesters arrested and jailed in the National Guard armories refused bail in order to deny the governor an easy way out. Because nuclear engineering is so highly technical, anti-nuclear groups needed scientists to testify at the AEC hearings. It often found these resources nearby, such as James Watson on Long Island, or within the AEC, such as John Goffman. A technical cause of the mass movement was the building boom for nuclear plants in the 1960s. And the electric power industry itself has been structured with giant monopolies that need big, expensive plants, dependent on either uranium or coal. The industry dependence on the AEC eventually meant many stages at which citizens could intervene.

Certainly, radiation dangers have produced a polarized situation to those for and against nuclear power. The life cycle of nuclear protest ran its course between the late 1960s and the early 1980s, ending in a victory for its opponents, and to continue the analogy of a life cycle, the movement is enjoying a quiet retirement.

The legacy of the movement is a series of citizen groups such as Ralph Nader's Critical Mass and local alliances such as Clamshell, Abalone, Catfish, and so forth. Because the economics have turned against nuclear plants, the industry side is quiescent. Industry realized that both high- and low-level waste needs permanent disposal. With the facility at Yucca Mountain semi-halted, electric companies continue to keep their spent fuel rods next to their reactors. As the amount piles up, some utilities are putting the older waste in concrete vaults on their property. This system of, in effect, doing nothing seems to produce the fewest objections. Plans to build regional dumps for low-level nuclear waste have been stymied by local citizens objecting to it being in their backyards.

Partisanship offers little understanding of policy on radiation today. In the 1950s, Democrats foresaw that nuclear energy would fit the New Deal framework hydroelectric power. By the end of the 1970s, the Democrats had backed away from the atom and tended to favor the environmental side.

Governmental procedures have had a great impact on radiation policy. During the thirty years when the AEC was "king of the hill" and the Joint Committee on Atomic Energy proclaimed the will of Congress, the nuclear industry was largely closed to the public due to secrecy and a general consensus to promote it. The public did not know what went on and could not intervene anyway. Once Congress passed the National Environmental Policy Act, the AEC could no longer maintain its secrecy. Citizens could intervene against permits for construction of and the operation of the plants. Splitting the AEC into the Nuclear Regulatory Commission and ERDA (later DOE) established an agency charged with protecting the public. At present, the most important nuclear issue is reducing the stockpile of nuclear weapons held by the United States and Russia. This situation naturally calls for a bureaucratic solution, not social movements, interest groups, or parties. Assuming the international agreement remains, it will call for experts to plan strategies, develop methods, improve techniques, and practice good engineering.

NOTES

1. John G. Fuller, *We Almost Lost Detroit* (New York: Crowell, 1975).
2. Catherine Caufield, *Multiple Exposures* (New York: Harper and Row, 1989), 239–240.
3. Roger M. Macklis, "The Great Radium Scandal" *Scientific American* August 1993, 94–99.
4. Jimmy Carter, *Why Not the Best?* (New York: Bantam Books, 1975), 59.
5. Jerome Rice, *The Antinuclear Movement*, (Boston, MA: Twayne, 1982), 4; Richard S. Lewis, *The Nuclear Power Rebellion* (New York: Viking, 1972).
6. Richard Corrigan, "Congress Takes a Chip Off Carter's Energy Block," *National Journal* (June 11, 1977), 890.

7. Mark Hertsgaard, *Nuclear Inc.* (New York: Pantheon, 1983), 213.

8. Zhores A. Medvedev, *The Legacy of Chernobyl* (New York: Norton, 1990); Nigel Hawkes et al., *Chernobyl* (New York: Random House, 1987), 101–103; Bernard L. Cohen, *The Nuclear Energy Option* (New York: Plenum, 1990), 109–112.

9. Edward L. Gershey et al., *Low-Level Radioactive Waste* (New York: Van Nostrand Reinhold, 1990); Raymond L. Murray, *Understanding Radioactive Waste* (Columbus, OH: Batelle Press, 1989).

10. Jeffrey S. Hill and Carol S. Weissert, "Implementation and the Irony of Delegation: the Politics of Low-Level Radioactive Waste Disposal," *Journal of Politics* 57 (1995), 344–369.

CHAPTER 6
PROTECTING THE ENDANGERED SPECIES AND THE WILDERNESS

The environmental problems addressed so far have been negative. Air and water are dirty, and radioactivity contaminates homes and buildings; in contrast, the problems in the next three chapters involve protecting positive features: saving birds, animals, and plants from extinction and preserving wilderness in the mountains, along rivers, and at the seaside. Guarding a species often has international aspects; saving tigers and whales from extinction cannot be accomplished within the boundaries of the United States.

The bald eagle—the symbol the founders of the Republic chose because of its majesty, its prevalence along the rivers and bays of the thirteen new states, and its bond to the ancient Roman republic—once faced extinction in the forty-eight states. In 1940, with the number of eagles falling and their symbolism rising with the war in Europe, Congress passed the Bald Eagle Protection Act. Nevertheless, the birds continued to decline. Only a thousand lived in the contiguous states by 1972. Rachel Carson pointed out how DDT was causing fragile egg shells and deformed chicks. In the rural west and Alaska, hunters shot the eagles for sport, going so far as to chase them in airplanes. Since then their numbers have grown to more than ten thousand. Increased awareness of ecology during the Environmental Decade revealed that many other birds, mammals, and plants were in danger, too. Overseas, leopards, rhinoceroses, and tigers face extinction. Under the seas, whales and porpoises are threatened.

Every year the earth loses 17,500 species forever. While most of them are simpler forms of life, such as bacteria, fungi, and algae, they are the base of the food chain that supports more complex forms of life. For example, the loss of an insect usually means the loss of the flower it pollinates. Under provisions of the Endangered Species Act, the U.S. Fish and Wildlife Service lists 753 native species: 320 animals and 433 plants. Additionally, it lists 522 foreign species, and a secondary category of 248 other threatened species.

Protecting a species, even eagles, often becomes controversial. Ranchers believe wolves kill sheep. Loggers and their employers believe saving the spotted owl prevents them from harvesting trees. In North Carolina, protecting the red cockaded woodpecker stopped construction of condominiums. In California, a butterfly blocked building houses. Today, scientists have become aware that trying to save a single species by itself is not enough. The spotted owl needs a rain forest in which to live. Their goal now is to save an entire habitat of forest, water, plants, and animals.

The problem of saving a habitat is even greater overseas than at home. The tropical rain forest presents the ultimate in biological complexity. An acre in Amazon Basin or Indonesia can be home to five or ten times as many species as an acre in a temperate climate. The total amount of biomass locked up in trees, ferns, bacteria, and animals is twice as great. The widespread burning of tropical forests releases so much carbon into the atmosphere that it accelerates global warming through the greenhouse effect. Moreover, due to this great diversity and mass, burning and clearing destroys opportunities to find new pharmaceuticals. Natural plants and animals are the original source of 40 percent of current drugs. Modern agriculture depends heavily on a few crops, leaving it vulnerable to disease, climate, or soil fertility. Of eighty thousand edible plant species, only twenty (like corn or wheat) supply 90 percent of the world's food. Cross breeding with wild species has reinvigorated domestic ones. Only a few thousand pygmy chimpanzees survive in the central African jungle. Also known as the bonobo, this closest relative of homo sapiens shares 99 percent of the same DNA and its social habits are much like humans. Anthropologists and zoologists fear it will become extinct before they can learn what light it sheds on human behavior, psychology, and physiology. Logging and warfare threaten it; the local people eat it, saying that bonobo meat is delicious.

Endangered species raise issues of environmental protection nearly opposite of air and water pollution or contamination from hazardous waste or radioactivity. In the cases of pollution, the danger is *to* humans, while in the cases of species and land, the danger is *from* humans. The issue also goes beyond health and science to raise questions of philosophy and religion. The sight of a soaring eagle lifts up the heart; the extinction of whales casts it down. Preserving wilderness raises similar concerns—safeguarding habitat for threatened animals and plants is one reason, but beyond that the reasons tend to be aesthetic, emotional, and spiritual. People have an innate love of nature, of mountain tops, and of pristine valleys. Most intriguingly, people's innate wish to protect the wilderness even extends to places they never have or never will visit personally. Heartfelt concern for the caribou range on the North Slope of Alaska is genuine and widespread.

People grow angry at the thought of lumber companies clearcutting in Oregon and Maine or motorcyclists tearing up the Mojave desert. The human love of the wilderness defies logic—it is a mystery.

BACKGROUND

Paleontologists calculate life began 3.7 billion years ago, a mere billion years after the formation of the planet itself. Multicelled plants and animals date back 570 million years. Plants emerged onto land four hundred million years ago and animals crawled out of the sea a hundred million years later. Evolution has not run a smooth course, however. The fossil record shows five mass extinctions in the past five hundred million years. During each of those episodes between 14 to 84 percent of genera (families of plants or animals) disappeared. The Permian Triassic episode 245 million years ago killed off marine invertebrates and terrestrial plants and insects. The Cretaceous Tertiary extinction sixty-five million years ago ended the age of reptiles; the dinosaurs were gone. A smaller extinction only eleven thousand years ago terminated one hundred species of birds and large animals in North and South America.[1] This period was also when the proto-Indians were crossing the Bering Sea from Siberia to Alaska and then southward. In Europe, it was the New Stone Age, with the earliest civilizations appearing eight thousand years ago.

For the past two million years, the earth has also suffered a series of ice ages. The periods of glaciation have lasted about one hundred thousand years each and the warm periods have lasted only ten to twenty thousand years. During the cooling, animals have retreated south to warmer climates. The same two million years have seen the evolution of humans from the australopithecus (the most famous of which is the Lucy fossil) to the beginning of the modern species, homo sapiens, two hundred thousand years ago. Archaeological exhumation of stone tools and meat bones demonstrate that humans hunted large animals one hundred thousand years ago in Africa and Asia. The impact was minor, however. Only seven species became extinct in Africa. Human impact appears to have been bigger in the Americas. The Pleistocene overkill theory maintains that human hunting wiped out the megafauna like mastodons, sabertooth tigers, and giant sloths. This theory answers the question of why the large animals perished, but not the small ones.[2] For example, before this extinction, the California condor, a scavenger recently down to its last two dozen survivors, lived all across the continent as far away as Florida. After the larger animals became extinct, they had less carrion to eat.

American Indians before Columbus changed the environment. Hunting, trapping, and fishing placed pressure on animal populations. Cultivation of maize and peppers depleted the soil. They lived along rivers where they disturbed the ecology. In the arid Chycaco Canyon of New Mexico, lived the Anasazi Indians. Although little is known about this mysterious people, one theory poses that they lived between 900 to 1150, and that they harvested ponderosa pine and piñyon for houses and firewood. The land turned to scrub, the soil eroded, and the water table sank.[3] In Ohio and Indiana, evidence indicates deliberate burning created small prairies, which the early European explorers assumed were natural. These American Indians set fires to clear land for agriculture and to improve hunting; whitetail deer frequented the edge of the woods to graze and were easier to hunt there than in the deep forest. Great Plains Indians started prairie fires to force buffalo into a canyon or over a cliff to be killed for food, and they hunted eagles and condors for their feathers. Although North America was close to natural when Columbus arrived on San Salvador Island, it was not pristine. The year 1492 cannot be the calamitous starting date for endangered species.

French settlement took hold only along the St. Lawrence River. The abundant French names for rivers, lakes, and towns memorializes their wanderlust, not their settlement. French trappers ranged as far west as the Rocky Mountains and as far south as the Ohio River, but their numbers were small and they mostly adopted native ways. With one exception, few animal species suffered. The exception was the beaver, which the trappers nearly wiped out. The European market for beaver hats first decimated the animals in Quebec and New York state, then on throughout the upper midwest. When European fashion finally turned away from beaver hats about 1830, the beaver had been so heavily depopulated in other regions of the continent that the trappers were trapping high up the slopes of the Rockies.

Along the Gulf coast and in the desert southwest, Spanish settlement was light. More settlers could find a livelihood in California along the coast and a few rivers. Giant ranches had thousands of cattle that grazed and overgrazed. The major product was hides, which sailing ships could carry thousands of miles, unlike beef, which could only be sold locally.

The impact of the American Indians, French, and Spanish was far less than that of the English colonists. The Virginia Company came to grow tobacco, mine metal, and collect fur. The Pilgrims and Puritans came to create religious communities safe from the Church of England. William Penn and Lord Baltimore founded their colonies to be religious havens. Settlers came to North Carolina for the tall trees to make masts and sap that was turned into turpentine for the Royal Navy. Whether the colonists came for natural resources or religion, very few valued or respected the natural environment. They believed the endless, dark forests were filled with danger from wild animals and American Indians that could kill them, so the early farmers cleared as much acreage as they could.

Pioneers in northern New England and the Allegheny Mountains scraped crops into the rocky, infertile soil only to later abandon them due to erosion. They shot and trapped animals without considering the consequences. Wolves, foxes, and bobcats were the settler's top targets because they killed sheep, cattle, and hogs. In the fertile limestone valleys in Pennsylvania, western Virginia, and later in Kentucky, Tennessee, and Ohio, they felled the trees and killed the animals. With little rain, the Great Plains were vulnerable. While building the transcontinental railway, the Union Pacific company hired William Cody, who earned the name Buffalo Bill because of the thousands of buffalo he shot to feed work crews. Once the railway opened, "sportsmen" arrived from the east coast and Europe to kill as many buffalo as possible merely for pleasure. Hunters would kill a buffalo, but only eat the tongue, leaving the huge carcass to rot. The orgy of bloodshed took its toll; the size of the great herds began to decline drastically. When the young Theodore Roosevelt heard this, he headed west to get his trophy while a few still remained.[4] His conversion to conservation came later.

RELIGIOUS VIEWS OF THE WILDERNESS

Protecting the wilderness has followed a track parallel to protecting plants and animals. Fascination with deserts, forests, and mountains shows in some of the most ancient writing of civilization. Certainly, it antedated the invention of writing. Genesis tells how Adam and Eve were created in a natural paradise. Later, it tells how Moses wandered in the wilderness to purify himself to lead the Hebrews out of Egypt and he climbed Mount Sinai to receive the Ten Commandments. The Hebrews wandered in the desert for forty years. Scholars point out how the Hebrews first worshiped the mountain itself, then began to conceive of God as existing everywhere they were, not just on Mount Sinai. Elijah exhorted the prophets of Israel on Mount Carmel and climbed Mount Horeb, where, after wind, earthquake, and fire, God spoke to him in "a still small voice."[5] David fled into the wilderness to prepare for battle against King Saul. Psalm 95 declares: "O come, let us sing unto the Lord; . . . / In his hand are the depths of the earth; the heights of the mountains are his also. / The sea is his for he made it; for his hands formed the dry land."[6]

John the Baptist wandered in the wilderness. Jesus, to prepare for his ministry, lived in the wilderness for forty days and returned to the wilderness before going to Jerusalem and his crucifixion. The gospels tell of his transfiguration on the mountain top, where he meets Moses and Elijah, both of whom wandered in the wilderness themselves. The Evangelist John sees a revelation of the mother (the church) and the young son fleeing to the desert. Early saints like Anthony and Basil the Great lived as hermits in the desert to avoid the corruption of cities. St. Benedict adapted much of the hermits' life in his monastic order. To the present day, monks and nuns, especially Trappists, continue this legacy.

When Columbus discovered America, he wrote to King Ferdinand and Queen Isabella that, according to his reading of theologians, the earthly paradise of Eden could be found in the New World somewhat to the south. The Church of England carried forward and enhanced the Catholic monastic Venite in its service of Morning Prayer.[7] Based almost verbatim on Psalm 95, the popular chant praises God for creating nature.

The Pilgrims and Puritans believed God called them to an Exodus to a wilderness more like Eden than Sinai. The prototype was John's vision of the woman who finds refuge in the wilderness.[8] The Puritan preacher John Cotton believed New England was "a Paradise, as if this were the Garden of Eden."[9] John Eliot was less glowing when he declared that God directed the Puritans to the Massachusetts wilderness instead of Canada with its lucrative fur trade, or Virginia with it warm climate, in order to avoid temptations. Roger Williams, the founder of Rhode Island, believe the wilderness clarified and purified the Christian mind. An election sermon preached in 1668 reminded voters that they were the seed God selected to grow in the wilderness. Cotton Mather declared that in New England "the blessed Jesus intended a resting place" for the reformed church. On the other hand, Mather noted that the wilderness was full of temptation and devils. As the thirteen colonies moved closer to rebellion against England, preachers identified America with the Exodus of Israel from bondage under the pharaoh.

German immigrants brought a legacy of mystical retreat to the wilderness. They reproduced the hermitages in the old country in establishing hermitages in Pennsylvania. Johann George Rapp's utopian community of Harmony in Pennsylvania and later New Harmony in Indiana are the best known. John Wesley translated and adopted five of these German hymns on the theme of wilderness. Quakers used the image of the peaceful wilderness as their goal of peace with the American Indians and with each other. Edward Hicks painted more than a hundred versions of "The Peaceable Kingdom," recalling Isaiah II: 6–9. For him, the scene represented the success of William Penn's colonization and, more generally, the Quaker goal of concord. John Chapman's wandering on the frontier in the guise of Johnny Appleseed came from his Swedeborgian theology.

The Plains Indians used to go alone onto the prairie to seek a vision. In a puberty rite, a boy would spend several days by himself until he saw his personal vision presaging his life as a man. Older men might go onto the prairie for renewal. On the other hand, American Indians did not necessarily consider the prairie or the forest to be wilderness; for them it was more like a park where they hunted, fished, and lived—the land was an extension of them, just as they were an extension of the land.

VOICES FOR PROTECTION

A few voices spoke out for the animals. Jean Jacques Audubon came to Pennsylvania from France in 1803 at age eighteen to escape conscription for the Napoleon's wars. Audubon continued his boyhood love of drawing birds while pursuing a living as a farmer, merchant, and investor. After his store and mill in Kentucky went bankrupt, Audubon embarked on drawing birds to earn money. He traveled to the Florida everglades, Missouri, and Newfoundland to portray the birds. (To get the exact details, he shot his specimens.) No American printer had the engraving skill or faith in sales so he travelled to Edinburgh and London to find a publisher for *Birds of America*. All the plates were drawn from nature and life sized. Known as the "Elephant Folio" because of its twenty-nine-inch by thirty-nine-inch size, each book had 435 hand colored prints, most of which are now unbound with individual prints in museums and private collections.[10] With

Two great crested flycatchers fight for dominance in John James Audubon's engraving. The artist, who drew birds from life, full-size, and exact in their anatomy and environment, published *Birds of America* between 1827 and 1838. The author's father purchased this print in 1935 for $25. Today, it is worth several thousand dollars.

the completion of *Birds of America,* the artist began its companion, *Quadrupeds of North America*, travelling as far as Fort Laramie in Wyoming to complete it.

By the 1850s, prosperous businessmen in the burgeoning cities took up hunting as a sport. Like many other trends in nineteenth-century America, this one copied the English upper class. Hunting clubs purchased preserves in the country where the animals could live before being shot. Sportsmen, as they called themselves, did not kill for food but for the contest. Clubs, which sprang up in every city, provided excursions that would test the men's strength and wits against the mountains and animals during the day, and that would allow time for sipping brandy and telling stories in the evening. The alternatives back in the city were female-dominated dinner parties and balls.

In addition to sport, the countryside fit into the Romantic movement of poetry and painting of Europe and in the United States. These were the years of the Hudson River School of Landscape Painting, of Constable in England, and of the Barbizon School in France. Beginning in 1829, George Catlin travelled in the west determined to paint the beauty of the land and the Plains Indians who lived there. The beauty of nature was an antidote for the artificial life in the city, while hunting re-created the pioneer spirit and brought a man closer to nature. Cities were getting smokier, dirtier, and more crowded with immigrants. The upper classes felt little in common with the new citizens, and resented the political bosses who dominated the cities with their votes. This period in history was the era of "machines" based on corruption and voting fraud.

The demise of the mighty buffalo awakened eastern concern. The railroads began the systematic slaughter, first to feed their workers, then by bringing sportsmen from the cities. The Army shot them in order to starve the natives into submission. And the invention of breech-loading rifles made the killing more efficient. George B. Grinnell, the editor of *Forest and Stream*, began a campaign to save the noble beasts. In 1887, he joined with Theodore Roosevelt, now less eager to kill, to form Boone and Crockett club that sought to protect animals and remote natural areas. Its members came from New York's upper crust. In 1908, Congress established the National Bison Range in Montana. The American Bison Society located thirty-seven bison to populate it.

Herons and egrets were bird species that were nearly annihilated because of the fad in women's fashion for big hats with plumes taken from these birds. In 1886, Grinell took the lead by establishing a society named after Audubon. As a boy he had lived on the late artist's estate in New York, where the widow, Lucy Audubon, taught him in elementary school.

Earnest Thompson Seton, later active in establishing the Boy Scouts of America, moved from the Romantic to the scientific in his hundreds of animal stores and books. He disliked hunters, often characterizing them as the villains in his writing. On behalf of a partridge caught in a snare, he asks rhetorically: "Have wild things no moral or legal rights?" Unlike most Romantics, Seton admired predators as well as their cuddly prey, accepting that killing for food was a law of nature. His contemporary, Charles Roberts, frequently made a wolf or a mountain lion the hero.[11]

During the 1870s, hunters and farmers did what seemed impossible: they drove the passenger pigeon to extinction. In Audubon's time its number was still astronomical as tens of billions lived in North America. During migration, the birds filled the sky, blocking out the sun. Their flocks could take three days to pass a single location; when they roosted for the night, trees crumpled under their collective weight. The birds could breed only when gathered in giant flocks, an avian orgy. Upon learning where the birds were congregating, commercial hunters would load railroad cars with stoves and jars to pickle the pigeons for shipment to the cities. This took its toll. After 1879, only a few thousand survived and the last one died in 1914 in the Cincinnati zoo. Although the passenger pigeon was neither very beautiful nor challenging to shoot, it seemed inconceivable that such a common bird could disappear.

In His Own Words: Theodore Roosevelt
Rancher, Hunter, Conservationist, and President

The extermination of the buffalo has been a veritable tragedy of the animal world.[1]

Ever since man in recognizably human shape made his appearance on this planet, he has been an appreciable factor in the destruction of other forms of animal life. . . . Never before were such enormous quantities of big beasts and large birds slain as in the nineteenth century.[2]

The true way to kill wolves, however, is to hunt them with greyhounds on the great plains. Nothing more exciting than this sport can possibly be imagined.[3]

The lion had come out on the left of the bushes. . . . Seeing Simba and me on foot, he turned toward us, his tail lashing quicker and quicker. Resting my elbow on Simba's bent shoulder, I took steady aim and pressed the trigger: the bullet went in between the neck and shoulder, and the lion fell over on his side, one fore leg in the air.[4]

The art and practice of photographing wild animals in their native haunts has made great progress in recent years. It is itself a branch of sport. . . .[5]

When governor of New York . . . I had been in consultation with Gifford Pinchot and F. H. Newell, and had shaped my recommendations about forestry largely in accordance with their suggestions. Like other men who had thought about the national future at all, I had been growing more and more concerned over the destruction of the forests.[6]

When I first visited California, it was my good fortune to see the "big trees," the Sequoias, and then to travel down into the Yosemite, with John Muir. . . . The second night we camped in a snow storm, on the edge of the canyon walls, under the spreading limbs of a grove of mighty silver fir; and next day we went down into the wonderland of the valley itself.[7]

I also appointed a Fine Arts Council, an unpaid body of the best architects, painters, and sculptors in the country to advise the government as to the erection and decoration of all new buildings. The "pork-barrel" senators and congressmen felt for this body an instinctive, and perhaps from their standpoint a natural, hostility. . . .[8]

1. "Hunting Trips of a Ranchman," Vol. 1, *The Works of Theodore Roosevelt, Memorial edition* (New York: Charles Scribner, 1923), 223.
2. Book review in *The Outlook,* January 20, 1915. Quoted in *Theodore Roosevelt: a Selection from his Writings,* Mario R. DiNunzio, ed., (New York: St, Martin's, 1994), 242.
3. "The Wilderness Hunter," Vol.2, *The Works of Theodore Roosevelt, Memorial edition* (New York: Charles Scribner, 1923), 368.
4. "African Game Trails," Vol. 5, *The Works of Theodore Roosevelt, Memorial edition* (New York: Charles Scribner, 1924), 73, 75.
5. Introduction to *Camera Shots of Big Game* by A. G. Wallihan (1901). Quoted in *Theodore Roosevelt: a Selection from his Writings,* Mario R. DiNunzio, ed., (New York: St. Martin's, 1994), 307.
6. "Autobiography," Vol. 20, *The Works of Theodore Roosevelt, National edition* (New York: Charles Scribner, 1926), 384.
7. Ibid, 311–312.
8. Ibid, 411.

GOVERNMENT SCIENCE

The federal government's role at the time was small. One of its few environmental actions was to ban hunting in Yellowstone National Park, which was home to a few remaining buffalo. In 1884, the Department of Agriculture established the

Office of Ornithology and Mammalogy, with a staff of two. (Soon renamed the Biological Survey, it eventually moved in 1939 to the Department of the Interior.) Congress wanted the office to give practical help to farmers, but the director kept pushing it toward science. Protecting ducks and geese during migration challenged the agency. Game departments in states that wanted to control hunting were powerless to stop the slaughter in lenient states. In 1913, Congress gave the secretary of agriculture authority over migration under the rationale that it was a form of interstate commerce enumerated in the Constitution.

The early mission of the Biological Survey was more to kill animals than to protect them. Early agricultural extension stations experimented to learn the most effective poisons and traps to control gopher, prairie dog, and squirrel populations; oftentimes, they gave farmers the poisons free of charge. The U.S. Forest Service hired trappers, soon called "gopher chokers." The Department of Agriculture also encouraged states to pay bounties for killing wolves, foxes, and coyotes. By the mid-1920s, wolves were wiped out in every state except Minnesota.

The goal of protecting animals generated some of the earliest scientific and lobbying associations that are so common today. In the early 1880s, the American Ornithologists' Union, an association of professional and amateur scientists, had lobbied Congress to establish the Office of Ornithology and Mammalogy. The Ecological Society of American first met in 1914.

From the late nineteenth century until about 1940, science evolved from amateur to professional. Factors promoting it were international journals, agricultural extension, land grant colleges, the introduction of universities on the German model, a government role in public health, and greater contact with European scientists. Many of the early zoologists were trained in medicine. Amateur and part-time scientists continued to contribute to "natural history" up to the end of this period mostly because museums were one of the few sponsors of scientific research. The advent of World War II evolved science into Big Science with atomic research, generous grants, the National Institute of Health, and the National Aeronautics and Space Administration (NASA). The day of the amateur was over.

The science of ecology arose during this time. In 1891, the Biological Survey began to classify the country according to life zones, based on its analysis of plants living on San Francisco Peak in New Mexico. These life zones, according to altitude, paralleled the terrain from the arctic to the tropics. The highest zone above the timberline was the tundra, much like the arctic where only moss and lichen survived. Below the timberline was a zone with stunted coniferous trees, then ponderosa pines, and so on down to the hot, arid desert. The next development was a theory of plant succession originating at the University of Nebraska. Assuming a beginning with bare ground, the first plants were grasses. Next came shrubs and cedars, followed by black cherry and pines, and so on until the land reached a climax stage. In the east and midwest, the climax was a hardwood forest of sugar maples and beeches. These species thrived with little sunlight, whereas earlier species like black cherry and pines could not sprout and grow in deep shade. The climax species have been permanent, unless a fire or windstorm sets back the clock of natural succession. The mix of climax species may be different in other locations. In the north or higher altitudes, the species may be spruce and fir. In arid western Nebraska, it might be grass with few trees, since trees require large amounts of water to survive. With time, the knowledge of plant ecology matched the goals of the Department of Agriculture. University of Chicago graduate students working at the Indiana Dunes branched out from plant ecology to study the animal life.[12] To this day, protecting the Indiana Dunes continues to be controversial.

While animal ecologists began to see the folly of poisoning, trapping, and shooting wolves, coyotes, and mountain lions, the Biological Survey continued to kill predators. Protecting the deer on the north rim of Grand Canyon in the 1920s proved to be a tragic failure. In 1906, the Agriculture Department designated the Kaibab National Forest as a wildlife refuge primarily for deer, and forbade hunting and cattle grazing. The deer multiplied rapidly, which appeared at first to mean the program was successful. By 1923, the deer were overrunning the forest and eating most of the undergrowth. The National Park Service in the Department of the Interior denied that the expanding deer population was a problem. The governor of Arizona did not want the national government overruling state game laws. During the winter of 1924 to 1925, cold, snowy weather, combined with the lack of food, left the large deer herds to freeze and starve. The following spring, deer carcasses were found littering the forest floor. In spite of this outcome, Arizona refused to cull the herd and sued to prevent the Forest Service from carrying out the action. The case went to the Supreme Court, which unexpectedly ruled against the state. Now the national government had the authority to override state game laws. The legal decision did not reverse the overall antipredator policy, however. Most game managers and hunters were not yet convinced.

Aldo Leopold joined the U.S. Forest Service in 1909, having graduated from the Yale forestry school. Assigned to Arizona and New Mexico territories, he labored to protect game by killing wolves and coyotes. His zeal to poison and shoot won him a gold medal in 1917. Over the next ten years, however, Leopold came to recognize that nature had a balance of its own. The disaster at the Kaibab National Forest was a prime example of game management gone wrong. His planning and supervising the establishment of Gila National Forest gave Leopold a broader perspective, which was also where he set up the nation's first wilderness area that was eventually named after him. His career moved on to the Forest Products Laboratory in Wisconsin to be an independent consultant and to be the University of Wisconsin's first professor of game management. Leopold took a prominent role in national policy and in writing the 1931 *Report on a Game Survey of the North Central States* and two years later *Game Management*. Franklin Roosevelt appointed him to the Committee on Wildlife Restoration. Leopold articulated his "land ethic" that extended the religious and social recognition that an individual is a member of a community: "The land ethic simply enlarges the boundaries of the community to include soils, waters, plants, and animals, or collectively: the land." After describing biological modes of cooperation, Leopold states: "The ecologist calls these symbioses. Politics and economics are advanced symbioses. . . ."[13]

Leopold was distressed that the few remaining wilderness preserves were found only in the Rocky Mountains, in isolated sections of the Great Plains, and in Alaska. He maintained that a man intuitively knows that wilderness "is something to be loved and cherished, because it gives definition and meaning to his life"—it has values for recreation, for science, and for wildlife. He observed that "in 1909, when I first saw the west, there were grizzlies in every major mountain mass, but you could travel for months without meeting a conservation officer."[14] Leopold was among the first to recognize that saving animals like the grizzly bear and the wolf demanded extensive land, advocating the need to combine national parks with surrounding national forests.

Others joined Leopold in recognizing that predator control was an exercise in futility. Survival of game birds, for example, depended more on food and habitat than safety from foxes. Observations of coyotes in Jackson Hole, Wyoming, showed they posed little danger to the elk herd (which the National Park Service continues to feed to this day). Study of wolves at Mount McKinley, Alaska, overturned the common wisdom about savage, "lone wolves." Both coyotes and wolves prey far more on the weak and starving elk and mountain sheep than on the healthy.

With more scientific understanding of ecology and the reformist impulse of the New Deal, the Park Service shifted its policies during the 1930s. It stopped poisoning coyotes in Yellowstone Park and created the National Park on Isle Royal in Lake Superior to protect a pack of wolves, almost the only ones remaining south of Canada. This did not mean fully accepting the natural order because the service continued to give extra protection to the more "cute and innocent" species. At the Grand Canyon it fed bears for the tourists to watch. Ecologists critical to this practice refer to bears, caribou, moose, tigers, and elephants as "charismatic megafauna."

Robert Marshall, born and raised in New York City, was another advocate of saving the wilderness. His father was a successful lawyer, a Jewish philanthropist, and a crusader for the Adirondack State Park, where the family summered. Joining the U.S. Forest Service, Marshall served in Montana, where he advocated protecting a million acres of wilderness. In 1930, he published a magazine article "The Problem of the Wilderness," soon called the Magna Carta of the movement. In 1935, he joined Leopold, Howard Zahniser, and five others to form the Wilderness Society, which he backed with personal donations eventually totaling $400,000. Marshall loved camping and hiking. The number of miles he walked was extraordinary; his standard mileage was thirty miles a day. When other campers were finishing dinner after a long day, Marshall would try to entice one or two companions to walk another five miles with him for exercise before bed. In fact, he was not a fast hiker, but shuffled along the trail.[15] The Bob Marshall Wilderness in Montana honors him.

142

THE WILDERNESS ACT

Zahniser left his job in the Biological Survey in 1945 to become the first full-time executive secretary for the Wilderness Society and to edit *Living Wilderness*, the society's magazine. Nicknamed the Wilderness Apostle, he came to believe Congress should enact a law to protect those areas. On behalf of his own society and in cooperation with others like the Natural Resources Defense Council (of which he was a co-founder in 1946), "Zahnie" lobbied and gathered support. The Wilderness Act was first introduced as a bill in 1962, its sponsor was Senator Clinton Anderson of New Mexico, formerly Truman's secretary of agriculture. In the Senate and more so in the House of Representatives, it encountered stiff opposition from the U.S. Chamber of Commerce and the American National Cattleman's Association. The legislatures of both Wyoming and Idaho sent resolutions in opposition. Representative Wayne Aspinall of Colorado resisted the bill from his powerful position of chairman of the Interior Committee. Aspinall believed in conquering nature, especially the Colorado River; during his twenty-four years in Congress, he sponsored more than a dozen dams and storage projects. Finally, in 1964 he agreed to a compromise in the wilderness bill by adding a commission to review all public lands. Zahniser's campaign for wilderness areas was succeeding as the bill neared passage in May. He had just completed an eleven thousand-word report for the Senate Interior Committee, when he suddenly died at age fifty-eight. Zahniser's martyrdom inspired Congress to pass the Wilderness Act. (His premature death by a heart attack paralleled two of his co-founders of the society—Bob Marshall died at age thirty-eight and Aldo Leopold at sixty-one.)

The act defined a wilderness "as an area where the earth and its community of life are untrammeled by man, where man himself is a visitor who does not remain." Furthermore, it is "primeval . . . with the imprint of man's work substantially unnoticeable" and has "solitude or a primitive and unconfined type of recreation." To qualify, it must be owned by the national government and be at least five thousand acres in size. The law immediately deposited nine million acres and followed with another fifty-two million acres later. In accord with the compromise with Representative Aspinall, the government began a ten-year review process and mandated that adding or removing land required congressional action. Senator Anderson wrote: "Wilderness is an anchor to windward. Knowing it is there, we can also know that we are still a rich nation, tending our resources as we should—not a people in despair searching every last nook and cranny of our land for a board of lumber, a barrel of oil, a blade of grass, or a tank of water."[16]

In 1968, Congress protected another sort of wilderness: rivers. Since colonial times, people had been damming streams and rivers to grind wheat or weave textiles. The government had begun damming them for irrigation and electric power with the Bureau of Reclamation in 1902. The New Deal marked the high point with the TVA, Bonneville in the Pacific northwest, and Fort Peck in Montana. As governor from 1929 to 1933, Franklin Roosevelt promoted the Power Authority

Scorecard for the ENDANGERED SPECIES and the WILDERNESS

LAWS
Endangered Species Act 1973. Bald and Golden Eagle Protection Act. Migratory Bird Treaty Act. Antiquities Act 1906. Wilderness Act 1964. Federal Land Policy Management Act (FLPMA) 1976. National Forest Management Act. Multiple Use Sustained Yield Act 1960. Resource Planning Act 1974. Alaska Lands Act 1980.

NUMBERS AND SIZE
858 endangered species in the United States and 521 abroad
Wilderness system grew from 10 million acres in 1970 to 100 million acres.

CONGRESS
House Committee on Resources (formerly Interior), subcommittees on Parks, Fisheries, Water, Energy, and Forests
Committee on Agriculture, subcommittee on Forestry
Senate Committee on Energy and Natural Resources (formerly Interior), subcommittees on Parks and on Forests and Public Land Management
Committee on Agriculture, subcommittee on Forestry

AGENCIES
Department of the Interior   Department of Agriculture   State agencies
• Fish and Wildlife Service   • Forest Service
• National Park Service
• Bureau of Land Management

INTEREST GROUPS
Audubon Society   Friends of the Earth
Ducks Unlimited   Logging companies
Sierra Club   American Forest and Paper Association
National Wildlife Federation   Mining companies
Wilderness Society   American Mining Congress
The Nature Conservancy   Ranchers
Greenpeace   National Cattlemen's Association
Natural Resources Defense Council

Source: EPA *25th Anniversary Report* 1995.

of the State of New York. The problem was that every dam flooded a valley, which displaced farmers and natural beauty. By the 1960s, environmentalists pushed for the value of leaving the rivers in their natural condition. Damming would prevent canoeing and trout fishing. Advocates of the dam had pointed out the recreational benefits of reservoirs; environmentalists countered that the country had enough flat water. It did not need more waterskiing and bass fishing. In fact, agencies like the Corps of Engineers were notorious for exaggerating the economic benefits of recreation when trying to justify their construction costs. For example, their embellished calculus assumed that swimmers would swim all the way into winter and that fishing poles would crowd every ten feet.

By 1972, the government recognized a new threat to the wilderness and other public land: five million motorcycles, snowmobiles, dune buggies, and jeeps. These off-road vehicles could penetrate remote areas, often damaging fragile terrain in just a few hours of joyriding. Motorcycles in the Mojave Desert in California chopped up the delicate soil and plants that would take fifty years to recover. A dune buggy on Cape Cod or the Outer Banks could hack off the grass that prevented the sand from blowing away. A snowmobile could travel undetected far into a mountain forest where the visitors might secretly shoot a wolf or trap a ferret. Rangers could not patrol all these remote locations.

DEEP ECOLOGY

For radical environmentalists, preserving wilderness areas is only the beginning. They despair of shallow programs like National Forests where logging and mining may be permitted, parks with hotels and trailer camp grounds, and protecting birds and animals because they are beautiful. Techniques that depend on scientific experts or allow a certain tonnage of sulfur dioxide to pollute the air are also shallow. Instead, they propose a Deep Ecology where the wilderness is once more the rule as it was in prehistoric times. This movement presents an alternative to the consumerism and materialism that devastates Mother Earth.

Arne Naess coined the term "deep ecology" in 1973 as a contrast to the shallow ecology of limited piecemeal programs, decisions such as denying a permit to one factory, or establishing a sanctuary for only one bird. Naess taught philosophy at the University of Oslo from 1939 to 1970 when he retired to devote full-time to the movement, which is based on religion, philosophy and non-violent persuasion (mainly Buddhism and Taoism, which contribute respect for all living beings, harmony, and reincarnation). Naess applauds the seventeenth-century Dutch philosopher, Baruch Spinoza, who set for a unified system weaving together God and Nature. Spinoza's philosophy influenced the nineteenth-century Romantic movement, and later Emerson, Thoreau, Cooper, and Muir. Naess also admires Gandhi and advocates non-violence.

Deep Ecology starts with a self-realization that extends beyond the individual or the family to encompass all of nature, not just humans. By maintaining the tenet that "the earth does not belong to humans,"[17] the movement holds that all animals and plants have an equal right to live and blossom, that is, to self-realization, and that humans have no authority to harm other animals and plants except for vital needs. The future, holistic world will be far different, by maintaining "a substantially smaller human population." Addressing the voracious appetite of the industrialized countries, Naess maintains the "population reduction must have the highest priority in those societies."[18] Humans will have to lower their material standard of living, thereby consumerism will disappear in favor of appreciation of life quality. The transformation will not be swift; instead, it will take hundreds of years. Spiritual life will dominate (although it will have little in common with institutional Christianity since most Christian theology, as characterized by Naess, presents "a crude dominating anthropocentric emphasis."[19]), and meditation will provide understanding and solace. The form will incorporate mysticism, much of it derived from Buddhism and Taoism, and a bit from Christian mystics.

Paul Shepard offers a more explicit and practical view of an ecological utopia of the future. He claims that the prehistoric hunter-gather of ten thousand years ago was more fully human than any time since. Shepard defends his belief by stating that humans at that time operated as small nomadic clans. They did not have to clear forests, change the flow of rivers, or drain swamps for cities or agriculture. They picked berries, dug edible roots, and killed just enough animals to meet their needs. Shepard believes that agriculture destroys both the land and the farmer, and that modern agri-business is the worst. He believes humans need wild animals in their habitats, and that domestic ones are pathetic substitutes. For humans to cause extinction of a species is a crime. While Shepard despairs that the total world population is far too big, he believes it cannot level off at fewer than eight billion people. In order to preserve wilderness areas in the interiors of the continents, humans will have to live in approximately one hundred sixty thousand cities, with each containing fifty thousand inhabitants located close to each other along the coastlines. Due to their high density, the architecture of the cities will be far from primitive or pastoral. The fifty thousand residents will live in high-rise apartment buildings connected with elaborately covered walkways. The next problem is how to feed them without advanced agriculture since hunting and small vegetable gardens will be insufficient. His answer is algae and kelp.[20]

Naess's version of a Deep Ecological utopia is not so grim. People would take up lifestyles of hunting and gathering similar to the American Indians or the people of the Bronze Age. This revolution in lifestyles assumes a much lower total population. The goal is not to be primitive for its own sake, but to live in harmony with nature, and the experience will be joyful. Although Naess does not offer this example, Sam Houston, the first president of the Republic of Texas, makes a good model. While a teenager, he ran away from home to live for three years with the Cherokee Indians in the Cumberland Mountains of Tennessee. He quickly grew to love the adventure, the forest, and the comradeship provided by the Cherokee.

THE ENDANGERED SPECIES ACT

In response to commercial killing of herons and egrets for hats, many states enacted laws to protect the birds, but found them hard to enforce because poachers quickly shipped the feathers across the state line. In the Lacey Act of 1900, Congress backed up the states by making it illegal to ship in interstate commerce feathers and pelts taken in violation of state laws. To provide a sanctuary in 1903, Theodore Roosevelt established the Pelican Island National Refuge, the first of fifty-one bird sanctuaries during his term.

146

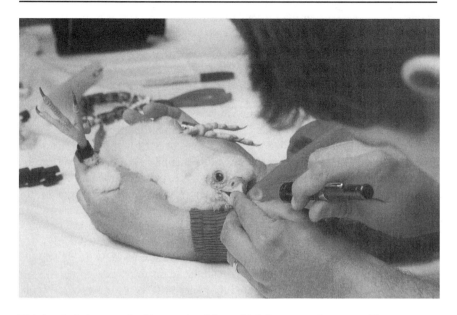

This banded, three-week-old peregrine falcon chick lives on a skyscraper. The endangered species has been introduced into cities, where it thrives by roosting on building ledges and hunting pigeons.

In 1913, Congresses passed the Migratory Bird Act giving the government jurisdiction over birds that migrated or ate insects, but the Supreme Court soon declared it was unconstitutional. The decision held because the framers in 1787 did not enumerate regulation of hunting in Article I, Section 8; therefore, Congress lacked the authority. Advocates for the birds circumvented the Court decision by negotiating a treaty with Canada (since many species of birds migrate north of the border), and persuaded Congress to pass the Migratory Bird Treaty Act, which the Supreme Court upheld in 1920 because under Article II of the constitution the president has clear authority to negotiate treaties. The strategy presaged the 1972 international agreement. The 1934 Hunting Stamp Act and the Pittman Robertson Act regularized funding for refuges, and that same year, the Fish and Wildlife Coordination Act required all agencies to consider the effect of their actions on wildlife.

The popular view of the federal government during the mid-1960s was more positive than any time since. The country was prosperous; wages were high and tax money flowed into Washington. Lyndon Johnson proclaimed that America could become a Great Society free of poverty and discrimination. During his administration, Johnson initiated 238 new programs. The 1966 Endangered Species Act gave the responsibility to the secretary of the interior and authorized the buying of land to protect habitat. An amendment in 1969 directed the Interior Department to promulgate a list of fish and wildlife in danger. In 1973, Congress expanded the program in the present Endangered Species Act to have a list of "endangered" and "threatened" species and of critical habitats, as well as a recovery plan to each species listed. In 1982, Congress added a program for critical habitat which applied to privately owned land.

Although the law is now a fact of life, criticism comes from both sides. Environmentalists complain that the very concept of saving a single species is flawed. By the time a plant or animal is discovered to be in danger, it is usually too late. The California condor, the largest and rarest bird in the world, was down to its last two dozen, mostly in zoos. Only a few survived in the wild. The population was so sparse that a male could not find a female for breeding. Ornithologists determined the only salvation was to capture birds for breeding in captivity, then release the fledglings. At present, about one hundred condors survive in the wild and in zoos. Captive breeding has saved other species as well. In 1880, the wild buffalo population was minuscule. Bulls and cows from a few captive herds and zoos supplied the stock later released in the wild. Many descend from a pair from the Bronx Zoo. Although these examples seem to be success stories, a single species cannot be saved without saving a habitat.

In 1941, only twenty-one whooping cranes still lived in the wild. These graceful birds, the tallest in America, overwintered in the Aransas Refuge in Texas. Because they migrated all the way to Canada, their chances of accident or being shot were high. The Fish and Wildlife Service hatched the chicks, then returned them to their parents. When this proved insufficient, the survey brooded the whooping crane eggs with sandhill cranes, a close relative. Although they grew into healthy adults, the foster children failed to return to their breeding sites. More serious, they became imprinted on their foster parents and were not successful in breeding with their own species. Today, the whooping crane population has grown to three hundred. Human intervention also restored the population of peregrine falcons, victimized by DDT. By 1964, not a single breeding pair lived east of the Mississippi River. These wanderers adapt well to city life, nesting in tall buildings and swooping down on squirrels and pigeons. The Fish and Wildlife Service situated a pair on top of the Interior Department headquarters. New York City claims the largest urban population.

The 1966 legislation recognized that saving a species often required saving its habitat, so the Fish and Wildlife Service was given authority to buy land. Habitat, however, is a tricky concept. It may need to be far larger than anticipated. An individual grizzly bear in a harsh environment like the North Slope of Alaska needs a home range of two hundred square miles, but in areas teeming with food, a grizzly may need only four square miles. A wolf pack may need up to six hundred square miles. For the grizzlies and wolves, attention has focused on Yellowstone Park. Ecologists recognized that the park by itself, with two million acres, is too small. The answer is the Greater Yellowstone Ecosystem which encompasses all of Yellowstone and Teton national parks, six national forests, and the elk refuge. Its total area is six million acres, and is home to 228 grizzly bears (only one thousand live in the lower forty-eight states, down from an estimated fifty thousand when Lewis and Clark explored the west). The Department of the Interior is currently reintroducing wolves into the Greater Yellowstone Ecosystem, a plan local ranchers vigorously oppose because they claim the wolves kill their lambs and calves.

Because the government owns nearly all the land in the Yellowstone region, a mega-habitat is possible. On the other hand, the purpose of a national forest is not the same as a park. A park is supposed "to preserve," while a forest has multiple uses of recreation, logging, mining, oil and gas drilling, and grazing for sheep and cattle. Loggers, miners, oil explorers, and ranchers oppose losing their opportunities to megahabits. Not surprisingly, other regions proposed as super-ecosystems have even more impediments than Yellowstone.

A further problem with preserving a habitat to protect a species is that it may in fact not be the optimal habitat. The red cockaded woodpecker is found chiefly on military installations in the south such as Fort Bragg, Fort Benning, and Elgin Air Force Base. These birds do not actually prefer living near artillery explosions, rifle ranges, and jet landings, but the military reservations are the only extensive land remaining with mature pines. Although the timber companies have millions of acres planted in pine, they harvest them after twenty years and the birds need older trees.

However, environmentalists have sometimes used the Endangered Species Act opportunistically. In 1963, the TVA proposed to build a dam on the Tellico River as it flowed into the Little Tennessee River. From the beginning many opposed the plan. Environmentalists wanted to preserve the river, economists pointed out that its cost-benefit ratio was ridiculously low, and Cherokee Indians wanted to preserve their ancestral graves. In spite of opposition, construction began in 1967. In 1975, just as other means to stop the dam fell away, a biologist serendipitously discovered a unique minnow: the snail darter. Biologists had no knowledge of any other snail darters that lived anywhere besides the Tellico River. On the other hand, it was really not a full fledged species but a subspecies closely related to other darters. Nevertheless, the U.S. Fish and Wildlife Service enlisted the minnow and the Circuit Court of Appeals issued an injunction to stop construction. The lawsuit went all the way to the U.S. Supreme Court, which ruled that the law clearly protected the minnow. Thus, the TVA could not close the gates on the now complete dam. The decision outraged many people in the Tennessee Valley. For them, it epitomized the ridiculous premise that minnows were more important than people. Around the country, it symbolized the absurdity of environmentalism. The Senate Republican leader, Howard Baker, who represented Tennessee and had long supported the TVA, vowed to reverse the Court. Calling in dozens of favors in the Senate and House, he persuaded Congress to pass a law exempting Tellico from the Endangered Species Act. A few years later snail darters were found in several other rivers.

American desire to protect endangered species extends overseas as well. The market for leopard skins, rhino horns, and elephant tusks is worldwide. In 1973, the United States called an international conference that negotiated the

Convention on International Trade in Endangered Species (CITES), which was signed in 1979. Encompassing 125 nations, this treaty outlaws trade for products of species threatened with extinction. Its primary list consists of about a thousand endangered species, virtually all animals. Its secondary list consists of those that look like the threatened ones, for example, common alligators whose skins resemble the rare African crocodile. Even though its premise appears solid, the success of CITES is limited. It only protects animals at the threshold of extinction and does nothing to protect habitat. Smuggling is easy. Although international trade in skins and ivory put many animals at risk, the loss of habitat is the chief danger. In 1994, Congress passed the Rhinoceros and Tiger Conservation Act to support international programs.

WHALES, DOLPHINS, AND SEALS

Since Herman Melville published *Moby Dick*, the whale has loomed as large in the American imagination as the mighty leviathan itself. In Melville's day, a sailing ship would spend three years and cruise fifty thousand miles to bring back thirty to forty whales. Now, a modern Japanese or Norwegian ship can catch that many in a single day, while the number of whales have declined rapidly—blue whales are only a tenth of their original population; humpbacks, 2 percent; and right whales, 1 percent.

To protest an American underground nuclear test in the Aleutian Islands of Alaska in 1971, some American and Canadian activists, who had met each other in the Sierra Club, sailed a ship, the *Rainbow Warrior*, into the forbidden zone. The following year, veterans of that voyage and others living in Vancouver, British Columbia, organized Greenpeace. Its mission was to take direct action against nuclear testing, and its chief tactic was to navigate the *Rainbow Warrior* into the forbidden test zone in the ocean. By exposing themselves to danger, the activists forced the American (and later the French) military to delay and sometimes to cancel the explosions. They described their actions as "the Quaker philosophy of bearing witness and trying to stand in harm's way,"[21] and consciously imitated the Civil Rights tactics of Martin Luther King.

While cruising the Pacific, the crew watched whales and porpoises that soon won their hearts and spontaneously convinced Greenpeace to add whale protection to its mission. The ship's First Officer, Paul Watson, was the most aggressive member. Like the other Greenpeace founders, he came from Vancouver and shared their background in journalism. He had also served in the Norwegian merchant marines and the Canadian Coast Guard. In 1975, he and the Greenpeace crew confronted a Russian whaler sixty miles off the California coast. Buzzing about in small speedboats launched from the *Rainbow Warrior*, they steered recklessly between the Russians and a dozen sperm whales the whalers were pursuing, making it nearly impossible for the harpooner to shoot. Not completely intimidated, the Russian gunner fired the harpoon into a whale; the cable splashed down only a few feet in front of the speedboat. According to Watson, as the whale died next to his little boat, the look in the whale's eye expressed solidarity and gratitude to his human defenders. Greenpeace captured the entire drama on video-tape, which was broadcasted on CBS's evening news program. Within days, the footage was seen around the world. The following year Greenpeace again took on the Russians, finding them north of Hawaii. Miraculously, this time the whaling fleet withdrew—their second encounter to save the whales was a victory.

Watson was too aggressive even by Greenpeace standards, so he was forced to leave the organization in 1977. He established the Sea Shepherd Conservation Society, which purchased a North Atlantic trawler, the *Sea Shepherd*, in England. Captain Watson's first target was the annual seal hunt in Newfoundland. For years hunters had been going ashore at the rookeries in March when the pups were only a month old and still had the prized soft white fur that would be used for women's coats. Because the seals had no fear of humans, the hunters could easily walk up to the pups and club them to death. The United States and the European Parliament have outlawed the purchasing of baby seal skins, effectively ending the commercial market, and Canada has permitted Canadian Indians and Eskimos to hunt the seals for their own use. By 1994, the Canadian Indian and Eskimo quarry secretly found its way into a commercial market again, now for a new product: Chinese men took to drinking a beverage made of dried and pow-dered seal penises to enhance their sexual potency. Mixed with tiger penises, the concoction sold for $8 a glass in Taipei. Chinese immigrants in Canada have formed a market closer to the source.

Watson began a military style campaign against whaling ships. His first tar-get was an outlaw ship, which had been illegally killing thousands of whales. For eleven years the ship had killed whales, ignoring the International Whaling Commission rules about endangered species, protecting nursing mothers, and no hunting zones. The *Sea Shepherd* tracked the whaler just west of the Portuguese coast and rammed it. The outlaw limped into port in Lisbon, where three myste-rious strangers later rowed out to it, planted a bomb underwater at its bow, then taxied to the railway station to catch the midnight train out of the country. The explosion sank the ship without injuring the forty-two crew members on board.[22] The Portuguese government declined to prosecute Watson. The next year the *Sea Shepherd* chased two illegal Spanish whalers into the port of Vigo, where later mysterious bombs sank them. In 1986, Watson took his ship to Iceland where it sank half of its whaling fleet. And even though he holds the rationale that sinking illegal whaling ships is merely enforcing international law, Watson does not have the authority to carry out his actions. However, the Portuguese, Spanish, Icelandic, and Canadian governments have either declined to indict Watson, found him inno-cent, or failed to sustain a conviction.

ANIMAL LIBERATION

Concern with endangered species stands in an uncomfortable relationship with the animal liberation movement. Peter Singer popularized the movement in 1972 with

A canoeist crosses Mendenhall Lake in Tongass National Forest in southeast Alaska. Behind him are the Mendenhall Glacier and Mount McGinnis. The Southeast Alaska Conservation Council opposes large-scale commercial timbering in this seventeen-million acre forest, which is home to grizzly bears, salmon, and bald eagles.

his book of the same name. Singer argues that an individual animal has rights, much like a person's civil rights. His inspiration came from the Civil Rights, Women's Liberation, and Gay Liberation movements. Singer traces the movement's rationale to the eighteenth-century political philosopher Jeremy Bentham, who predicted a future when animals will gain rights then denied by tyranny. The justification will not be because they are rational (even though a full grown horse or dog is more rational than a one month old infant), but because they have a sentience to pain. Obviously, dogs, cats, and higher mammals can suffer; they can also think, communicate, and experience emotions. Scientists have taught language to chimpanzees and apes. Moreover, when humans feel intense emotion, they frequently abandon language and logic for more primitive, simian communication.

Some advocates for animal rights argue for extending animal rights much farther down the evolutionary chain, although Singer concedes that the connection becomes poorer. They employ the term "speciesism" to place guilt on humans for tyrannizing other animal species. It is like racism, and its worst manifestation is laboratory experiments on non-humans. Psychologists force mice to choose between starvation or electric shocks; neurologists amputate chimpanzees' arms to study pain. These experiments, which guarantee suffering, produce so-called scientific results that are frequently trivial or have obvious outcomes. More significantly, animal liberation opposes raising animals for meat. In the past, humans hunted for food, but today's farming is ruthless, they argue. Farmers keep chickens in tiny cages, inject cattle with hormones, and box in calves so as to not spoil the veal.

Animal liberation fits with environmentalism, but not very much. The liberationist concentrates on the individual animal and the environmentalist concentrates on the species. Captain Watson campaigns to save whales, often individual ones. He reports feeling an emotional connection to the whale who looked him in the eye and seemed to say "thank you." Others feel that way about a wolf, a grizzly bear, or a whooping crane. Ecologists, on the other hand, reject this outlook as sentimental and maudlin because animals, insects, and plants prey on other animals, insects, and plants, and as a result, the population of species is controlled. The chances of an individual animal dying of old age are small. Most will perish in the mouth of another; that is the way of nature.

THE ENDS OF THE EARTH

Today, any true wilderness of great size has nearly disappeared from the earth. The 1966 legislation defines it "as an area where the earth and its community of life are untrammeled by man, where man himself is a visitor who does not remain." Finding a place that meets the legal definition of being "primeval . . . with the imprint of man's work substantially unnoticeable" calls for a journey to the ends of the earth: the Arctic, the Antarctic, and the Himalayas.

The Arctic

The Arctic National Wildlife Refuge covers fifteen thousand square miles on the North Slope of Alaska, extending from the Arctic Ocean south one hundred miles to the Brooks Range and east one hundred fifty miles to the Canadian border. The delicate tundra consists of moss, flowers, and dwarf birch. The refuge proper and an adjoining strip along the coast is home to four hundred thousand caribou, the remanent of the millions that used to live across the northern country. The only human residents of this permanently frozen landscape are two hundred Eskimos. The winter temperature dips to 35 degrees Fahrenheit below zero in the winter and climbs to 65 degrees Fahrenheit during the short summer when the whole tundra blossoms. The Canadian government has proposed to manage it jointly with a national park in the Yukon Territory, making the combined area the largest protected wilderness on earth. It will provide a haven for caribou, moose, bears, and wolves. To the west, past the eight hundred-mile elevated oil pipeline, the borders of the Arctic National Park and the Noatak National Preserve extend three hundred miles nearly to the Bering Straits.

The threat to the Arctic Refuge comes from the oil reserves that lie thousands of feet underneath. Petroleum geologists estimate these reserves may contain as much as four to eight billion barrels of crude oil, which would be comparable to the Prudhoe Bay oil field. The Reagan administration tried to open the refuge to petroleum exploration and, even today, the proposal remains on the table. Although the value of this oil is huge, the refuge would suffer environmental damage that would last for decades; for example, tracks remain from Army maneuvers during World War II because the short growing season forces vegetation to take many years to regenerate. On one hand, the refuge is so remote and cold few will ever visit. On the other hand, hikers and rafters already pose a danger to its delicate condition. Thus, by constructing a road for petroleum drilling tourists would gain more access.

The Antarctic

At literally the opposite pole, the Antarctic continent remains pristine. The industrial countries can keep the continent wild or they can scar it. Although Antarctica is not owned by any country, the United States has the greatest single voice in its future. The American role does not come from the old validations of international law: discovery, settlement, or conquest. Indeed, the United States, along with eleven other countries, renounced sovereignty in the Antarctic Treaty of 1961, which proclaims that the southern continent will be managed cooperatively "for the benefit of all mankind." It guarantees the freedom for scientific investigation and forbids military operations, nuclear explosion, and the dumping of nuclear waste. (A few years later the United States, the Soviet Union, and several other countries signed a treaty on sovereignty of the moon that replicated many of the Antarctic provisions.) American influence over Antarctica comes from its scientific might and logistic support by the Air Force and Navy. The U.S. Navy has maintained a year-round research station at McMurdo Sound continuously since 1957 and Scott Station at the South Pole soon after.

So far, Antarctica is too remote for commercial exploitation, but that day will come. While the mineral resources are barely explored, geologists have discovered coal, cobalt, chromium, and manganese. They believe platinum, gold, and diamonds may also exist there. Petroleum companies already have the expertise and equipment to work in the Arctic and in the North Sea. Strip mining requires few workers, and underground mining would have the overburden to keep the miners warm. Currently, with forty-two nations as members, the Antarctic Treaty group has an unofficial moratorium on mining and mineral exploration. Australia and France have suggested the frozen continent should become a "world park." Tourists have been flocking to Antarctica; in one year alone there were eight thousand tourists. Luxury ships anchor near Cuverville Island and Port Lockroy, sending their passengers ashore to visit the penguin rookeries. Airlines bring in tourists via Chile, Argentina, and New Zealand. The treaty group has adopted guidelines for ecotourism, but since the treaty itself outlaws sovereignty, no country has jurisdiction to enforce those guidelines. Even though diminished numbers of whales and the international moratorium have ended whaling, fishing for fish and krill continues to be the biggest industry in the oceans surrounding Antarctica.

The Himalayas

The Himalaya Mountains extend for fifteen hundred miles through Pakistan, India, Nepal, Bhutan, Tibet and China. Crowned by Mount Everest, which reaches 29,028 feet above sea level, the range has 110 peaks above twenty-four thousand feet. Each year thousands of climbers attack the summits and thousands more come to hike and photograph. In the high mountains much of the terrain remains unspoiled mostly because it is so rocky, cold, and distant that it sustains little farming. Yet, every year more visitors come and the Nepalese and Indians who live at the base of the mountains have been "bitten by the bug of materialism." The population is growing rapidly and Sherpas have been cutting down the forests for farming. The wilderness worthy of protection extends below the highest mountains, for the slopes are covered with forests that contain tigers, monkeys, and birds unique to this region.

The conjunction of isolation, concentration, and a harsh climate makes litter a major problem. Since Sir Edmund Hillary in 1953, hundreds have "conquered" Mount Everest, but few of them have taken their trash away when they left. The trail and campsites are fouled with old equipment, tin cans, plastic cups, and other garbage. In 1996, a band of environmentalists formed an expedition just to clean the litter. The Roof of the World, however, can expect more and more pressure. At present, the backwardness of the People's Republic of China protects the north side by default. Although China permits a few climbing expeditions, it does not welcome ordinary tourists. With the deaths of the aging Communist leaders, however, the lure of the dollar, deutschmark, and yen is sure to increase mountaineering and tourism.

War is a further danger to the Himalayas, though not to the highest peaks, which are too formidable. India fought China in this region in 1962 and Pakistan in 1965. The beautiful Kashmir province has witnessed almost constant bloodshed since 1947 when the British withdrew as the colonial power, while the Afghan War, which lasted from 1978 to 1985, threatened the western portion of the region. As if war has not already made the political balance surrounding the Himalayas unstable, China, India, and Pakistan also maintain nuclear warhead arsenals. If wealthy industrial nations have been unable to fully protect the Arctic and Antarctic where virtually no one lives and no national boundaries are disputed, with five countries and fifty million people in the area, the Himalayas are more vulnerable.

Only a few other wilderness areas of great size remain on earth such as the Andes Mountains in South America, the fourteen thousand-foot high peaks in New Guinea, and the rain forests in Brazil. In New Guinea, a foreign company mines on mountains so remote that it uses helicopters for exploration.

155

Encouraged by the Brazilian government, settlers cut down the Amazon rain forest for farms, but the natural balance is too delicate, besides the fact that the soil lacks nutrients for crops. In the lower forty-eight states, potential wilderness areas exist in the Cascades, the Sierra Nevada, and the Smokies.

The only wilderness that remains largely untrammeled is the ocean. The U.S. Park Service has an underwater nature trail at Buck Island Reef on the Virgin Islands. In spite of limited protection by individual nations, damage to the oceans has been limited. "Pirates" rob the South Pacific reefs of corral, which take years to regrow, to sell for jewelry. Oil drilling rigs dump lubricants into the ocean and the oil itself pollutes ocean habitats.

THE PROS AND CONS OF PROTECTION

Concentrating on endangered species and wilderness areas demonstrates the issues—political, emotional, and religious—at both ends of the spectrum. In fact, animals and plants are worth protecting, even when not immediately threatened by extinction, and land is worth preserving, even when not pristine. The definition set forth by the Wilderness Act that a wilderness should be "untrammeled by man" makes it logically impossible for more than a few people to visit and for any to stay in hotels or drive on roads. Still, the wilderness areas come the closest to pure nature. Few of these living paragons are left, and once they are gone, they cannot be replaced. Preserving them, however, does not preclude preserving less pure areas in parks and government-owned forests.

Viewed more generally, the American endangered species policy appears to lack consistency. Its goals are contradictory and without broad support. Its most successful role is a bit duplicitous: to give environmentalists a powerful weapon to fight development as demonstrated with Tellico Dam. Environmentalists opposed the dam from the beginning and discovering a subspecies of the darter minnow was a lucky break, albeit not lucky enough.

The National Wildlife Federation gives four practical reasons to protect endangered species: medicine, agriculture, commerce, and ecology. Forty percent of all prescription drugs are either based on or synthesized from natural compounds. Digitalis, a heart medicine, is one of the better known prescription drugs. Not only do these species save lives, they contribute to a pharmaceutical industry worth over $40 billion annually. Unfortunately, only 5 percent of plant species have been screened. Of the eighty thousand edible plants in the world, only twenty species such as wheat and corn provide 90 percent of world's food. Wild relatives of these common crops furnish a genetic reservoir for new pest- and disease-resistant strains. Wild species may contribute new strains that can grow in poor soils or drought-stricken areas to help solve the world hunger problem. Genetic material from wild corn in Mexico was used to stop a leaf fungus that had previously wiped out 15 percent of the American crop. Some wild species are even harvested commercially. Salmon fishing in the Northwest provides sixty thousand jobs and $1 billion annually in income. The tourist industry, not confined to ecotourism, depends on clean air and water. Every year one hundred million Americans spend $60 billion on travel, lodging, equipment, and food to fish, hunt, and photograph.

The Wildlife Federation goes on to state that diverse species make up the fabric of healthy ecosystems such as coastal estuaries, prairie grasslands, and ancient forests, all of which purify the air, clean the water, and supply food. When species become endangered, it indicates that the health of these vital ecosystems is beginning to unravel. The U.S. Fish and Wildlife Service estimates that losing one plant species can trigger the loss of up to thirty other insect, plant, and more complex animal species. Pollution off the coast of Florida is killing the coral reefs along the Florida Keys, which serve as habitat for hundreds of species of fish. Not surprisingly, catches of commercial fish species have begun to decline. The key species may not be one with dignity or beauty—the humble and hidden earthworm cultivates the soil for farmers.

The rationale that the rain forests and tundra hold plants and animals that will yield valuable pharmaceuticals is true, but may be exaggerated. It overstates the medical benefits from exotic plants. Famous medicines like digitalis and aspirin were developed fifty to one hundred years ago. Today, pharmacologists can synthesize drugs. With respect to aspirin, scientists did not systematically search for it, but listened when the Indians of South America explained how to chew a willow branch. Although Sir Alexander Fleming discovered penicillin from mold, the spores came from the polluted air of London, not a rain forest. The future appears to lie in manipulating DNA, instead of harvesting plants from the South American rain forest. The most efficient way to advance medicine may be to expand research at the National Institutes of Health and universities.

The troublesome reciprocal of discovering a cure in the tropical rain forest is unleashing an epidemic like AIDS or ebola, both of which came from central Africa. Scientists have determined that AIDS was present in monkeys, but either had never spread to humans or was confined locally. The increase of truck traffic on new highways spread the disease throughout the continent. Once established in the major cities, it could literally be transported to America or Europe at jet speed. Ebola was unknown until an outbreak in 1976, after which it disappeared until 1979 and then disappeared again until 1995. Victims can die within days or even hours. So far it has not spread so widely as AIDS, but the danger still exists. The fact that it thrives in conditions of poor sanitation makes it less likely to spread to America or Europe, but Asia is still at risk. Additional plagues in Brazil and Indonesia may be waiting for increased human contact. Unknown diseases may also afflict domestic animals or key crops.

The sister rationale for protecting tropical rain forests for future cures is that plants not yet discovered may help to improve agriculture. This line of thought appears to have more basis because agriculture is overly dependent on a limited number of species. Yet to insist on 100 percent protection seems extreme from an economic standpoint. First, a species going extinct nearly always has many closely related cousins. Second, the crops in which farmers overly depend are

157

chiefly grains such as corn, wheat, and rice. This suggests the need to protect grasslands, but not particularly rain forests or tundra.

The third problem with the Endangered Species Act is its focus on species that are at the brink of extinction. For them, it is usually too late. Dramatic interventions like robbing the nests of the California condor, then breeding the eggs in a laboratory rarely succeed. When successful, as with the whooping crane, the effort may take many years—in this case, sixty years. Taxpayers may be willing to support a long-lasting project for a tall, beautiful bird, but they are not likely to do the same for a minnow.

The rationales for protecting endangered species that rest on practicality— medicine and agriculture—are two-edged. If they cannot pay their way, the practical response is to terminate the program. Yet, a purist view that preservation is important, even if impractical, may be too great a luxury. Does the United States really want billions of passenger pigeons? With eight hundred thousand species of beetles in the world, are they all necessary? A program of extreme protection may create a dusty museum with two million curiosities. Although, to allow extinction of a beetle, while protecting a colorful bird is anthropocentric. If these types of judgments are made, these natural species are being treated like pets and potted flowers. Soaring hawks and furry seals warm the heart, regardless of their place in evolution.

The impossibility of protecting endangered animals and plants when they need intensive care directs reformers toward saving entire habitats. The spotted owl cannot survive without forests. For a few species at the top of the food chain, the habitat may need to be several thousand acres. The wolf and the grizzly bear will perish without wilderness and buffer zones like the Greater Yellowstone ecosystem. (And currently, four other giant ecosystems are proposed in the Rocky Mountains.) Other endangered species need far less and may even live compatibly with humans. At the Pinehurst Resort in North Carolina, red-cockaded woodpeckers share the fairways with golfers, while the peregrine falcon adapts well to life in the city. Ironically, the spotted owl does better in new growth forests than in old growth ones.

CONCLUSION

Programs to protect endangered species and wilderness areas enjoy widespread popular support. Public opinion polls and letters to members of Congress attest to this. Yet, this support tends to be a vicarious experience because how can the masses ever encounter such rarity? Americans want to save the Alaskan tundra and Brazilian rain forest even though they will never have the opportunity to visit. The emotional and zealous side of the movement has its spiritual dimension that both recalls religion and, for some, substitutes for it. Zahniser's wilderness philosophy and Leopold's land ethic are creeds. And while protecting species and wilderness came to prominence due to pre-conditions, the technical factor was the science of ecology such as studies of the San Francisco Peak, the Indiana

Dunes, and the Kaibab National Forest. The chief structural factor was the settlement of the west; people were turning the mountains and prairies into mines and ranches. After 1945, prosperity and improved education permitted attention to and protection of nature that previously had been a luxury. Viewed in terms of its life cycle, the protection movement seems no where near its end. Its popularity continues to grow. As a vicarious movement, it thrives on television programs, magazines, and Internet chats with heroes like Captain Watson. Prosperity and cheap air fares foretell more eco-tourism.

To a large extent the founders of the movement recognized the importance of lobbying for interest groups. Grinnell established the Audubon Society; Leopold, Marshall, and Zahniser founded the Wilderness Society; and Brower revitalized the Sierra Club with the aim of political action. All were well educated, sophisticated men accustomed to the levers of power in Washington and New York. Their connections and resources stand in contrast to those of Lois Gibbs. Today, those three societies (as well as others devoted to protecting species and wilderness) are well financed, well led, and well connected. The other active interest groups, of course, are businesses. Real estate developers do not like to see their golf courses and condominiums blocked by endangered birds and butterflies, and mining and logging companies do not want forests and mineral deposits off-limits.

Partisanship has little importance for protecting species and wilderness. While the GOP does lean toward business, the effect is modest. Many of the leaders of the big nature organizations are wealthy and influential Republicans in the mold of Russell Train.

Government science has led in protecting both species and wilderness. The Biological Survey of the Department of Agriculture pioneered in safeguarding migratory birds. Carson and Zahniser worked for the Biological Survey, and Leopold and Marshall worked for the Forest Service. In fact, the protection of species and wilderness is probably the area most indebted to bureaucrats.

NOTES

1. Richard Leakey and Roger Lewin, *The Sixth Extinction* (New York: Doubleday, 1995).
2. Ibid., 173–184.
3. U.S. House of Representatives, Committee on Resources, *Science and the Endangered Species Act*, 1995, 29.
4. Thomas Dunlop, *Saving America's Wildlife* (Princeton: Princeton University Press, 1988), 7.
5. 1 Kings 18:20 and 19: 8–12.
6. Psalm 95: 1, 4–6.
7. George Williams, *Wilderness and Paradise in Christian Thought* (New York: Harper, 1966), 73.
8. Revelations 12:6.
9. Quoted in Williams, 100.

10. Reproductions are available from Houghton Mifflin in 1940 and 1966, Abbeville in 1981 (edited by Roger Tory Peterson) and MacMillan in 1937 and 1950.
11. Dunlap, 25.
12. Ibid., 45.
13. Aldo Leopold, *Sand County Almanac* (New York: Ballantine, 1966), 239, 238.
14. Ibid., 266–267, 269, 276–277.
15. Donald Dale Jackson, "Just Plain Bob Was the Best Friend the Wilderness Ever Had" *Smithsonian* 25 (August 1994): 92–100.
16. *American Forests*, July 1963.
17. Arne Naess, "The Deep Ecological Movement: Some Philosophical Aspects," *Philosophical Inquiry* 8 (1983): 10–31.
18. Ibid.
19. Ibid.
20. Paul Shepard, *The Tender Carnivore and the Sacred Game* (New York: Scribner's, 1973).
21. Philip Shabecoff, *A Fierce Green Fire* (New York: Farrar, Straus and Giroux, 1993), 122; David Day, *The Whale War* (San Francisco: Sierra Club Books, 1987).
22. Lecture by Captain Paul Watson, Earth Day Lecture (Toledo, OH: University of Toledo, April 22, 1995).

CHAPTER 7
PROTECTING THE PARKS

In the structure of this book, parks fit between the wilderness "where man is a visitor" and the forests used for lumber, grazing, or mining. Every year seventeen million people visit Shenandoah National Park, five million visit Cape Cod National Seashore, and millions more go to other national and state parks. Visits to city parks are countless: to play ball, to watch birds in Washington's Rock Creek Park, or to watch people in New York's Central Park. Parks range from neighborhood playgrounds to the new Wrangell-St. Elias National Park in Alaska with eight million acres. While a few of the biggest like Sequoia and Death Valley include wilderness areas, most are too developed. National parks have a mission to preserve and protect, but virtually all of the older ones have welcomed tourists to hotels and restaurants since they began. Smaller ones lack the acreage for a wilderness.

To the other side of the continuum, national forests and land under the jurisdiction of the U.S. Bureau of Land Management are supposed to be used more intensively. Preservation and recreation must balance against grazing, logging, and mining. Wildlife refuges are more likely to preserve and protect, at least their birds and animals. Because nearly all the national parks outside Alaska were frozen in size and boundaries long ago, the national forests have more potential for change, including creating new wilderness areas.

BACKGROUND

Urban parks and gardens are as old as civilization. Archaeologists found them when they excavated the ancient city of Ur and the Hanging Gardens of Babylon, both of which are famous to this day. A new theory explains this in terms of biophilia, a term defined as an inborn human love for plants and animals. In its evolution, homo sapiens developed a brain "hardwired" to favor a natural setting like the east African savanna in which the species developed. Primitive humans survived best on an open plain with flowing water, flowering plants, and shading trees. Predators could not sneak up because visibility over the grass was good. Water was available to drink, to grow plants, and to attract animals, thus making hunting easier. Flowers showed the location of edible plants. The trees provided shade. Although, compared to a savanna, a forest contains more biomass per acre, the floor is shady so it lacks plants to eat, and predators can hide more easily. Protohumans walked upright three million years ago, so grassland was optimal for running after prey and away from predators. An arid desert does not have enough food, even though it has the advantage of being open.[1]

The biophilia hypothesis maintains that the human predisposition to the African savanna continues to this day. Controlled experiments demonstrate that people prefer a daily environment with grass, scattered trees, water, and flowers. Indeed, they use the word "park-like" to describe it. Suburban housing epitomizes the preference for grass, trees, and flowers. The biofilia hypothesis suggests that the suburbanite's desire for a lawn and shade trees is biologically determined by evolution. The chief modern benefit of the savanna is to reduce stress—people feel at home biologically, therefore they relax. A further benefit may be that people are more creative in this setting.[2] The trend of corporations building a headquarters "campus" with grass, water, trees, and flowers in preference to the old fashioned downtown skyscrapers affirms this benefit. The greatest benefits of parks appear to come from outdoor recreation; studies specifically of wilderness areas have proven that people place the reduction of stress as a high priority. An experiment on stress reduction demonstrates that a vigorous forty-minute walk in a park is a quick and healthy way to relax.

Most colonial towns lacked parks, presumably because America had plenty of nature close by. The exception was Savannah, Georgia, which began with a city plan calling for one block of park for every eight blocks of buildings. James Oglethorpe, the reform-minded founder, considered the parks to be important. Although less extensive, William Penn's plan for Philadelphia had many parks. Following European custom, these colonial parks were formal and symmetrical; they were designed for viewing and walking. Flowers were rare. Meanwhile, in Britain, fashion turned to a naturalistic style with random pathways and incorporating existing rocks and streams. International commerce in flowering plants and advances in the science of botany spurred the fad. The Dutch imported the tulip from Turkey and bred strains with bigger and brighter blossoms; their biggest customers were the English.

The leading American exponent of the English style of parks was Frederick Law Olmsted, with his English partner, Calvert Vaux. When Olmstead won the competition to design New York's Central Park in 1857, he emphasized the natural features and at the same time created more grassland than was normal for an eastern hardwood forest. His relationship with the city government was stormy (he resigned twice). Even after the park was complete, Olmsted resisted (unsuccessfully) building baseball diamonds and the zoo. In spite of his misgivings, Central Park was a resounding success, so much so that his landscaping architecture business won clients from all over the country. He designed Prospect Park in Brooklyn, Fairmont Park in Philadelphia, the Capitol grounds in Washington, Belle Isle in Detroit, and the Stanford University campus. In fact, his design of the Niagara Falls park influenced that state to preserve the area and inspired more state parks. And from 1864 to 1890, he served as the first chairman of the Yosemite Park commission.

The flourishing of parks in the late nineteenth and early twentieth centuries was part of the City Beautiful movement. Its most prominent advocates were wives of the new "Captains of Industry." The captains themselves had lost interest in city improvement as railroads, canals, and coastal shipping linked cities together. In the colonial period and up to the Civil War, few businesses extended beyond a single city and its hinterland, therefore, a business leader was a civic leader as well. One reinforced the other. For example, even Benjamin Franklin, the most cosmopolitan American of his day, had difficulty expanding his printing business beyond Philadelphia in those days before railroads and telegraphs. Thus, because his business was largely limited to the city, he focused on Philadelphian politics and philanthrophy. He founded the fire department, the hospital, and the predecessor of the University of Pennsylvania. Nineteenth-century railroads transformed business and industry. By 1889, Andrew Carnegie shipped his steel to New York and Chicago and operated mills in Pittsburgh, Philadelphia, and Cleveland. Of course, many of the Captains of Industry had no interest at all in philanthropy, but when they did, it was not confined to a single city. This left the cities orphaned.

Their wives picked up the slack, promoting libraries, museums, and parks. These improvements appealed to the new bourgeois middle class that never existed before industry grew to need accountants, salesmen, and engineers. The other component was the politicians. When the Captains of Industry lost interest in city politics, their replacements were party bosses, who usually came from immigrant groups like the Irish, Germans, Italians, and Poles. The wives and the bourgeoisie felt little in common with the new citizens and resented the political bosses who dominated the cities with their votes. The bosses loved beautiful buildings. Erecting an elegant court house or city hall with a copper dome glorified their success. Besides, building a magnificent edifice was a good way to disguise paybacks to campaign donors. A further goal in creating a park might have been to get rid of a dump, squatters' shacks, or a red light district. Other times, a city located a park at a site that was too rocky or too swampy for agriculture. New York's Central Park was stony and barren. Boston's Back Bay was too filled with gullies for houses, and Chicago's South Park was a wetland.

The wives of the rich and the new middle class envisioned the parks for strolling about, playing croquet, or riding horses. Their benevolent purpose was to refresh the worker's spirit after a week confined in factory or an office. The purists frowned on horse race tracks, but they were popular with both the upper and lower classes. They tried to discourage drinking and team sports by installing water fountains and not allowing playing fields. The assumption was that the family took its pleasure together. These parks had a further purpose of cleaning the air, in particular of malaria, which physicians erroneously thought was due to "bad air," not mosquitos.

By the turn of the century, reformers began to capitalize on the parks as a tool for social improvement. Jane Addams of the Hull House worried that children got into trouble without adult supervision. Cities hired athletic directors to organize the children and young men (women were rarely included). Recreation was no longer a family affair, but segregated by sex and age. The model was the Young Men's Christian Association (YMCA) and the German sport clubs. The reformers seemed to assume that the lower class could not organize its own recreation; therefore, the directors hired staff members who would set a good example in morality and education. Athletics, however, was only one form of recreation that would improve the lower class. Band concerts and folk dancing were viewed as other recreational improvements, which were held in the parks. Reformers preferred to discourage regular dancing. When unavoidable, chaperones and a small admission fee helped control rowdy behavior. Garden plots, craft classes, and branch libraries became common, while shelter houses were available for public meetings.[3]

Public health officials recognized the benefits of the outdoors. Tuberculosis was the leading killer of the era. While physicians did not know the cause was bacteria, they did know that fresh air decreased its prevalence. Sunshine prevented rickets. Personal hygiene improved health, so besides the opportunity for recreation, swimming pools and beaches had the advantage of cleaning the "great unwashed" lower classes. Parks built locker rooms for changing and showering for athletics. More directly, cities built bathhouses in the parks.

The New Deal poured money into parks, municipal as well as rural, and unemployed men and women could find endless work maintaining and improving them. The Works Progress Administration (WPA) spent millions of dollars building swimming pools, shelter houses, and zoos. However, when normal life resumed after World War II, municipal parks headed two directions. One was a general aggrandizement with more and fancier facilities. Now the swimming pool could be indoors and the baseball field would have a grandstand. The other direction was toward the suburbs. Although the residents had their own yards and needed fewer parks, suburban towns built thousands of new parks as their population grew. The negative side was the decline of the central city. The decrease in the tax base and the flight of the middle class hurt. The reforms of the first half of the century were worn out, while racial desegregation brought further controversy. Throughout the south and border states, cities frequently closed their parks rather than integrate them. Swimming pools provided the most bitter fights.

Scorecard for PROTECTING the PARKS

LAWS
National Park Service Organic Act 1916. Alaska National Interest Lands Conservation Act 1980. Antiquities Act 1906. Yellowstone Park Act 1872, and other laws for individual parks.

SIZE
The national park system nearly tripled since 1970, from 30 to 83 million acres.

CONGRESS
House Committee on Resources (formerly Interior), subcommittee on Parks
Senate Committee on Energy and Natural Resources (formerly Interior), subcommittee on Parks

AGENCIES
National Park Service
City park departments
State park departments

INTEREST GROUPS

National Parks and Conservation Association	League of Conservation Voters
National Wildlife Federation	Greater Yellowstone Coalition
Sierra Club	Save the Dunes Council of Indiana
Appalachian Club	Real estate companies
The Nature Conservancy	Mining and timber industries

YELLOWSTONE AND YOSEMITE NATIONAL PARKS

Far from the industrial cities in need of parks and beautification, the American pioneer was running out of land for farming. He still had plenty of land in the west, but it was too dry for crops. The Census Bureau announcement that a frontier no longer existed came in 1890, but by 1870, land that would grow corn and wheat without irrigation was nearly gone. The historian Frederick Jackson Turner earned fame for explaining the American character as a result of having a frontier. It fostered optimism and waste because the pioneer could always move on. It promoted democracy because wealthy landowners could not indenture the poor as tenants as they could in Britain and Europe. When the frontier ceased to be an outlet, American attitudes toward exploiting the forests and mines did not necessarily change. Nevertheless, Americans began to recognize the need to protect and conserve.

In 1870, a group of nineteen men settled near Bozeman, Montana, felt they were sufficiently established and prosperous to amuse themselves by exploring the territory to their south at the headwaters of the Yellowstone River. No white people lived in the inaccessible land and, because it was not on the trail to Oregon or on navigable water, no one knew what was there. Its inhabitants were the mild Bannock Indians, whom the fierce Flathead Indians chased into the mountains. The only known white explorers to have seen this area were John Colter and Jim Bridger, both reputed to be two of the biggest liars in the history of the "Tall Tale." These mountain men claimed to have seen boiling mud, steam that shot into the air, and a mountain of glass. Nineteen men rode their horses into the magnificent wilderness of mountains, and of valleys, discovering for themselves the fountains, geysers, and a cliff of obsidian. The beauty and uniqueness fascinated them all. Legend tells how on the last night camping before they headed home, these pioneer ecotourists talked of the wonders and vowed to create a national park. The concept sprang full blown and, incredibly, within two years Congress established it. Yellowstone became the first national park anywhere in the world and remained the largest in the world for 108 years.

Once convinced of the park's desirability, Congress found implementation easy because the land was already in the public domain as part of the Louisiana Purchase and the treaty with Britain settling the Oregon Territory. Soon the Northern Pacific Railway had built its line to the north entrance at Mammoth Hot Springs—passengers could board a Pullman in Chicago and step off at the park. By 1890, thousands of visitors arrived annually. They travelled by stage coach to first class hotels at Old Faithful and Mammoth Hot Springs. The men hunted elk, cougars, and the few buffalo remaining outside captivity. At its low point, only twenty-two survived in the Yellowstone herd.

A thousand miles to the west in California, Yosemite had a similar history. Its existence was also a mystery. American Indian tales reported a secret valley with walls rising straight up into the sky, sparking waterfalls, and giant trees. Rediscovered by white settlers almost by accident in 1851, the tourist promoters began advertising it in a magazine within five years of its exploration. The Interior Department transferred ownership of the valley and the grove of giant sequoia trees to the state of California in 1864, and retained the mountains and meadows surrounding it for homesteading and grazing sheep and cattle. This included the Hetch Hetchy Valley, a slightly smaller sister to Yosemite located fifteen miles to the north. In 1868, its most famous resident arrived: John Muir.

Born and raised in Scotland until the age of eleven, his family emigrated to Wisconsin. In 1861, Muir entered the University of Wisconsin, where he studied botany, mechanics, and literature. His favorite authors were Henry David Thoreau and Ralph Waldo Emerson. Fearful of being drafted into the Union army and feeling still more a Scotsman than an American, he "skedaddled" to Canada, to use his own terminology. Returning to the United States after the war, Muir worked as a millwright in Indianapolis, quitting when an industrial accident temporarily blinded him. Resolving to study his first love of nature, he walked the thousand miles to Florida. During that trek, he hiked across the Cumberland Mountain wilderness (the first mountains he had seen), camped out in a Confederate cemetery when his money ran out, and avoided alligators in the swamps. The following year he sailed for California via Panama. Arriving in San Francisco, he did not tarry, but headed out of town for the famous Yosemite Valley he had read about.

The next summer Muir found a sympathetic rancher who hired him to herd sheep in the Yosemite Valley and the alpine meadows surrounding it. The rancher gave him time off to hike and climb mountains. Muir recognized that ancient glaciers had carved the valley, a phenomenon recently discovered in Switzerland. For the next several years he supported himself in the valley running a sawmill to build tourist cottages and an addition to a hotel. Muir explored every niche of the region, sleeping on the ground with a fire for warmth. In fact, his camping skills were notoriously poor. He neglected to prepare, failed to bring enough blankets, and ate only oatmeal, when trout leapt from the streams and game was abundant.

Muir's intelligence, knowledge of science, and quaint habits soon made him a popular guide for visitors. He acquired admirers, typically middle-aged women, who sent him more visitors and published stories about him in newspapers and magazines. Muir had an innate talent for publicity and attracting influential people. In 1871, his hero Ralph Waldo Emerson came to the valley and sought out Muir. Completion of the transcontinental railroad two years before made travel from coast to coast in first class splendor possible in only ten days. Emerson and

In His Own Words: John Muir
Naturalist, Publicist, and Founder of the Sierra Club

Arriving by the Panama steamer, I stopped one day in San Francisco and then inquired for the nearest way out of town. "But where do you want to go?" asked the man to whom I had applied for this important information. "To any place that is wild," I said. This reply startled him. He seemed to fear I might be crazy, and therefore the sooner I was out of town the better, so he directed me to the Oakland ferry. . . .

Looking eastward from the summit of the Pacheco Pass one shining morning, a landscape was displayed that after all my wanderings still appears as the most beautiful I have ever beheld. At my feet lay the Great Central Valley of California, level and flowery, like a lake of pure sunshine, forty or fifty miles wide, five hundred miles long, one rich furred garden of yellow compositae. And from the eastern boundary of this vast golden flower bed rouse the mighty Sierra, miles in height, and so gloriously colored and so radiant, it seemed not clothed with light, but wholly composed of it, like the wall of some celestial city. . . .[1]

In my first interview with a Sierra bear we were frightened and embarrassed, both of us, but the bear's behavior was better than mine. When I discovered him, he was standing in a narrow strip of meadow, and I was concealed behind a tree on the side of it. After studying his appearance as he stood at rest, I rushed toward him to frighten him, that I might study his gait in running. But, contrary to all I had heard about the shyness of bears, he did not run at all; and when I stopped short within a few steps of him, as he held his ground in a fighting attitude, my mistake was monstrously plain. I was then put on my good behavior, and never afterward forgot the right manners of the wilderness.[2]

1. John Muir, "The Yosemite," 1912 reprinted in *The Eight Wilderness Discovery Books* (Seattle: Mountaineers, 1992).
2. John Muir, "My First Summer in the Sierra," 1901, reprinted in *The Eight Wilderness Discovery Books* (Seattle: Mountaineers, 1992).

Theodore Roosevelt and John Muir at Glacier Point in Yosemite Valley. Muir's writing, advocacy, and friendships with powerful people advanced the conservation movement and protected natural areas throughout the west. He also founded the Sierra Club.

Muir rode horses together to the Mariposa Grove where the poet and essayist named a giant sequoia. They corresponded the rest of Emerson's life.

Basing his personal philosophy on that of Emerson's and Thoreau's philosophies, Muir moved beyond the Transcendentalists to equate God with Nature (using a capital N). He believed he had a mission to "preach Nature like an apostle," and Nature was a unified whole: "When we try to pick out anything in Nature, we find it hitched to everything else in the universe." Muir also advocated the purest protection; forests were not to be preserved because people might need their lumber, but because they were part of nature. His beliefs were romantic and mystical. While he was on the forefront of science, accepting the then novel theories of glaciation and evolution, he insisted nature was benign. In place of Charles Darwin's struggle for survival, Muir envisioned "the essential kindliness." Nearly a century later, Howard Zahniser of the Wilderness Society pointed to Muir as the movement's prophet.

Muir operated on a sweeping scale and enjoyed wide success. Early in his career he hiked all over the Sierras, climbed Mount Shasta, sailed to the Bering Strait, stopped off in Siberia, and visited Switzerland. Later, he travelled to

168

Russia, China, Egypt, and the Amazon. In India, he saw the Himalayas. In 1892, Muir helped organize the Sierra Club and became its president, serving the rest of his life. He modeled it on the Appalachian Mountain Club founded in Boston sixteen years earlier. On one hand, the club's purpose was for recreation: hiking and camping. On the other, it was political: to safeguard Yosemite and to protect other parts of the Sierra Mountains. Muir published articles in magazines like *Harper's*, *Atlantic Monthly*, and *Century*, and wrote eight books. He lobbied Congress and the secretary of the interior to take over the Yosemite Valley from the state of California, which had failed to protect it, and to establish a park with the surrounding mountains and alpine meadows it already owned. Muir's rough charm captivated many politicians, the most famous being Theodore Roosevelt. Muir persuaded the president to camp out for three nights under the stars, and, as it turned out, under four inches of snow. Roosevelt proclaimed the trip was "bully." Muir's tour for President William Howard Taft six years later was not so rigorous, but the president accepted his advice on the park.

The controversy over the Hetch Hetchy Valley tormented Muir in his later years. About two-thirds the size of Yosemite Valley, it too was glacial in origin. Granite cliffs rose straight up for two thousand feet and waterfalls spilled down. Ominously, the city of San Francisco wanted to dam the valley to supply water and generate electricity. Suffering under the monopoly of a private water company, the city wanted an alternative. San Francisco, however, could not erect a dam without approval of the secretary of the interior. Progressive political leaders of the period tended to favor municipal water systems. It seemed good use of natural resources and would strengthen municipalities. Muir and the preservationists managed to hold off the demands for Hetch Hetchy during the Roosevelt and Taft administrations, but with the inauguration of Woodrow Wilson in 1913, the balance shifted. California had voted for Wilson and he intended to thank the state. His secretary of the interior was from San Francisco and favored the dam. The project needed a vote of Congress. Muir and the preservationists lobbied to save the valley, but lacked enough support. Moreover, Muir's rigidity and self-righteousness was beginning to offend many Congressmen. Already an old man, he grew depressed and died the next year.

Yellowstone, Yosemite, Grand Canyon, Grand Teton, and other large western parks are the major parks of the system. Since Congress organized the Park Service in 1916, they have been the focus. Purists inside the service and in interest groups like the National Parks and Conservation Association, the Sierra Club, the Wilderness Society, the Audubon Society, and the Nature Conservancy consider the "Crown Jewels" the genuine parks. Indeed, this focus is a frequent criticism of the Park Service. The service tends to ignore other units like the historical parks, recreation areas, and urban sites like Independence Hall and the Statue of Liberty. Typically, the rangers who have reached the top of the bureaucracy have spent their careers in the big western parks. They often consider the other parks to drain resources from the Crown Jewels, thereby justifying their proposals of turning the lesser facilities over to cities or states.

The purists are most offended by the National Recreation Areas. Gateway Area in New Jersey and New York and Golden Gate in San Francisco seem unworthy of inclusion. A Resources for the Future author writes that "the entire urban wing of the National Park System was, in essence, an experiment . . . and the [service should] write off the failures. . . . Indiana Dunes is probably such a failure. Fire Island is also without doubt a failure."[4] In 1988, the conflict over Manassas Battlefield Park in Virginia earned the title, the Third Battle of Manassas, to follow the first two battles during the Civil War. By that time, suburban development from Washington had sprawled over countryside to impinge on the site known to Yankees as Bull Run. Real estate developers proposed to build a shopping mall adjoining the National Park where twenty-five thousand soldiers died in 1862. To prevent this dishonor, the government bought six hundred acres. Six years later, the Walt Disney company announced plans to invest $650 million to build a theme park four miles away comparable to Disneyland and Disneyworld. The Virginia government was to subsidize the project with $163 million. The amusement park would have an historical theme, perhaps saving people the need to visit the real thing. Historians, environmentalists, and local home owners opposed Disney and were outraged that the state would subsidize it. The company quickly abandoned its plan.

Five thousand miles to the north, plans to establish parks in Alaska were unresolved for twenty-one years. When Congress admitted the forty-ninth state in 1959, it delayed settling claims for land. Demands by Eskimos, American Indians, Aleuts, whites, corporations, the state, and the Park Service overlapped. The tundra and boreal forest could not be farmed. Natives needed hunting territory and every one wanted the mineral wealth. Following well honed skills at avoiding conflict, Congress postponed the decision. In 1971, Congress returned to the issue in passing the Alaskan Native Claims Settlement Act. (This law introduced the terminology "Native American" to encompass the three aboriginal races.) Still facing ambiguities on specific pieces of land, Congress provided that within seven years the president could withdraw up to eighty million acres for parks. A few days before the deadline was set to expire in 1978, Congress had not yet approved the last forty-seven million acres. To avoid the deadline, Carter used his authority under the Antiquities Act of 1906 to withdraw the land. Eventually, Congress straightened out the muddle in the Alaskan National Interest Lands Conservation Act of 1980. The Park Service now had six new parks, two of them bigger than Yellowstone.

ADIRONDACK STATE PARK

The establishment of the Adirondack State Park in northern New York paralleled and drew inspiration from Yellowstone and Yosemite. The same year Congress created Yellowstone, the New York state legislature took the first steps in creating a park in the northern mountains. The most important reason to protect the wilderness was to ensure its water supply for the Erie Canal and the upper Hudson River. Cutting the timber wiped the mountainsides bare, which caused the soil to erode. Moreover, much precipitation came not as rain, but from the leaves and needles combing the moisture out of the clouds as they drifted over the mountains. Recreation was also an important justification—economic prosperity (plus steamboats and railroads) enabled the wealthier classes to take vacation in the north country. Even though agriculture and poor enforcement of game laws had already depleted the moose and cougars, the park was still expected to sustain hunting. With these reasons in mind, the New York City Chamber of Commerce began lobbying for the park.

In 1882, the legislature established the region as a forest preserve and ten years after that as a park. The 1894 state constitution declared the Adirondacks "shall be forever kept as wild forest lands." The law drew a "Blue Line" around three million acres of public and private land, making it larger than Yellowstone's two million acres. Later additions doubled the size. It remained the largest park in the United States (indeed, in the world) until 1980. The Adirondack Park always included privately-owned land. In the east where farms, sawmills, and villages already existed, the state had no other choice but to allow private ownership. On the other hand, the steep, barren land was poor for agriculture, its population was already declining by 1872, and nearly all the virgin timber had been harvested.

The foresight and large scope of the Adirondack Park exemplified the high quality of New York state government. In grasping the potential for good, employing high-caliber civil servants, and utilizing the most up-to-date technology, New York led other state governments and was at least on a par with the national government. (Public health and education were other areas in which it excelled.) Its park system, with shelter houses, picnic groves, and hiking trails, extended across the entire state from Montauk Point on the eastern tip of Long Island to Niagara Falls and Chautauqua Lake. Its governorship earned the nickname of the "stepping stone to the White House" because of its progressive government as well as its large number of votes in the electoral college. Governors who stepped to the presidency, or at least their party's nomination, were Tilden, Cleveland, both Roosevelts, Smith, and Dewey, while Rockefeller came close. Many of Franklin Roosevelt's New Deal innovations were simply state policies he took to Washington. In fact, the New Deal copied the TVA almost directly from the Power Authority of the State of New York.

The problem of balancing privately- and publicly-owned land inside the Blue Line flared in 1971. Governor Nelson Rockefeller proposed legislation to increase regulation of private property because the presence of outsiders threatened the park. Tourists were building thousands of vacation homes in the park; gas stations, amusement parks, and night clubs catered to visitors; traffic overloaded the narrow highways and polluted the air; poor construction eroded soil, and ugliness sprawled across the landscape. However, many regular residents encouraged this growth. They needed to make a living, and catering to tourists brought in the money. State ownership of the preserve property kept it off-limits for economic development, therefore timbering and mining were not allowed—

the state seemed to be saying: "mustn't touch." Nevertheless, the permanent residents were outnumbered by the 1.2 million summer people. When a museum exhibited photographs designed to cause alarm at the commercial blight, the local people admired the economic success portrayed.[5]

The governor and the environmentalists persisted, and, with many compromises, the legislature passed the law creating the Adirondack Park Authority. One concession to local communities was to give them several months of delay during which they could approve subdivisions for vacation homes. The authority master plan divided the park into seven regions with categorizations ranging from wilderness to intensive use, with the first region covering nearly one million acres. Overall, the plan favored the environmental side.

The difficulties in matching local business profit to preservation goals have not been confined to the Adirondacks. Gateway towns like Gatlinburg, Tennessee, are eyesores. Situated at the west entrance to Smokey Mountain National Park, Gatlinburg contains eight amusement parks, dozens of fast food restaurants, miniature golf courses, video arcades, and the Cupid Chapel of Love that advertises "No tests, no waiting." Visitors at the Rocky Mountain National Park get a jolt of commercialism at Estes Park, which is actually one of the better gateway towns. Jackson Hole, just south of the Grand Teton National Park is, by these standards, charming. The sore point from the environmental perspective is the airport, located within the park boundaries. On Friday evenings, a procession of jets roar in from Salt Lake City, Los Angeles, and Chicago. Although the airport location within the park boundaries offends, expelling it would make little improvement because it would still be in the valley.

THE SIERRA CLUB REACTIVATES

The political side of the Sierra Club lay dormant from Muir's death until 1952, when it flared to life again to oppose the Bureau of Reclamation proposal to dam the Green River in Echo Park Canyon in Dinosaur National Monument. Few people even knew of the existence of this park on the tributary of the Colorado River spanning the states of Colorado and Utah just south of the Wyoming border. In the early 1900s, paleontologists discovered a rich bed of dinosaur fossils, which gained federal protection in 1915. Only a handful of visitors ventured beyond the fossils to the remote canyons with their spectacular rock formations. The bureau proposed two dams which would raise the water levels by five hundred feet, flooding the most dramatic scenery. Local people wanted the irrigation and the jobs during construction, but the Sierra Club, the Wilderness Society, and the National Parks Association opposed the dams. Even so, the remote location and relative insignificance made Dinosaur Monument hard to defend.

Harry Truman favored the dams both because he liked big government water development in general and because Democrats in the western states believed it would gain votes. His secretary of the interior faced internal conflict with his biggest bureau, Reclamation, which championed the dams, and another big bureau, the Park Service, which opposed them. Summoning his political skills, he delayed the decision. After Dwight Eisenhower's victory in 1952, the new administration decided to build the project. The new secretary, Douglas "Give Away" McKay, asked Congress to authorize it. Although the states of Colorado, Utah, and Wyoming had a total of only nine representatives in the House, they held key positions on the Interior Committee. In the Senate they had six senators out of ninety-six and half the seats on the Interior Committee. By then, environmentalists had stimulated strong popular opposition. In a single month, the House Interior Committee received five thousand letters against the dams and only fifty-three in favor. After another year of wrangling, the committee gave up the plan.

In igniting the flame of opposition, the Sierra Club transformed itself from an outdoor club into a political force. Much credit goes to its executive director, David Brower, who grew up near Berkeley, California. He loved to hike and camp; he was inspired by Muir, Leopold, Marshall, and Zanheiser. During World War II, he joined the 10th Mountain Division that trained in the Rocky Mountains and fought in the Italian Alps. Soon, after becoming the Club's first executive director in 1952, he learned of the dam proposal and convinced the board of directors to fight it. Senators and representatives from the region favored the dam for its electricity and irrigation, but a flood of protest from environmentalists persuaded Congress not to authorize it. As the lobbying success of the club became apparent, clouds appeared. The Internal Revenue Service concluded that the club's lobbying violated conditions for its tax exemption. Eventually, conservative board members, who sought to return to its non-political days, forced Brower to resign. In 1969, he organized Friends of the Earth, whose chief purpose was to influence policy. Eventually, this organization also proved to be too passive for Brower, so he moved to his third organization, the Earth Island Institute. In his old age, Brower reconciled with the club and rejoined its board, where he backed the election of Adam Werbach to be president. Werbach, who was only twenty-three, had organized the Sierra Student Coalition.

MUNICIPAL PARKS

The outstanding accomplishments of the City Beautiful Movement parks of the turn of the century failed to keep pace with suburban growth from 1945 to the present. Two factors contributing to this were the limits on municipal annexation and disinterest by suburbanites. The magnificent, large parks that ring many downtowns exist because farsighted commissions purchased or received as donations a selection of farms and estates dating from the end of the nineteenth century. For the next half-century, houses and businesses grew up to surround the parks. Most cities in the east and midwest found themselves blocked from further annexation by the 1950s or 1960s. Suburban towns chose to remain independent, often to avoid social problems in the central city. Racial integration of schools in the 1960s and 1970s further discouraged annexation. Small suburbs also lacked the critical mass necessary for planning ahead to acquire land for future parks. The second factor was that the suburbanites had their individual quarter-acre or half-acre lots and did not feel the pressure for parks that city dwellers living in row houses and apartments did. The biophilia hypotheses perhaps deserves a corollary that homo sapiens may need grass, shade trees, and flowers, but that a quarter-acre of it is enough.

One way to meet demand for suburban parks was to set up an intergovernmental agency to buy and maintain parks. An individual suburb was too small to do this on its own. These parks serving the entire metropolitan region (and frequently named Metroparks) could capitalize on the aggregated tax base and wide geographical area. For example, the Toledo Metropark System has eight properties surrounding and outside the incorporated city, properties that are as large as three thousand acres. The members of this district are the city, seven suburbs, and the country government. The Metropark Authority is supported by a small tax on property. With their large size, the Metroparks are not convenient for neighborhoods—they are more like miniature state parks. They chiefly offer hiking, nature museums, and educational programs, and three have camp sites.

Traditional municipal parks have been moving toward natural habitats. Greater interest in ecology is one reason, while saving money is another. For example, in Toledo's Ottawa Park, designed by Frederick Law Olmsted, the park department converted land that had consisted of mowed grass and shade trees, and proclaimed that it would become natural. (One reason was that more unmanicured woods would attract birds. School children planted saplings, all native species.) Allowing this section to return to woods permitted a link between two wooded sections so birds and mammals could move between the them. Another reason for the change was that less mowing and tree trimming saved money; nearly every city in the northeast and midwest faced a severe shortage of tax funds when a series of economic recessions struck in 1974, 1978, and 1981.

STATE PARKS

State parks lagged behind both national and municipal parks. Aside from New York, few states had programs prior to the 1920s when the automobile stimulated demand. Now, millions could get out of the cities for a few hours of driving, thus popular demand caused many early parks to be designed for tourist camping. A 1921 National Conference on State Parks spurred many to develop systematic plans. The state parks' role was to be miniature national parks located in rural areas of natural beauty. Accessible by auto, they rarely were wildernesses. Most states did not own unsettled public domain like the national government did and purchasing sites was expensive. The chief source of land was by donation from a wealthy person or a company, and the goal was often to encourage tourism.

Perhaps because it manufactured so many automobiles, Michigan was quite explicit in developing land for state parks. Of its first sixty-four state parks, fifty-nine started with donations. For example, from their motor car fortune, the

Dodge brothers gave ten properties. Michigan suffered typical partisan problems of the time. The first director, who was a crony of the governor, earned a reputation of doing favors and of mismanagement. The next governor developed a remedy: establish a commission whose unpaid members had their own expert knowledge, could check on each other, and could better represent conservationists, hunters, and fishermen. Commissions were a favorite panacea of the reform era, however, they could become inbred and unresponsive to new policies. In this case, the commission fired its first director after eight months because he would not abrogate regulations protecting game when hunters wanted more quarry. On the other side, interest groups like the Friends of Native Landscape and the Detroit Women's City Club lobbied to establish parks. Later, the chief group was the Michigan Parks Association.

Genevieve Gillette devoted over fifty years to lobbying, organizing, and haranguing for parks. Gillette, who was the first woman to graduate from the Michigan State University program in forestry and landscape architecture, took instinctively to influencing policy. In her effort to establish more state parks near Detroit, she first persuaded the Conservation Department to install temporary exhibits in the city, then pressured the department to make them permanent. Gillette earned her living as a florist, so she promoted parks at flower shows with displays, photographs, and films. At a Boy Scout exhibition, she induced the department to set up an "indoor state park" and, at another demonstration, the department transplanted real trees and gave away pine seedlings. Gillette promoted the Sleeping Bear National Lakeshore and served on the first Wilderness Advisory Board.

For twenty-nine years of her unpaid lobbying career, Gillette targeted Percy Hoffmaster, who served as park superintendent and director of the conservation department from 1922 until his death in 1951. Today, such a long career at the top of a bureaucracy is unheard of; however, it was common then. Hoffmaster served under eleven governors, at least one of whom tried hard to fire him, but the commission members shielded him. As park superintendent, Hoffmaster honed his skills in stretching a dollar. He would concoct deals to acquire land for a new park. For example, he would take a piece of property that escheated to the state for non-payment of taxes but was not suitable for a park, then trade it for the land he wanted. He was frequently at odds with the state or county highway departments that wanted to build a road through a park. Hoffmaster, however, was more favorable to development than environmentalists were. Hotels, restaurants, and ski slopes seemed ways to him to make a park better.

Protecting the Porcupine Mountains in the Upper Peninsula was a project important to Hoffmaster and Gillette for many years. Only a few states east of the Rocky Mountains possessed extensive wilderness regions. The Porkies, as they became known, still contain the largest virgin hardwood and hemlock forest remaining east of the Rockies. The state toyed with protecting it as far back as 1925. In 1944, demand for lumber for the war brought the axe and saw to its border. A national outcry finally prompted the legislature to purchase it. Its preservation was only partial, however, because lumber companies asked for permission to cut the timber. Upper Peninsula politicians favored this in order to create jobs. The exhaustion of the remaining timber and the end of copper mining meant unemployment was high. Some members of the Conservation Commission proposed building a ski resort with a hotel, while another proposal was to allow dog racing in state parks. No law protected the wilderness, only by the vote of the commission could a park or region be protected. To remedy the vulnerability of the Porkies, environmentalists asked for legislation, which finally passed. In contrast with state parks, for national parks, the Park Service is required to "preserve" them. Moreover, they tend to be more spectacular, which enhances the opportunities to get publicity and find citizen support. Environmentalists trying to safeguard state parks typically have a harder job.

State and local governments benefit when Congress creates a national park. First of all, it gives them all the advantages of a state park without the expense. In 1959, the National Park Service identified Sleeping Bear Dunes on Lake Michigan as a possible site. It was one of the few coastlines that remained undeveloped. The area was fifty-seven thousand acres of white sand dunes that shifted from year to year and patches of forest and grass. Wind sweeping across Lake Michigan carved sand and gravel cliffs from the glacial moraines, which rise five hundred feet directly up from the surf. Atop the most beautiful moraine perched a small wooded dune that an American Indian legend told was an exhausted mother bear curled up asleep after swimming across the lake to save her cubs from a forest fire in Wisconsin. Alas, her cubs had drowned and the Great Spirit had turned them into two islands off shore. A small state park occupied the point near a Coast Guard lifesaving station. Vacationers were buying lots and building cottages. A private company gave auto tours, where for $5 it drove the visitor in a late model convertible with oversized tires across the fragile sand dunes, leaving ruts and killing the sparse grass. At a stop within the mother bear dune boundaries, the driver would warn against picking flowers, then, on the return drive, go down the biggest dune as fast as possible. The tourists, of course, were thrilled.

Local residents and summer people fought the Park Service proposal. At a hearing at Frankfort, 1,480 of the 1,500 people in attendance were opposed. They feared losing their houses or cottages, which was a legitimate fear since the Park Service proposed to buy private holdings, although usually giving back the right to occupy them for the residents' lifetime. The *Detroit Free Press* editorialized that "if they can get away with this steal, this blatant land grab, no home in America is safe from the bureaucrats."[6] One local resident claimed the government must be communist if it could take private land away. Those who valued privacy feared hoards of tourists.

Then "coho madness" broke out. During the 1950s, lamprey eels, accidently introduced up the St. Lawrence River, killed nearly all native game fish. State and provincial governments finally brought the eels under control by erecting weirs on every tributary of the Great Lakes. To restock Lake Michigan, the Conservation Department in 1965 chose the coho salmon, largely because its run took place in

September so fishermen would extend the tourist season by a month. The salmon, which were hugely successful, brought people in from Detroit, Chicago, and elsewhere. The people spent their money, drove automobiles all over private property, and drank whiskey in the evenings. Eventually, ugly motels, bars, and parking lots sprang up to meet the needs of the growing number of tourists. Now a national park did not seem like such a bad idea.

Congress passed the Sleeping Bear Park Act in 1970 after adding provisions to provide extra protection for property owners. The final boundaries excluded houses and cottages surrounding the picturesque Glen Lake in the heart of the park. Their owners were often articulate, well-connected lawyers, businessmen, and physicians from Chicago, Detroit, and St. Louis who had made it a point to write their Senators and Representatives. Purchase of property actually within the park boundaries proceeded slowly, while those owners who kept their property at Glen Lake or near the other boundaries found themselves in a much better position than before the park was created. Currently, the Park Service preserves the region from further development and provides two museums, picnic sites, and a scenic drive. Owners no longer worry about a condominium or an amusement park spoiling the neighborhood. The Park Service has been known to use a heavy hand at times; after condemning cottages and evicting the owners, it tried to rent the cottages.

The coho salmon success, however, developed a sinister side. Being at the top of the food chain, the fish accumulated mercury and heavy metals from their prey, as such, the EPA determined they were toxic. Today, the Department of Natural Resources, the successor to the Department of Conservation, recommends eating only one fish a month.

HISTORICAL PRESERVATION

A movement to preserve history has run parallel to the environmental movement for the past three decades, and the two have proven quite compatible. With American independence, the patriots were eager to preserve battlefields and sites of the Revolutionary War. In 1827, Jews in Newport, Rhode Island, rebuilt their Touro Synagogue, the first building restored in the United States. Philadelphia purchased and restored the old capitol, better known as Independence Hall. The architect contracted to do the restoration paid homage to the hall's history by reconstructing the ruined tower in the original style. In 1850, New York state purchased and restored the Hasbrouck House in Newburgh that George Washington had used as his military headquarters. Within days after the Battle of Gettysburg ended in 1863, local citizens proposed a park to commemorate the victory and honor the dead.

In 1853, Ann Pamela Cunningham of South Carolina organized the first historical society that set the model for much of today's effort. When real estate promoters tried to purchase Mount Vernon, Cunningham was distressed that neither the national nor Virginian governments would step in to buy Washington's home, by then rather run down. She boldly appointed herself national regent of the Mount

Vernon Ladies Association. As regent, she next appointed state regents throughout the south and later the whole country. Women from all over the country contributed money to purchase and restore the house, a campaign that was entirely private. The nineteenth-century preservation groups chose their sites based on the buildings' connections to famous patriots and leaders. Architectural merit was secondary. Mount Vernon combined both and had the additional benefit of having been "preserved by neglect"—no one had spoiled the original structure by adding rooms or remodeling. The Ladies Association continues to own and manage it.

Even though business, profit, and modernity dominated the Gilded Age from the Civil War until the Great Depression, a few tiny sparks for preserving old houses flickered. In 1891, the private Trustees for Public Preservations organized in Massachusetts, a state always in the forefront of the past. The group inspired the British National Trust three years later, but the idea could not be brought back to the United States at a national level until 1949. In 1925, the Metropolitan Museum of Art opened its American Wing of twenty-five rooms in colonial and federalist styles. At the same time, the Philadelphia Museum of Art took over surviving old houses in Fairmont Park.

In 1926, the rector of the Burton Parish Church in Williamsburg began his campaign to save the colonial capital of Virginia. Like Mount Vernon, it was "preserved by neglect." He envisioned restoring the town as an outdoor museum, faithfully adhering to its architectural integrity. He found a patron in John D. Rockefeller, Jr., son of the Standard Oil Company founder and father of the future governors of New York and Arkansas. Williamsburg would present a real, complete town, where Washington, Jefferson, and Patrick Henry lived and legislated. With only a few modern buildings needing to be removed, the majority of the older ones had changed little since the colonial era. Williamsburg became an immediate success, attracting historians and tourists alike. Government had almost no role; the money and planning came from the Rockefeller family. Like Mount Vernon and the Hasbrouck House, Williamsburg continued the path of preserving buildings associated with famous people.

Private preservationists finally organized nationally in 1947, when the National Park Service sponsored a conference. They established the National Trust for Historic Preservation, with authority to own and manage property. Although closely tied to the Park Service, it was a private organization that was dependent on donations and promoted by the American Association for State and Local History. Participants tended to be from families who were wealthy or who could trace their ancestry to the colonial period, however, the two elite characteristics did not necessarily overlap. As the membership grew to one hundred thousand, Congress authorized it to accept government grants.

At the same time as the National Trust enjoyed modest success, the larger economic and political forces were destroying historic houses and neighborhoods. Suburbanization, amplified by the veterans mortgages and the automobile, pulled young families out of their old neighborhoods that they might have maintained and improved, far out of the city. In turn, the commuters needed highways that governments often constructed by tearing down old neighborhoods. The Interstate Highway Act of 1956 accelerated the demolition by giving the state highway departments grants for 90 percent of the cost instead of 50 percent under the old method. The Housing Acts of 1949 and 1956 provided millions, eventually billions, of dollars to clear slums. The earliest projects resembled wartime bombing; nothing old remained. For example, southwest Washington, D.C., extends from Capitol Hill to the Potomac River, about twelve blocks by nine blocks. It contained many of the city's oldest buildings, although not the most important ones. After "renewal," only three old buildings remained standing. Contemporaneously, an additional twelve square blocks were cleared for a freeway. Even city planners recognized this was excessive.

By the 1960s, other forces converged pointing to the benefits of historic preservation. European cities bombed during World War II restored many of their oldest buildings. London, Amsterdam, and Brussels painstakingly rebuilt their churches, bridges, and guildhalls. Warsaw restored its Market Square from Nazi and Russian bombing. In fact, European countries had laws protecting historic buildings dating as far back to the Swedish laws in 1066 and 1630. The oldest modern preservation program began in 1819 in the Papal States. France had a preservation commission in 1837. Modern Greece, whose war of liberation owed much to American independence, enacted legislation in 1839.

Advocates of preservation grew concerned during the late 1950s that the National Park Service showed little interest in projects outside its bailiwick. Not all historic buildings, however, could become museums. Many needed to be used as residences, offices, hotels and restaurants, a concept labeled "living history." Attention to historic preservation fit the ambitious plans of Lyndon Johnson because the Great Society needed to be beautiful as well as everything else. His wife, Lady Bird Johnson, who had a particular interest in this, chaired a White House Conference on Natural Beauty. While most groups were concerned parks and environmental protection, a division on Townscapes recommended legislation enhancing the National Trust with grants and controlling highway and urban renewal programs that destroyed historic sites.

To increase support for the bill, a housing lobbyist, Laurence Henderson, suggested to Representative Albert Rains the stimulus might be a trip of prominent leaders to visit preservation programs in Europe. The U.S. Conference of Mayors agreed to sponsor the trip, and the Ford Foundation agreed to pay for it. The Rains Committee travelled to eight countries. Members were from the Trust, the Department of the Interior, a governor, a mayor, a representative, and a senator. Perhaps inevitably, the senator was Edmund Muskie. These influential men and women returned convinced the government needed to do more. The European countries recognized private donations were not enough. Upon its return, the Rains Committee drafted a proposed bill, which Muskie introduced in March 1966. Its four elements were a National Register of Historic Sites, grants to state agencies, opportunity to stop action by other federal agencies that would harm a registered site, and an Advisory Council on Historic Preservation. Six months later, Congress passed the National Historic Preservation Act and Johnson signed it, rapid progress by today's measure, but typical of many laws Johnson promoted for his Great Society.

In 1906, Representative John Lacey, author of the 1900 Act to protect birds, persuaded Congress to pass the Antiquities Act. The first two sites were the Petrified Forest in Arizona and the Cliff Dwellers ruins near Santa Fe, New Mexico. Prior to its protection, robbers looted the ancient rocks and artifacts. Since then, the law has protected two hundred sites. Jimmy Carter's maneuvering to save land for the six Alaskan parks was the most creative. During the 1996 campaign President Clinton used the law to preserve 1.7 million acres in southern Utah as the Grand Staircase-Escalante National Monument. His designation won praise (and presumably votes) from environmentalists around the country even though it infuriated Utah's political leaders, who were all Republicans. Senator Orin Hatch declared "there's going to be hell to pay." The move blocked plans by a Dutch company to mine coal worth as much as $1 trillion. President Clinton made the announcement in Arizona, staying clear of Utah. He calculated he could win in Arizona and California, two nearby states more favorable to the environment, and wrote off Utah as hopeless. The November results proved him right.

NEW TRENDS AND PARKS OVERSEAS

The other trend for national parks and preserves in the last three decades has been to nail down a few large areas notable for their natural beauty and significance. Ten huge parks and refuges in Alaska cover a combined total of fifty-two million acres. The Mojave National Park in California covers 1.5 million acres of desert protected from motorcyclists, Army tanks, and real estate developers.

Popular concern with racial and ethnic issues have touched the parks only lightly. In 1980, Congress renamed Mount McKinley Park in Alaska to the American Indian term "Denali," which means Great One. It kept the old name for the mountain, however, to continue to honor the twenty-fifth president. (Ohio representatives and senators object to altering the memorial to the state's native son.) In 1991, Congress renamed the Custer Battlefield in Montana after the Little Bighorn River and authorized erecting a monument to the Sioux and Cheyenne who died there battling the Seventh Calvary. In 1994, the Park Service added, albeit reluctantly, the Boston African American National Historical Site on Beacon Hill, a neighborhood once the center of the black community.

Establishing these last big parks exhausts the possible sites in the entire United States. Virtually no large regions remain unclaimed. Yet, many National Forests contain mountains, forests, and lakes of stunning beauty and biological importance. The continuing conflict between the National Park Service in the Department of the Interior and the Forest Service in the Department of Agriculture precludes converting National Forest land to National Parks. The split dates back to the very first reservation a century ago. While the Forest Service resists transferring land, it is willing to establish the equivalent of parks.

The greatest opportunities for parks today are overseas. East Africa, the Amazon rain forest, and Papua New Guinea face dangers of overdevelopment and poaching. With poetic, perhaps ironic, justice, the savannas of Kenya and Tanzania, where homo sapiens evolved for three million years, still inspires people. From the biophilia perspective this inspiration is only natural because humans are hardwired to appreciate their ancestral home. These African plains today still display great diversity of life. While North America could claim billions of buffalo or passenger pigeons but not much variety, Africa features a hundred different species mixed together. Foreigners are surprised to see zebras, giraffes, wildebeests, and ostriches mingling together. Additionally, the savanna is home to the largest animals and most famous predators: elephants, rhinoceroses, lions, and cheetahs.

During the colonial period, the British established national parks at Tsavo, Serengeti, and Athi plains. These were very much like the big parks being created contemporaneously in the United States and England. After independence, Kenya and Tanzania continued and improved the parks. Kenya earns much of its foreign exchange from tourists who come to see the animals and the savanna. Yet, it faces pressure from its citizens who need land for farming because its population has doubled in two decades. Poachers threaten the big game since ivory from elephants is worth thousands of dollars per tusk. Residents living near Tsavo or Serengeti probably gain little advantage from the tourism, while being forbidden to hunt or graze their cattle, and many resent the parks.

Rhinoceroses face a greater threat. Superstitious Chinese men believe drinking a potion of their powdered horn will increase their sexual performance. Poachers typically maim the rhinoceroses, saw off their horns to smuggle them overseas, and leave the wounded animal to die slowly. One remedy is for game wardens to capture the rhinoceroses with a tranquilizer gun and saw off their horns—sacrificing the horn removes their commercial value and the only harm is cosmetic.

Chinese also seek tiger bones and penises for a brew they believe enhances their sexual potency. A single male tiger may be worth $20,000 for his bones and penis and his skin can be sold for as much as $15,000. Although the Convention on International Trade in Endangered Species (CITES) forbids trade in tigers, the black market price encourages poaching, even though the peasant who shoots the animal may receive only a few hundred dollars. The species is extinct or nearly extinct everywhere except in India and Bangladesh, where about four thousand survive, while another thousand or so live in southeast Asia.

Attempts to protect species can have perverse consequences, however. In 1989, CITES prohibited trade in rhinoceros horns and elephant ivory. During the ban, the population of black rhinos in Zimbabwe fell from six thousand to three hundred, and the number of elephants grew to sixty-five thousand, twice the number the land could support. Poaching has decimated the rhinos and lack of culling has overprotected the elephants. Excess elephants tear apart trees, destroy the savanna, and eat agricultural crops. In eight years, Zimbabwe and its neighbors Botswana and Namibia accumlated a 120-ton stockpile of tusks from elephants that died of natural causes. Eventually, the members of CITES voted to permit the three countries to sell this ivory, which is worth millions of dollars, to Japan. Led by Secretary of the Interior Bruce Babbitt, the American delegation supported lifting the ban.

CONCLUSION

The great national parks like Yellowstone began as local movements. The ranchers and settlers, who explored the land of geysers and steam vents in 1870, spontaneously conceived of a totally new concept and soon convinced Congress to make it a reality. In a similar fashion, historic preservation began as a grass roots movement typified by the Mount Vernon Ladies Association. The City Beautiful movement was more self-conscious of its mission, which combined naturalistic urban parks with Progressive ideals of health, cleanliness, and wholesome fun. While the dynamic era of parks is over within the United States, the situation overseas remains fluid. Americans are now aware of how war, poverty, and disease in Africa damages the environment and the wildlife there. Poaching and habitat loss are now only part of the African problem. The Amazon Basin, the Himalayas, and the Antarctic are next in line, and the mass movement aspects to save these regions will be largely vicarious, just as is the case for endangered species and wildernesses.

Yosemite Park has been the heart of the Sierra Club ever since John Muir founded it. This quintessential interest group now has over half a million members, a large, paid staff, and a budget in the millions of dollars. The club enjoys high prestige, a record of outstanding directors, and its political skill is legendary. Many other well-organized interest groups work on behalf of parks at the national and state levels, such as the Michigan Parks Association.

The Democratic and the Republican parties differ on parks. Jimmy Carter and the Democratic-controlled Congress added six giant national parks in the Alaskan Lands Act, while Republicans were unenthusiastic. The Reagan administration cut the budget for the National Park Service and ended grants to states for their own parks. President Clinton and the Democratic members of Congress created the Mojave National Park and added land to the Death Valley Monument. At the height of the campaign in 1996, Clinton declared 1.7 million acres of Utah as a National Monument, often the first phase in establishing a park and one the president can take without needing the approval of 'Congress. During the 1995 to 1996 budget battle between the Republican Congress and Clinton, the National Park Service was a major target.

Critics accuse the Park Service of being rigid and over centralized. In fact, since its duties have changed little in recent years, this may be inevitable. It is not a dynamic area and budget cuts have hurt. Rigidity may deserve more criticism in historic preservation programs because builders and homeowners are often stymied by rules that block or add expense to remodeling. Specialization and regulations can be dysfunctional.

NOTES

1. Edward O. Wilson and Stephen Kellert, eds., *The Biophilia Hypothesis* (Washington, DC: Island Press, 1993).
2. Robert S. Urlrich, "Biophilia, Biophobia, and Natural Landscapes," in Wilson and Kellert, eds., *The Biophilia Hypothesis* (Washington, DC: Island Press, 1993), 100–103.
3. Galen Cranz, *The Politics of Park Design* (Cambridge, Massachusetts Institute of Technology Press, 1982), 77.
4. Ronald Foresta, *America's National Parks and their Keepers* (Washington, DC: Resources for the Future, 1985), 239.
5. Frank Graham, *The Adirondack Park: A Political History* (Syracuse, NY: Syracuse University Press, 1978), 239.
6. Quoted in Claire V. Korn *Michigan State Parks* (East Lansing: Michigan State University Press, 1989), 115.

CHAPTER 8
PROTECTING THE LAND

Managing land is a traditional function of local and state government. Counties record deeds, and states enact laws for rights and transfers. The national government does not provide these functions; instead, its importance comes from being a giant landlord. It owns nearly seven hundred million acres, chiefly left over from the donation by the thirteen original states, the Louisiana Purchase, conquest from Mexico, and so forth. From the environmental perspective, controlling government-owned land presents different issues than controlling privately-owned land. Of the entire public domain, the Bureau of Land Management (BLM) of the Interior Department owns 270 million acres and the Forest Service owns nearly two hundred million acres. The BLM land, often called "the land nobody wanted," is the residual of the original 1.2 billion acres that no one purchased, homesteaded, paved for highways, turned into a park, or declared a National Forest. The National Forests were selected for transfer to the Department of Agriculture because they were valuable. Forty-eight state governments combined own only a few acreage. Texas and Alaska, however, are exceptions. When the Republic of Texas entered the union, it kept its public land, while Alaska received millions of acres from the federal government, mostly from the 1971 and 1980 laws.

Although states, counties, and municipalities do not own much land, their influence is great. Nearly all cities and urbanized counties are zoned, meaning they have zones restricted to residential, commercial, or industrial uses. Moreover, many have more extensive plans for use. Now, rural counties are also becoming zoned or adopting plans. At the state level, the trend for the past thirty years has been for states to establish plans for land use. Many states have laws preserving farms threatened by suburbanization. States use their traditional authority on property law in imaginative ways to deal with environmental problems. Lastly, states administer a series of delegated national programs, such as protecting coastlines, regulating wetlands, and reducing factory emissions. Delegated responsibilities under the Clean Air and Water Acts frequently determine how land is used along rivers and lakes.

Governments have always recognized that land is a unique form of property: permanent, immovable, and affecting its neighbors. Because people die but the land remains, governments have far more detailed requirements for transferring it than for personal property like furniture, tools, and automobiles. The term "real estate" or "real property" recalls the original royal role. How an owner uses his property affects his neighbors, because a drainage ditch can cause erosion, a dump can be a nuisance, and a brush fire can spread.

BACKGROUND

Surveying tools found in archeological digs of ancient Egypt testify to both its mathematical skills and the local governmental function of managing property rights. Throughout the entire kingdom, officials administered irrigation from the Nile River, successfully managing a larger, more fragile area than any until modern times. The Babylonians built tunnels and canals for irrigation extending dozens of miles. The ancient Greeks, whom political science glorifies for their philosophy and democratic institutions, ranked near the bottom in land management. By 300 B.C., they had chopped down their forests and eroded their farms.

Europeans of the early medieval period lived in forests with rain and good soil. By 1400, Europeans had turned their forests into farms. Italy had decimated its forests a century earlier. After reunifying the British Crown after the War of the Roses, King Henry VII invaded Ireland. To secure his conquest, he encouraged the English and Welsh to emigrate there. Later, Scots settled. His son Henry VIII's separation of the Anglicans from the Roman Catholics gave England further reason to encourage settlement across the Irish Sea. The Irish patriots rejected the Church of England and sought alliance with France. To a certain extent, the British colonization of Ireland set a pattern for its colonization of North America.

The purpose of the Virginia Company was purely commercial. The settlers were to hunt and trap animals for fur, grow tobacco, mine for lead and gold, and trade with the American Indians. While the Pilgrim and Puritan settlers in Massachusetts sought to establish a society based on religious principles, they too planned to hunt, fish, farm, and trade with the American Indians. Like the Virginians, they exported goods to England. Although they may have been fascinated by the testing and bounty of the wilderness, they did not intend to keep it wild. Upon arrival, the colonists laid out lots for houses, fields for crops, and common pastures for grazing. The Boston Commons, now a downtown park, retains its original name of a field owned in common for grazing sheep and cattle.

The most important feature of land in America was its democratic owner-ship, in contrast to the Old World, where nearly everyone working the land was a tenant of the lord of the manor. In the New World, nearly everyone owned their own farm. The effect on government was immense. The American farmer could now enjoy autonomy that had been impossible previously in Europe where the lord would evict tenants who refused his requests. Known as a yeoman, meaning a farmer who owned his land, this farmer was the backbone of democracy. The alternative term, freeholder, continues in use. For example, New Jersey counties are governed by a Board of Chosen Freeholders (a board elected from among men who own property). Indeed, until about 1820, most states required voters to own property. Thomas Jefferson believed ardently that the yeoman farmer was the best guarantee of liberty; he considered cities and manufacturing a threat. Agricultural policy up to the present aims to protect the family farm.

Americans had the luxury of land ownership because there was so much of it. The frontier offered endless acreage; people only had to move west. If they could not afford to purchase it from the colonial government, they could settle illegally as a squatter. Eventually, most squatters converted their land to legal ownership. The frontier also solved social problems. An impoverished family could go there to start over. Mentally ill people could retreat beyond the stress of civilization. The frontier's existence moderated the abuse of indentured servants, because a disgruntled servant could run away and easily disappear from view. Many of the founding fathers also sought to develop the western land. George Washington earned a living as a surveyor and led expeditions as far as Lake Erie. He owned thirty thousand acres on the Ohio River at the Kanawha River and many smaller parcels closer to home.

During the movement towards independence, one of the patriot complaints against the British Crown was its restriction on settlement. By 1770, the growing population pressured the pioneers to move across the Allegheny Mountains to the rich soil of Kentucky and Ohio. The British government, looking at the big pic-ture, realized settlement west of the mountains would bring conflict with the American Indians, so they forbid it with the Line of Demarcation. Parliament passed the Quebec Act which extended that colony's boundaries to the Ohio and Mississippi Rivers, territory Americans considered to be theirs. The patriots of the Second Continental Congress specified it as one of their grievances against King George in the Declaration of Independence.

After its victory at Yorktown, the young Republic turned its attention to managing its Northwest Territory. The thirteen states relinquished their claims to the land that stretched to the Spanish territory of Louisiana west of the Mississippi River. Kentucky was already organized as a county of Virginia, and Tennessee was part of North Carolina. In three laws passed during 1784, 1785, and 1787, the Continental Congress organized the land north from the Ohio River to the Great Lakes and west to the Mississippi. Thomas Jefferson drafted the original bill in 1782 while serving as a delegate to the Continental Congress. Jefferson was influenced by ideas of the Enlightenment typified by technology and of representative government. The Northwest Ordinances of 1784 and 1787 dealt with establishing government and the process of petitioning for statehood, and the latter provided for schools. Each township received property to sell or rent in order to build a school house and pay a teacher.

The Ordinance of 1785 directed the national government to survey the land into ranges, townships, and sections along the key lines of latitude and longitude. A township would be six miles by six miles forming thirty-six sections of one square mile. Each section, having six hundred forty acres, would be sold for $1.25 per acre. Later, Congress extended the system to the Louisiana and Oregon Territories, giving the midwestern and the plains regions their characteristic grids, quarter-section farms of one hundred sixty acres, and roads running north-south and east-west. No other law passed by the Continental Congress continues to have so great an influence on national policy today.

PRIVATE PROPERTY AND THE FAMILY FARM

The Northwest Ordinance guided land policy with little change for seventy-eight years, and its effects remain to this time. The price of $1.25 per acre proved too expensive for many pioneers, especially since they had to purchase a full six hundred forty acres. Companies bought the land and subdivided it, provoking accusations of speculation and manipulation. The government granted free land to veterans of the Revolutionary War and, later, of the War of 1812 and Mexican War. Overall, the system worked well in promoting agriculture in the relatively flat, fertile, and rainy midwest. The settlers chopped down the hardwood forest, planted corn, and fattened cattle and hogs. The family farm fit with the land.

In Alabama and Mississippi, which were settled later than Tennessee and Kentucky, Congress made similar provisions to the Northwest Territory, but unfortunately, the land was less fertile so the single family farm was less productive than farther north. The soil in the southeast did not have the benefit of ancient glaciation, and the heat quickly decomposed organic material. The most productive crop was cotton, which was most efficiently raised on large plantations with slave labor. At the eve of the Civil War, only a few pioneers had settled beyond the Missouri River. The pioneers were still in land that could be farmed by individual families and without irrigation.

The Department of the Treasury conducted sales directly from its headquarters until 1812, when it set up its General Land Office. In 1849, Congress separated it to be the core of the new Department of the Interior, and the Land Office constituted most of the new department. It continued as a bureau within the Department of Interior until merging with the Grazing Service in 1946 to become the Bureau of Land Management.

Nineteenth-century voters saw the benefits of free land, of course. In its visionary electoral platform for Abraham Lincoln in 1860, the new Republican party promised a homestead law, which was enacted in 1862. A settler could receive one hundred sixty acres of the public domain in return for building a house and a barn and living on the property for five years. The rationale behind the law (besides getting votes) was that empty land had little value and only once it was improved would it be valuable. The Homestead Act dominated federal land policy for half a century and continued until Franklin Roosevelt ended most of it in 1935. As pioneers moved onto the Great Plains, the lack of rainfall meant the one hundred sixty-acre limit was too small. Wheat, where it would grow, needed a bigger farm to be efficient. West of the 100th meridian, only grazing was possible and the rancher needed several sections. Congress amended the law to allow for an increase in acreage. It also raised the number of school sections in a township to two and later three. The old fashioned family farm was no longer compatible with the land. This fact was also true in Alaska where most of the terrain was too cold for farming and ranching.

A second progressive plank in the 1860 Republican platform was the promise to build a railroad across the continent that would serve the new homesteaders and link the country to California. Free land was the incentive dangled before the railway companies. The 1862 law gave alternate sections to the railway and kept the remaining ones for settlement. The pattern was like a checkerboard. At first, the alternate sections extended out one mile, but the land proved so poor that the railways demanded sections out for ten miles and eventually twenty miles. The railways recognized the most valuable resource was not farmland, but coal and minerals. Surveyors for the first transcontinental line, the Union Pacific, chose a route considerably south of the Oregon Trail in order to mine coal deposits to supply its locomotives. The Railway Act required companies to establish a town every fifty miles, but one hundred miles was a more suitable distance to fit the technology of the steam engine. Therefore, the companies partly ignored the act. For example, these towns, located along the original Union Pacific line are about one hundred miles apart: Julesburg, Colorado; Cheyenne, Laramie, Rawlins, Rock Springs in Wyoming; and Logan, Utah. Although most of the land given to railways was in the west, millions of acres were in northern Michigan, Wisconsin, and Minnesota as well. Developers could reap fortunes from the timber. The tracks and bridges they built were cheap and flimsy because the railway never foresaw much potential in transportation by itself; the profits were in harvesting the trees. They cut down the virgin forests and did not replant them.

To further encourage development, Congress in 1866 and 1872 passed laws legitimating mining on the public domain. Prior to these laws, miners were technically trespassing. After these laws, any person or company could get the mine for a small fee by staking a claim. As with homesteading, the rationale was that the land was worthless unless developed.

The idea of protecting the environment or the taxpayers' mineral assets did not occur to Congress. Even so, most mining techniques of the period did little damage. Mining was either underground, or it disturbed only a small surface area. Hydraulic mining in California and Arizona was not so benign, however. As early as 1850, gold miners would dam creeks and use pressurized hoses to wash

Scorecard for PROTECTING the LAND

LAWS

Homestead Act 1862. General Mining Law 1872. Mineral Leasing Act 1920. Taylor Grazing Act 1934. Federal Land Policy Management Act (FLPMA) 1976. National Forest Management Act. Multiple Use Sustained Yield Act 1960. Surface Mining Control and Reclamation Act (SMCRA) 1977. Resource Planning Act 1974. Alaska National Interest Lands Conservation Act 1980. National Historic Preservation Act.

OWNERSHIP *(in millions of acres)*

Bureau of Land Management (DOI)	329
Forest Service (USDA)	190
Fish and Wildlife Service (DOI)	85
National Park Service (DOI)	71
Department of Defense (DOD)	30
Water and Power Resources Service (DOI)	7
Department of Energy (DOE)	1
Tennessee Valley Authority (TVA)	1
All other U.S. government	1
Total	715

CONGRESS

House Committee on Resources (formerly Interior), subcommittees on Parks, Fisheries, Water, Energy, and Forests.
Committee on Agriculture, subcommittee on Forestry
Senate Committee on Energy and Natural Resources (formerly Interior), subcommittees on Parks and on Forests and Public Land Management
Committee on Agriculture, subcommittee on Forestry

AGENCIES

Department of the Interior
• Bureau of Land Management
• Fish and Wildlife Service
• Office of Surface Mining
• Water and Power Resources Service (formerly Bureau of Reclamation)

Department of Agriculture
• Forest Service
• Natural Resources Conservation Service (formerly Soil Conservation Service)

Army Corps of Engineers
County and city zoning commissions

INTEREST GROUPS

American Forests
The Nature Conservancy
Sierra Club
Natural Resources Defense Council
Friends of the Earth
Southeast Alaska Conservation Council
Logging Companies
American Forest and Paper Association

Ketchikan Pulp Co.
Mining companies
National Coal Association
American Mining Congress
Ranchers
National Cattlemen's Association
Real estate companies
NIMBY groups

Source: National Park Service, "Acreage of the National Park System," http://www.nps.gov/.

away the overburden. Elsewhere, the cumulative damage from hundreds and thousands of small mines is still visible in spoil piles along creeks. Miners also used mercury to help extract gold and silver from the ore; this poisonous liquid metal still remains in the mountain soil and rivers. The 1872 law remains in force for certain mining today. Clinton's Secretary of the Interior Bruce Babbitt has campaigned for Congress to amend the law, which in 1994 obligated him to turn over gold reserves worth $10 billion to a foreign corporation. The next year he had to give away copper and silver reserves in Arizona worth $3 billion in return for a fee of $1,750. Babbitt asked rhetorically: "When will Congress end this form of corporate welfare?"[1]

THE CONSERVATION MOVEMENT

Toward the end of the nineteenth century, a handful of Americans grew concerned with the waste of natural resources. In 1871, a giant fire burned 1.2 million acres of Wisconsin timber and killed more than a thousand people. Loggers had carelessly left stumps, sawdust, and chopped-off limbs where they became tinder in the hot and dry fall. To save themselves, survivors waded into rivers and lakes, and in Peshtigo, hundreds boarded a steamer that headed out to Lake Michigan. Ironically, at the same time, the city of Chicago burned, killing two hundred fifty people. Besides the human losses, the conflagration in Wisconsin destroyed millions of board feet of lumber.

Among the first Americans concerned with forest destruction was Franklin Benjamin Hough. Trained as a physician, as were so many naturalists, he turned to geology and forests while he practiced medicine in Somerville, New York. In 1855, the state government hired him to conduct a census involving data on agriculture and population. His report highlighted damage to forests. After serving in the Civil War, Hough directed a census of the District of Columbia and was superintendent of the national census of 1870. Gaining the support of the American Association for the Advancement of Science, Hough conducted a national evaluation that persuaded Congress to create a Division of Forestry in the Agriculture Department. He headed the division from 1876 to 1883, then returned to New York to successfully lobby for the state Forestry Commission. In turn, the commission developed the Adirondack Forest Preserve.

Although America offered no academic training in forestry, the discipline had been developed in Germany and France. The orientation of the continental schools was commercial: how to grow and harvest trees efficiently—the environmental aspect of forestry came much later. Bernhard Fernow was the first to bring German technology to American forestry. Born in Germany and educated at the Hanover-Muenden Forest Academy, he began his career in the Prussian Forest Service. Romance and marriage brought him to the United States in 1876, where he first worked in Pennsylvania managing fourteen thousand acres that supplied charcoal. In 1882, Fernow organized the American Forestry Congress, and President Cleveland appointed him chief of forestry four years later. Fernow professionalized the Forestry Division by hiring experts, implementing scientific methods, and lobbying Congress.

In 1891, Fernow and other trained foresters persuaded Congress to pass the Payson Act, named for the Illinois representative who sponsored it. Two previous laws actually had increased destruction, and the Supreme Court had just ruled that citizens had a fundamental right to exploit government land. The act gave the president authority to withdraw forested land from the public domain. This method had the advantage of no cash cost. The government already owned the land; the president merely shifted it from one classification to another. The disadvantage was that the government already had sold or given away many places that needed protection most, but there were no funds to buy them back. Within a month, President Benjamin Harrison withdrew a forest next to Yellowstone Park, and before leaving office, he withdrew another thirteen million acres. Cleveland withdrew twenty-one million acres and Roosevelt withdrew one hundred fifty-nine million acres. Only seven million acres have been added since.

Fernow's successor in 1898 was Gifford Pinchot, the most famous forester in American history. After graduating from Yale University, he attended the French National School of Forestry and traveled to Switzerland, Germany, and England. Upon returning, he managed the reserves on the Vanderbilt estate in North Carolina. During his time in office the number of national forests increased from 32 million to 139 million acres. His division gained ownership of the National Forests from the Interior Department and the division was elevated to become the U.S. Forest Service. Pinchot organized the Society of American Foresters, the Public Lands Commission, the Inland Waterways Commission, and the Governors' Conference on the Environment (an early use of that word). Later, the voters of Pennsylvania twice elected him governor. Because they shared a love of the outdoors, Pinchot and Theodore Roosevelt developed a close friendship. Pinchot believed the purpose of forests was to supply lumber; he did not accept the idea of preservation for a wilderness or a park, which brought him into conflict with men like John Muir.

Pinchot was energetic and self-confident. He believed he knew the answers to most questions and did not need much advice from others. President Taft fired him for insubordination in 1910 for demanding a more thorough investigation of land fraud in Alaska. The controversy pitted Taft against the progressive wing of the Republican party, led by Theodore Roosevelt who was, by then, out of office. The dispute between the progressive and conservative Republicans expanded, and by 1912, the split was complete. Roosevelt tried to prevent Taft's renomination and when that failed, he withdrew to form the Progressive party. When asked whether he was healthy enough to run for president again, Roosevelt replied that he was "as strong as a bull moose," giving the new party its popular name of the Bull Moose party.

Pinchot and Roosevelt epitomized the conservation movement of the turn of the century. Its tenets were protection of American natural resources for enjoyment and use. The establishment of national and state parks was one side of the movement (essentially equivalent to today's environmentalism), while managing forests, minerals, and wildlife efficiently was another. Bitten by the lure of western adventure as a young man, Roosevelt had purchased a ranch in the Badlands of North Dakota where he tried for three years to make it a financial success. Poor land and the Blizzard of 1888 wiped out his investment, but not his love of adventure. Returning to New York City, he founded the Boone and Crocket Club and continued to camp, hike, and ride. In fact, at the time President McKinley was shot, Vice President Roosevelt was camping in the Adirondacks, and upon receiving the telegram, drove all night in a buckboard to reach a railroad.

THE NEW DEAL

Franklin Roosevelt's election brought important changes to land policy, just as it did in so many areas. The Dust Bowl in the Great Plains was the biggest land problem he confronted. In the late 1920s, five years of extreme drought had eliminated much of the moisture. Unfortunately, five extremely wet years at the beginning of the century had encouraged farmers to settle on land that was not suitable in the long term. Climatic vagaries had given them the worst of both— farm crops had destroyed the native plants that protected the soil, and with the drought, the strong plains wind stirred up the dust and blew it for miles. A dust storm could strip one county and blow the dry soil to another where it buried crops and penetrated into houses and machinery. Oklahoma suffered the worst damage. Farmers could no longer raise crops or pay their mortgages, so many gave up, loaded their clothes and dishes into a Model T, and headed for jobs they heard about in California.

Soil erosion was a problem in the south as well. Cotton depleted the soil, and crop rotation and alternatives like peanuts were not yet popular. Once farmers abandoned cotton, the bare topsoil eroded into gullies. Scientists in the Department of Agriculture had monitored the problems. In 1935, Congress established the Soil Conservation Service (SCS), which employed Civilian Conservation Corps (CCC) workers to quickly extend its program nationwide at a minimal cost. Two years later it expand to protect watersheds and to construct ponds and reservoirs. Eventually, the service grew to three thousand local districts and covered more than two billion acres. A board of farmers and the Department of Agriculture staff run each district, while the staff also advises individual farmers. Later legislation made the board responsible for improving water quality and protecting wetlands. Now renamed the Natural Resources Conservation Service, the agency's environmental role has expanded.

Roosevelt wanted to help the farmers who were forced off their land by the Dust Bowl. The fact that large regions could never again support crops was apparent, and that leaving them barren would perpetuate the dust storms. Part of the solution was for the Agriculture Department to purchase the abandoned farms and ranches and return them to prairie. The job went to the Forest Service, which named them National Grasslands since most had scarcely a tree. This was

An Oklahoma ranch about to be engulfed by a dust storm in 1935. Aggravated by drought, uncontrolled soil erosion during the Depression years stripped the land of top soil in one county and buried crops, machinery, and property in another.

not virgin sod with healthy, native grasses so thick it was hard to plow; it was the waste from overly optimistic planting and years of drought. These grasslands are some of the few places where the federal government acquired new property by purchase, rather than merely retaining it from the public domain.

The president's compassion for the poor took a similar form in the east, where the government purchased marginal farms in the Appalachian Mountains. These were usually tiny: a plot of land with a few cows and hogs. In the Blue Ridge Mountains of Virginia, the government patched the former farms together to create the Shenandoah National Park. Hikers today know that when they spot an apple tree, they can find the stone foundations of a house and a barn nearby. To crown the park, the WPA constructed a scenic highway along the highest ridge: Skyline Drive. For seventy-five miles south from Front Royal the spectacular road twists through the mountain tops. While in 1939 it seemed the acme of a park, changing concepts of protection would appall current environmentalists if it were proposed today. This was the same period that Mount Rushmore was decorated with the faces of Washington, Jefferson, Lincoln, and Theodore Roosevelt.

On Catoctin Mountain near Thurmont, Maryland, Roosevelt took a personal interest in the WPA-CCC project. From colonial times, the mountain had supplied charcoal for iron furnaces, and farmers and lumber companies had cut down the trees, leaving only scrub and saplings. The farmers had abandoned their holdings. CCC workers labored to plant trees, build paths, and stop erosion. In 1942, the war caused Roosevelt to change his weekend custom of relaxing aboard his yacht cruising the Potomac River or the Chesapeake Bay. German submarines were sinking ships off the east coast and had put saboteurs ashore in Long Island and Florida. Another potential threat was a seaplane launched from a ship disguised under a false flag. The American bombing raid on Tokyo from an aircraft carrier pointed out the danger. Roosevelt decided on Catoctin Mountain. The Navy built a few bungalows and a bomb shelter (which the president named Shangri-La, a utopian land depicted in James Hilton's *Lost Horizon*). The hideaway did not suit Harry Truman, but Dwight Eisenhower liked it and renamed it after his grandson: Camp David.

During the New Deal, Representative Edward Taylor of Colorado sought to reform the careless use of the public domain for livestock. He understood the damage unregulated grazing did to the western range, and that any rancher was legally entitled to feed his sheep or cattle with no charge and no responsibility. Sheep ate the grass down to a nub, and cattle damaged streams and increased erosion. The Taylor Act created a grazing service in the Interior Department that was to rent the rights for a fee. In 1946, the service merged with the General Land Office to become the Bureau of Land Management.

While the Taylor Act greatly improved the previous situation of no management, the fees were too small and the pressure to open land was too great. During Lyndon Johnson's administration, the Bureau of the Budget (later the Office of Management and Budget) tried to increase the fee to closer to what a private landowner would charge. The attempt was only the beginning of at least three decades of battle between economic rationality and the political power of ranchers. The Budget Bureau advocated that the ranchers pay the full cost of grazing and not leave the BLM to pick up the extra costs of damage to the range and water. The fee a private owner charged was a logical yardstick. For their part, the ranchers wanted to maintain their beneficial arrangement. Their arguments were that it was traditional, that BLM costs were exaggerated, and that private owners provided additional services, such as repairing fences. Mostly, their argument was that senators from their states held powerful positions on the Public Lands Committee.

Created by the Senate in 1816, the Public Lands Committee was always a top choice for western senators and held little appeal to those from other parts of the country. The western states contained large amounts of government land and needed water for irrigation. They amended laws on minerals, coal, oil, and gas to pay half the royalties to the state governments. Eastern senators had many other committees of more interest such as banking, commerce, or labor. Midwesterners also sought positions on these committees as well as on the Agriculture Committee. Many western states have low populations, so they do not have many representatives in the House. In virtually every Congress for a century, western senators have constituted half the committee members. The committee changed its name to the Interior in 1948 and to the Energy and Natural Resources in 1977.

Although western senators dominate the committee, a number of members have been dedicated to environmental values, including Henry Jackson. Jackson began his career working for the New Deal Federal Emergency Relief Agency in Everett, Washington, then won election to the House of Representatives at the age of 29. In 1952, he was elected to the Senate, where he joined the Interior Committee. Jackson became chair in 1964, serving until his death in 1983. While chair he guided the Wilderness Act, the Land and Water Conservation Act, the National Wild and Scenic Rivers Act, the National Trails System Act, and the Alaska Lands Act. Additionally, he sponsored the National Environmental Policy Act. No senator was a better friend to the land than Jackson. He also supported projects in water, defense, and agriculture for the benefit of his home state.

SURFACE MINING

Technology for mining coal and minerals changed by 1950. Giant electric drag lines and shovels made it cheaper to dig up coal by removing the soil overburden than by tunneling underground. Deep mining demands huge investments in tunnels, tracks, and electricity, and most of the investment cannot be reused when the deposit is depleted. Stripping grew cheaper each year, and the company could move its equipment to a new site. Environmentally responsible stripping requires replacing the overburden, keeping out water that will leach the acid, saving the topsoil, and replanting the surface with trees or crops. Unfortunately, many companies have been irresponsible by leaving the spoil ungraded, neglecting drainage, and discarding the topsoil. In 1946, the state of Pennsylvania passed a law to regulate the damage, and West Virginia and Montana passed laws a few years later. From the operators' perspective, every dollar spent for reclamation was that much less for profits. If they reclaimed, they lost customers to competitors who took shortcuts. The Pennsylvania law put all operators in the state in the same position, but those in more lenient states like Virginia and Kentucky could produce the coal more cheaply.

Representative Ken Heckler of West Virginia realized the environmental standards would have to be uniform for all states that mined coal in order to prevent this competition in leniency. A native of Long Island, Heckler studied political science at Swarthmore College and Columbia University. Always vigorously engaged in life, he held junior positions in the New Deal, fought in World War II, and served as assistant director of the American Political Science Association. Heckler moved to Capitol Hill to work for a representative and decided he wanted to be one himself. Scouting for a possible seat, he moved to West Virginia in 1957 and won election to Congress the following year. His district was in the heart of the coal fields, and suffered from strip-mining with barren pits, acid draining into the creeks, and landslides. The state found it difficult to stand up to the coal companies. Heckler overcame this problem of a single state trying to regulate by introducing a bill to regulate strip-mining on a national level.

Like virtually all major pieces of legislation, this one required years of debate

Since the development of larger equipment, this surface-mining operation in eastern Kentucky can remove the entire top of a mountain instead of a small strip around its edge. When Congress debated the bill, environmentalists opposed mountain-top removal, but compromised so the National Coal Association would support the bill.

and polishing in committee. In 1968, the Interior Committee was satisfied, and, for the first time, recommended the bill to the whole House. When Heckler left the House, Morris Udall of Arizona took up the banner. He was a dedicated environmentalist whose brother served as secretary of the interior under presidents Kennedy and Johnson. First chair of the subcommittee responsible for the bill, Udall moved up to chair the entire committee in 1977. During its fifteen years of debate, the bill took various forms. At one point it outlawed all strip-mining, until engineers and biologists demonstrated that reclamation could be just as good for the environment as underground mining. At another point it included all minerals, not just coal, until the horde of opponents became overwhelming.

During the last week of the session in 1972, the House of Representatives passed the surface mining bill for the first time, but it died when the Senate adjourned without debating. Two years later, the Senate passed the bill, and, the following year, the House passed it. After a conference that lasted until

December, both houses approved the compromised version of the bill and sent it to President Ford for his signature. Ford was of two minds. He wanted to continue Nixon's environmental policies that pleased Republican voters. His EPA administrator, Russell Train, argued for it. Yet, he worried about inflation. His secretary of the treasury argued against it. Moreover, the Democrats controlled both houses of Congress, so they would get much of the credit if it became a law. In the end, finance won over nature. Because Congress already had adjourned, Ford did not have to veto it, but merely refused to sign it so it died as a pocket veto. The following spring, Congress again passed the Surface-Mining bill. This time Ford did not equivocate; he vetoed it promptly. In 1976, the Democratic supporters of the bill did not waste their efforts passing it a third time, but persuaded their nominee for president, Jimmy Carter, to declare his support in a campaign speech in September. Congress passed the bill again in 1977, and Carter signed it into law.

The Surface-Mining Control and Reclamation Act (SMCRA) was in two ways the ultimate environmental law of the Environmental Decade, meaning both the last and the most refined. Because it was the last environmental law, Congress had the benefit of experience with the Clean Air and Water Acts along with a half-dozen less prominent ones. By 1977, Congress had refined the structure of a delegated program. Because twenty-two states already had their own strip-mining laws, a central program was not possible, nor was a centralized program the custom since before the New Deal. The form improved on earlier environmental laws. Clean Air Act delegation went by program so a state might have one for mobile and another for stationary sources; or it might have one, but not the other. The Clean Water Act delegated some responsibilities to a state while it gave others to cities. A further problem was that a state's authority might be uncertain, resting on agency regulations and contracts. SMCRA regularized this. It delegated the program as a whole—either a state had primary regulatory authority, or it did not. The act also required a state wishing to take the program to enact a law so authority would have a clear legal basis within the state.

Although in the end the coal industry finally gave nominal support to the SMCRA bill in order to avoid worse provisions, its attitude ranged from hostile to grudging. For their parts, the interest groups that had lobbied for the law were in no mood to compromise. The Carter team at the Department of the Interior shared the environmental view. A number of environmentalists received appointments there in the new administration. SMCRA established the Office of Surface Mining (OSM) to implement the law, and key staff of the new bureau strongly supported the law. The first director, Walter Heine, had testified in its favor in hearings in his former post as head of the Pennsylvania agency. Within the OSM, the environmentalists were clustered in the division that determined whether state proposals should be approved. Legal staff were not in the OSM itself, but in the departmental Office of the Solicitor. These lawyers were eager to bring industry into line—the deputy assistant secretary in charge was a no-nonsense woman who personally wrote most of the interim regulations.

In view of his background as an engineer, Heine aimed for technical simplicity. He believed that if the OSM would issue standards telling exactly how to design the mines, the operators would conform. This would be the quickest and surest route to implementation. The alternative was to issue standards for how a mine was to perform, in which case the engineering would be uncertain. For example, in its regulations to prevent a mine from discharging polluted water, the OSM regulations told exactly how to build a sedimentation pond. A performance standard would have been to monitor the end of the pipe to see that it met a certain level of quality. While the engineers liked this simplicity, the mine company owners considered it too expensive.

To coal industry leaders, Ronald Reagan's candidacy for president in 1980 answered their prayers. They agreed that the government regulated too much, they liked his promise to "get the government off the backs of the American people," and many had supported him in the primaries. After their election victory, the Reagan team swept into the Interior Department and the OSM determined to roll back the program. Secretary James Watt appointed leaders in the department and the bureau who reversed direction. Within days, they began to suspend regulations promulgated under the Carter administration. As is customary, the Carter political appointees had already resigned.

The new secretary of the interior, James Watt, previously had opposed SMCRA, while directing the Rocky Mountain Legal Foundation and remained an implacable foe of the OSM. His director and assistant director of the bureau believed their mission was to stop the OSM from hurting the coal industry, so they issued lenient regulations and approved weak state programs. However, the Watt team did not wholly succeed in aiding industry due to the strength of the law, the survival of many of the Carter administration regulations, and lawsuits by the National Wildlife Federation and the Environmental Policy Institute. The Watt appointees also lacked management skills, which reduced their effectiveness in undermining the law.

The OSM's mismanagement became an embarrassment. Watt's first director resigned, and he had a difficult time finding a replacement. Then Watt, himself, had to resign. By 1985, the worst was over at the OSM. This recovery paralleled other environmental agencies like the BLM, the Forest Service, and the EPA. A new director with able management skills took over. The aim of catering to every whim of the coal industry diminished, and OSM returned to enforcing SMCRA, albeit weakly.

MULTIPLE USE AND WISE USE

Gifford Pinchot's approach to forestry at the turn of the century was not to protect trees, but to use them efficiently. His famous quarrel with John Muir set out the contrast between managing and preserving nature. Conservationists like Pinchot spoke of "wise use": prevent fire from destroying timber, harvest it when mature, clear cut to maximize profit, replant with the fastest growing species, and so forth. In the same forest, lumberjacks can harvest timber, cattle can graze, and petroleum companies can pump oil. Foresters refined the concept under the label of "multiple use" and Congress set it into law in the Multiple Use Sustained Yield Act of 1960. The desired uses were timber, mining, oil and gas, grazing, water production, and recreation. A 1964 law directed the BLM to do the same. With increasing concern about the environment, Congress amended the law to add fish, wildlife, and wilderness. Obviously, the last two goals are not fully compatible with the first four goals. Sustained yield means that when a company cuts timber, it must replant or leave a few trees standing for reseeding. To illustrate multiple use, the BLM points to places that have coal, oil, grazing, and potential for a dam. The sensible plan is to mine the coal, drill the oil wells, then construct the dam for both irrigation and electric generation.

Forest Service timber sales continue to generate controversy. At present, very little government-owned land outside the Pacific northwest has trees worth harvesting. Compared to privately-owned land, government forests are much lower in value. With the easy-to-reach timber gone, the remaining timber is on steep slopes or remote spots where harvesting is expensive and erosion is more likely to occur afterward. Timber companies need trees to stay in business, and the sales (supposedly) generate money for the U.S. Treasury. The Wilderness Society and other critics rebut that the Forest Service is too anxious to please the companies and manipulates its accounting methods. According to the Forest Service, timber sales made a net profit of $1 billion in 1992, but according to the Wilderness Society, they lost $244 million. The Forest Service counted a company's expense for building logging roads as part of the money it paid. The rationale is that the roads give greater access for recreation, but the Wilderness Society counters that too many roads already criss-cross the forests. Hikers and campers do not want any more roads. Moreover, the Forest Service often closes the roads, making a lie of the pretended benefit. When the service constructs its own roads, it does not enter the cost of the road base itself and uses excessively long periods for amortization for bridges, culverts, and surfaces.

Most of this controversy centers on the old forests in Oregon, Washington, and Alaska. These are temperate climate rain forests comparable to the tropical rain forests in Brazil. The amount of biomass far exceeds other forests outside the tropics, and the carbon locked in these trees counters global warming. The ancient forests contain the world's most diverse giant evergreens: cedar, Douglas fir, true fir, pine hemlock, and spruce—some of which are eight hundred years old. The forests are also home to two hundred species of fish and wildlife, including two dozen endangered or threatened species. Although the amount of lumber cut is rising, employment declines, because automation makes fewer workers more productive. Exports of logs have increased to 24 percent, and go to sawmills and wood factories overseas, many in Japan. The lumber corporations find it more profitable to shift to the southeast states, like Georgia and Alabama, where a warm climate makes the trees grow faster. The Pacific northwest has lost twenty-six thousand timber jobs since 1979.

Covering seventeen million acres, Tongass is the largest of the 156 U.S.

National Forests. It spreads across 80 percent of southeastern Alaska. In the 1950s, the Forest Service signed a fifty-year contract giving favorable terms to two corporations, which would export the timber to Japan. The hope was to stimulate the local economy and to rebuild the Japanese economy after World War II. In 1980, the Forest Service granted even better terms as part of a compromise on the Alaska National Interest Lands Conservation Act. Section 705a guaranteed 4.5 billion board feet every decade and free road building. The quantity proved crippling for the environment. The timber companies clearcut, ruining salmon breeding and harming wildlife, such as the bald eagle and the grizzly bear. Alarmed, Congress amended the law in 1990 to rein in the worst abuses.

Senator Frank Murkowski of Alaska favored the logging industry. He owned shares of the parent company of the Ketchikan Pulp Company, which was the only remaining large buyer of Alaskan timber. He also owned more than a million dollars worth of shares of the First Bank of Ketchikan, whose profits depended on the timber economy. Murkowski became chair of the Energy and Natural Resources Committee when the Republicans won control of the Senate in the 1994 election. The other Alaska senator, Ted Stevens, supported his fellow Republican and repeatedly attempted to influence the Forest Service management of Tongass. When Senator Murkowski became chair, he introduced a bill directing the Forest Service to provide enough timber to support twenty-four hundred jobs, even though no other national forest has a harvest level set according to employment. To shepherd the bill through the Senate, Murkowski hired an industry lobbyist to work on his committee staff.[2] Other Alaskans opposed the bill—fishermen feared the decrease in salmon, hotel owners and outfitters feared the loss of tourists, and conservationists wanted to preserve the natural condition. To support their efforts, they created the Southeast Alaska Conservation Council. The Democratic governor of the state opposed the bill. When many opponents flew to Washington to testify against the bill, Murkowski canceled the hearing.

Murkowski and Alaska's representative, Republican Don Young, both introduced bills to extend the Ketchikan Pulp Company's fifty-year contract another fifteen years. The company argued it needed the extension to finance pollution control equipment. One year, the company pleaded guilty to fourteen criminal counts of violating the Clean Water Act. The state filed a complaint for multiple violations in air emissions, and the EPA considers Ketchikan Pulp Company the second worst toxic polluter in the Northwest. When it came time to vote, the Alaskan member of Congress ran afoul of their fellow Republicans who realized the huge subsidy the company received: $102 million. Young chaired the House Resources Committee, formerly known as the Natural Resources Committee until he dropped "Natural" from the name. (Its older name was the Interior Committee.) Meanwhile, the Clinton administration was seeking a way to protect the Tongass Forest. It began negotiations with the pulp company's parent company, Louisiana-Pacific, and arranged to buy out the contract for $140 million. While the amount seemed high, it would actually save the government money by ending the subsidies.

THE SAGEBRUSH REBELLION

Western resentment towards national government boiled over during the 1980s. The movement proclaimed itself to be the Sagebrush Rebellion. Nevada fired the first shots in 1979 when its legislature took up Assembly Bill 413, which asserted that the state, not the national, government controlled the public lands within its boundaries. When the territory became a state in 1864, its constitution relinquished those claims, but A.B. 413 intended to take back the land unilaterally. Although virtually no one with legal training believed it was legitimate, it demonstrated western resentment over the pervasive (and sometimes arbitrary) power of Washington. The Bureau of Land Management owned forty-eight million acres, nearly four-fifths of the state. Nevada's bold stroke inspired Arizona, New Mexico, Utah, and Wyoming to pass similar legislation, while Alaska, California, Colorado, and Montana contributed money to support the rebellion. In the presidential campaign the following year, Ronald Reagan announced "count me in as a Rebel," and James Watt also proclaimed his support.

Watt's slant on public lands differed, however. He proposed to sell or give them to private owners, not to the state governments. This proposal was his personal preference and the recommendation of the economists who staffed the new administration's planning office in the Interior Department. Their reasoning was that a private owner would seek the most efficient utilization of the land, which might be farming, lumbering, mining, or building ski resorts or vacation homes. Advocates of this rather standard economic argument often make the case for it by presenting the hypothetical example of how the Audubon Society would use a piece of donated land. If the property were not suitable for a bird sanctuary, the society would sell it and buy another piece that was more suitable. This way, the bird lovers would get the best sanctuary and the buyer from the Audubon Society could put the original property to its highest use, which might be housing or grazing. Many of the Sagebrush rebels did not like this turn of events within the Interior Department. They wanted the land to remain public, but under state ownership. Watt tried without success to advance his privatization scheme. The environmentalists fought it, and the true rebels were unenthusiastic. Once Watt resigned a year later, the proposal withered. His successors, William Clark and Donald Hodel, preferred not to antagonize their opponents, and, while never formally abandoning the privatization proposal, did not move it forward.

Another side of privatization is the extent to which government reduces the value of private property by regulating it. When government takes control of property, its legal right to do so is clear. Governments have been condemning property since time immemorial to provide fire breaks in medieval cities, to build roads, and to erect buildings. First, a government agency tries to negotiate a mutually agreeable price, and, if the parties cannot agree, the agency sues in court to determine a price. The agency then pays this amount and takes the title to the land. The situation is less clear when the government reduces the value of a piece of property, but does not take possession. Generally, courts have favored the government in these cases. As long as the property can still be used for its original purpose, no compensation is required. A marsh at the edge of a lake serves as an example—if a county designates that it is to remain wetland, the owner has no right to compensation simply because the property can no longer be sold for condominiums. The rationale is that the owner can still use it for pasture, duck hunting, or whatever the original use was.

Coal mine owners in Virginia sued the Office of Surface Mining soon after Congress enacted the SMCRA, claiming that the law reduced the value of their coal deposits. The basis of the case was the Fifth Amendment of the Constitution, which guarantees that "No person shall . . . be deprived of . . . property without due process of law, nor shall private property be taken for public use without just compensation." The Supreme Court ruled, however, that as long as the coal had some value, the OSM had not "taken" their property.[3] More recently, courts, including the Supreme Court, have shown more favor towards the property owner. A government agency must demonstrate a relationship between its regulation and its purpose. In one case, a city sought to protect a flood plain, but also required property owners to make space for a bicycle trail. The court ruled that the trail did not add anything to protecting the flood plain—its purpose was recreational.[4] A number of state legislators have introduced bills to compensate property owners generously. If passed, they will either require counties and towns to pay a high price, or will chill their willingness to regulate and zone to protect the environment.

States have taken various approaches to the rights of property. South Carolina enacted legislation in 1988 to discourage resort construction on its barrier islands. Under natural conditions the fierce winter storms and relentless summer waves push the islands back and forth over the decades. Therefore, to build a house on this sand is to bet against the ocean. The objective of the state is to avoid pressure to build bridges, roads, and jetties. The law provided that if a storm destroyed a building, the owner could not rebuild it. Only a year later, Hurricane Hugo struck, demolishing hundreds of houses and buildings. Montana, Louisiana, Mississippi, North Dakota, Texas, and Florida have passed laws allowing landowners to sue the state for compensation. While it is too early for agencies and courts to work out implementation, anxiety over possible liability has a chilling effect on environmental policies. For example, in Florida, Palm Beach County planned to reduce the building allowed near the Everglades, but backed away for fear of a lawsuit under the new state law.

Framing the issue in terms of property rights instead of the environment bolsters the owners' argument. The reasoning is that the government should not take private property except in the most extreme cases. Taking property, in this case, is defined more broadly than mere possession; it implies its potential wealth. For example, county zoning that prevents building vacation condominiums on a steep hillside decreases the value of that land. Planners in Flathead County, Montana, near Glacier National Park, clashed with property owners over zoning that set a minimum size for lots that needed a septic system. Eighteen states, pri-

In His Own Words: Ron Arnold
"Father of the Wise Use Movement"

Although it would be rash to propose wise use's articles of faith—it is a diverse movement—some of the following principles would probably find wide agreement . . .:

1) Humans, like all organisms, must use natural resources to survive. . . . If environmentalism were to acknowledge our necessary use of the earth, the ideology would lose its meaning. . . .
2) The earth and its life are tough and resilent, not fragile and delicate. Environmentalists tend to be catastrophists, seeing any human use of the earth as damage and massive human use of the earth as a castastrophe. . . . Wise users, on the other hand, tend to be cornucopians, seeing themselves as stewarding and nuturing the bountiful earth as it stewards and nutures them. . . .
3) Our limitless imaginations can break through natural limits to make earthly goods and carrying capacity virtually infinite.[1]

We are beginning to notice the organized environmental movement in a new way. We are beginning to notice that it has grown immensely rich and powerful, funded by big industry, big foundations and big law firms. . . . There is no way the air can ever be clean enough, the water pure enough, the land ever perfect enough. We always need a new law to make it cleaner, purer, better. We are beginning to notice that our old friends the Sierra Club and the Audubon Society and the Natural Resources Defense Council are shifting steadily to the left. . . . We see that every place where people want to make a living is suddenly recognized as the habitat of The Last Big Old Tree or The Last Cute Little Animal or even The Last Ugly Bug. . . . We are beginning to notice that the big mainstream environmental organizations have lost their way, no longer just *identifying* crises, but *fabricating* them so there will be something to do with all their large fund-raising infrastructure.[2]

Environmentalism is the new paganism, trees are worshipped and humans sacrificed at its altar. . . . It is evil. . . . And we intend to destroy it.[3]

1. Ron Arnold, "Overcoming Ideology," *The Wolf in the Garden*, Philip F. Brick and Robert McGreggor Cawley, eds., (Lanham, MD: Rowman and Littlefield, 1996).
2. Ron Arnold and Alan Gottlieb, *Trashing the Economy*, 2d ed., (Bellevue, WA: Free Enterprise Press, 1994), 6–7.
3. *Boston Globe*. January 13, 1992.

marily in the west, have passed laws against "takings." In the south, Louisiana, Mississippi, and Florida have "takings" laws.

Today, the terminology of "Sagebrush Rebellion" has fallen into disfavor; the "War on the West" is more popular now. Its advocates have revitalized the term of wise use, which Gifford Pinchot and other foresters popularized at the turn of the century. The tenets of wise use start with the assumption that the key is an economic evaluation. The environment seldom ranks high by this standard because it has a large collective goods component.

Ron Arnold is the most fervent advocate of "wise use." In essence, the movement paints an exaggerated picture of environmental zealots and juxtaposes it to its own combination of optimism and faith in the free enterprise system. Arnold, a journalist and advocate, co-founded the Center for the Defense of Free Enterprise—one of the few organizations opposed to protecting the environment. Critics consider the center a sham, mere camouflage for the timber and mining industries, which contribute money to it. Arnold, in turn, confronts the environmentalists aggressively with stories of citizens and private companies being abused by big government and leaves little middle ground for compromise. He tells how the Forest Service claimed the land of a rancher in California by asserting that the survey, completed decades earlier, was in error and how restricting logging causes unemployment.

RIGHT-WING UTOPIAS

A few westerners take the more extreme position that government cannot interfere with their lives. Starting in the 1950s, independent-minded people began to settle in remote areas of western Montana and in Idaho, particularly in the Bitterroot Valley. The early ones earned the title "survivalists" because they expected nuclear war was likely and intended to survive by living as remote from civilization as possible. They stockpiled food and clothing and armed themselves with guns. They were hardy and self-sufficient, building cabins high in the mountains and living off the land. In many ways the survivalists lived in harmony with nature. They hated and feared communism, and held ultra-conservative views. If the Red Army invaded after the nuclear war, the survivalists intended to fight a guerrilla war.

Even though the Soviets never launched intercontinental ballistic missiles or invaded the United States, the number of survivalists increased. As the communist threat receded, they turned their hatred toward the American government, which they believed was infringing on their rights. Other westerners in rural areas, although not holding extreme views, shared the belief that the government infringed on their property and their rights. The moderate conservatives believe that government regulation is excessive, and the BLM and Forest Service are arrogant in dealing with them.

Randy Weaver and his family became the most famous of the extreme group. Leaving Iowa in 1984, they built and settled with their children in a cabin at Ruby Ridge, Idaho, on the Montana border. Their goal was a miniature utopia where they could practice their fundamentalist Christian beliefs and minimize their contact with the secular world. Considerably more religious than her husband, Vicki Weaver believed that Christ would come soon to proclaim his kingdom and save the faithful, who were people like themselves. Before leaving Iowa, they had visited the Amish to learn about their philosophy and self-sufficiency. The Weavers lived in harmony with the environment—hunting game and growing vegetables. Their circumstances were close to the ideal of the Deep Ecologists. A few years after moving to Idaho and at the urging of an undercover Bureau of Alcohol, Tobacco and Firearms agent, the family combined a camping vacation with the

205

Aryan Nations Congress, an assembly of white supremacists. Still later, the ATF informant asked Weaver to spy on the Aryan Nation. When he refused, the ATF agent arrested him for possessing illegal weapons, after the agent had asked Weaver to saw a quarter-inch off a shotgun. Weaver ignored the summons to court and more than a year after he had failed to appear in court, U.S. marshalls surrounded the Weaver cabin with rifles, pistols, and surveillance cameras. By now, the Weavers were celebrities, hounded for television and newspaper interviews. The bizarre circumstances inflamed Vicki Weaver's belief the world would end soon.

After withdrawing for several months, the marshals returned in August 1992, reinforced by the FBI and the National Guard. As the federal agents snuck up the road, the family dog detected them, sparking gunfire that killed the Weaver's 14-year-old son, a marshall, and the dog. (Later on, the autopsy revealed that the boy was shot in the back as he ran away.) The next day the agents surrounded the cabin. Trying to negotiate, the agents drove to the cabin in a National Guard armored personnel carrier, but the Weavers refused to surrender. At 6:00 P.M., snipers wounded Weaver, his wife (while she was holding their baby daughter), and a young hired hand, yet, they managed to retreat to the cabin. The agents again asked for surrender, which the Weavers refused again. Five days later, Vicki Weaver died of her wounds. During a truce, the seriously wounded hired hand surrendered, while Weaver remained holed up with his sixteen-year-old daughter and his baby for nine more days before surrendering.

By the time Weaver and the hired hand stood trial, the wind had shifted. Although they were charged with murder in the first degree and conspiracy, the jury found them innocent. It declared that the ATF had entrapped him into sawing off and selling the shotgun. The jury did convict Weaver of failing to appear in court two years earlier and of possessing firearms while on bail, for which he served two years in prison. The U.S. Department of Justice later reviewed the episode, concluding that the agents had overreacted. The Senate Judiciary subcommittee investigation reached the same conclusion, and the FBI disciplined twelve agents. To compensate Weaver and his daughters for the deaths of the mother and son, the government paid $3 million. In spite of the retribution paid to the Weavers, the U.S. Marshals Service gave five of the marshalls its highest award for valor.

More organized groups of government resisters often describe themselves as Freemen, who claim allegiance to the Posse Comitatus and advocate government under Common Law. These assertions are based on a twisted understanding of medieval British institutions: no government should exist above the local level, because the national and state governments usurp local authority. The Freemen believe they can establish their own government and laws under the authority of the ancient British forms and of the Bible. They are less likely than the Weavers to withdraw to isolated areas in the mountains and live off the land. More commonly, they are ranchers and farmers, often those unable to make a profit. A favorite tactic of the Freemen is to file legal motions in court alleging that a bank fraudulently induced them to borrow money, therefore they do not have to repay the loan.

Another tactic is to refuse to pay income tax to the Internal Revenue Service. The movement originated in Tigerton, Wisconsin, where it uses the name of the Family Farm Preservation.

The Freemen who holed up in their ranch near Jordan, Montana, for two months in 1996 held these anti-government beliefs rather than the more utopian ones of the Weaver family. The Branch Davidians, followers of David Koresh, at Waco, Texas, were even more extreme. While the Freemen may be wiley and greedy, they are only partially out of touch with civilization. Publicly owned forests are a favorite playground for gun lovers and amateur soldiers as well as for hikers and campers from the Appalachian or Sierra Clubs. The Michigan Militia implicated in the bombing of the Oklahoma City Federal Building practiced its maneuvers in the forests on weekends.

FIRES

Government policy regarding forest fires has shifted over the years. Foresters like Pinchot considered fire an enemy that destroyed a valuable commodity—trees that burned could never be harvested. As early as the 1920s, however, a forest ranger realized that the absence of fires could also damage the forest. His view went against the official dogma that took half a century to reverse. The first principle of the new philosophy is that fires occur naturally, started by lightning. When a forest burns periodically, no single fire does much damage. The flames advance along the ground consuming dry grass and underbrush, but mature trees, protected by their height and bark, suffer little harm. Ash from the fire enriches the soil. Indeed, the reproductive cycle of jack and lodgepole pines depend on fire. Their cones enclose the seeds tightly for many years until the heat of a fire causes the cone to open, releasing the seeds. The seedling sprouts and grows quickly because grass and shrubs do not choke it out. The problems begin to occur when a forest does not have periodic small fires, because underbrush accumulates. In a forest that has not burned in years, when a fire does start, it is much hotter and reaches higher. The hot temperatures burn through the bark to the living part, and flames reach high to the leaves or needles. The heat bakes the soil, destroying its fertility.

Even though some foresters became aware of the dangers of suppressing forests fires, fighting them remained the official policy until 1971. Environmentalists applauded the change because it was closer to the natural situation, favored native species over exotic ones, promoted diversity, and increased the bird population. Suppression can alter the mix of trees. In New Mexico and Arizona, for example, conifers have replaced aspens. Lumber companies wanted the foresters to continue to fight fires because, by their reckoning, it destroyed trees they might have harvested. When a fire did occur, the companies often asked permission to salvage the wood that remained. Although the salvaging did yield wood, it made natural rejuvenation impossible, because the soil required nutrients contained in the ash. Residents living near the forests wanted

A firefighter stops to look for hot spots in the aftermath of the Lewis Lake fire in Yellowstone National Park in 1988. The Yellowstone fires prompted the Department of the Interior to reverse its "let them burn" policy, but the issue remains controversial. Environmentalists tend to favor not controlling lightning fires, because of the natural regeneration that follows. The general public, however, may become outraged when fires—especially those caused by humans—takes lives or destroy real estate.

to suppress the fires to protect their houses, cottages, or ski lodges. In California, forest and brush fires occur frequently.

Public outcry over the 1988 holocaust in Yellowstone Park and surrounding National Forests challenged the policy of letting fires burn. Because Yellowstone is the biggest jewel in the park system crown, it garnered more attention than fires in national forests or less prominent parks. Nevertheless, the issues were identical. The policy had been to suppress manmade fires and to allow lightning fires to burn. By the end of the hot, dry summer, the park had had fifty-one fires, which burned eight hundred thousand acres—40 percent of the park. Although several of the fires were lightning related, investigation showed that an arsonist had set one of the worst. By mid-summer, the Park Service reversed course and began fighting all fires, even though several of the biggest were hopelessly out of control. Some fires burned until snow fell in September, and by then, the park appeared devastated. Television and magazine photographs displayed miles of blackened ground and charred, leafless trees. The following spring, the Department of the Interior announced it was formally reversing its "let them burn" policy dating back to 1972. Ironically, by that time grass and wildflowers sprouted all over and charred trees burgeoned with new leaves and needles.

With each year that followed the Yellowstone fires, the Park Service and the Forest Service eased back toward letting the lightning fires burn. The professional staff believed this to be scientifically best and environmentalists supported them. Yet, the general public was not so technically sophisticated. When fires remained too small to capture widespread attention, the professionals prevailed, but when a newsworthy fire struck, the public demanded suppression. Members of Congress often lead the demands. During the Yellowstone fire the senator from Wyoming, Alan Simpson, cried the loudest that the Park Service should fight the fires. When, in 1994, a deadly wildfire killed fourteen young smokejumpers on Storm King Mount in Colorado, the public again clamored for fire prevention. Reaching the contrary conclusion, the Department of Agriculture and Forest Service concluded that a series of small fires over the years would have prevented the inferno. On a related aspect, the Forest Service and Park Service more thoroughly investigated arson and human-caused fires, and they prosecuted an arsonist at Yellowstone. They sent a bill of $2.8 million to a camp outfitting company and its client whose carelessness started the Hellroaring Canyon Fire. In 1993, the Park Service sent a bill to a couple who began a fire in Idaho.

ZONING

Local land policy has little in common with national government land management. Until eighty years ago, municipalities did little after laying out streets and lots at the time a town was founded by colonists, pioneers, or a railway company. Only exceptional cities like Philadelphia and Savannah started with planned sites for markets and parks. Counties did virtually nothing. Today, nearly all cities, suburbs, and metropolitan counties zone areas to be residential, commercial, and industrial. Many have more sophisticated master plans. The popularity of zoning and planning extends to many rural counties, especially ones with tourism and vacation homes.

Zoning sprang up suddenly around 1910 and quickly spread nationwide. Prior to then, real estate developers had achieved much the same benefits with covenants in the deeds that restricted use. The pattern of detached houses on quarter-acre lots appeared around 1850 in an era of prosperity and streetcars. The attraction of houses with a bit of land, shade trees, grass, and flowers suggests the innate human sense of biophilia. But, this luxury required money and transportation.

The ambience of a residential development would be lost if one's neighbors spoiled it with a boarding house, a livery stable, or a garbage dump. Real estate developers wrote restrictions into the deeds, such as the owner would not keep farm animals, conduct a business, or further subdivide the lot. To achieve elegance, covenants might require houses to be set back thirty-five feet from the street, cost a minimum amount, and provide a garage for an automobile. The object was that each resident could share the benefits of a dignified, spacious neighborhood. The covenants were perpetual. Frequently, the real estate developer sought to ensure the future value of the houses by forbidding sale to "a member of the Negro or Jewish race." Racial covenants continued until 1948 when the Supreme Court ruled them illegal.

Restrictive covenants could not solve all problems. They could only be established when the property was subdivided, and modification was not possible at a later time. They were expensive to enforce. If an inconsiderate neighbor kept a cow or built an addition too close to the lot line, the only way to enforce the covenant was to sue in court, an expensive and uncertain method. The solution was to zone the entire city. New York City began in 1916, and zoning soon swept the country. At first, doubts existed about its legality until 1926 when the U.S. Supreme Court upheld it in the *Village of Euclid* v. *the Ambler Realty Co.* The usual method to zone was to hire an outside expert to draw a map dividing the city into three categories—residential, commercial, and industrial. Each of these categories was further divided into three or four levels. For example, R-1 would be for apartment buildings, R-2 for row houses, R-3 for duplex houses, and R-4 for detached houses with lots of a certain size. Commercial would be divided for small shops, office buildings, and so forth. A permanent zoning board could change the plan as necessary or permit a single variance.

Zoning worked well. It enhanced property values by guaranteeing stability and freedom from unwanted neighbors, yet changes were possible upon application to the board. The new system did not completely replace restrictive covenants in the deeds, however. A real estate developer could insert provisions for fences, uniform styles, and so forth. Nevertheless, zoning has its disadvantages. For example, a municipality that wants to maintain a low total population to keep its budget low for services like police, fire, and garbage, may forbid lot sizes smaller than five acres. Big lots also keep the school population low. Some towns that did not want the expense of building a new school were notorious for their requirements for new apartments. Each one had to have at least one thousand-square feet, but with only one bedroom. The effect was to shift the child population to less strictly zoned municipalities, often in existing cities. The rich school districts got richer. More generally, suburbs learned to zone out poor people. A second disadvantage is that zoning takes many years to have its impact. Typically, a municipality zones when the land is empty and waits for construction. The technique is passive and cannot change houses or buildings already built. The construction boom after 1945 fit the movement perfectly. Suburbs that collected an income tax on their residents learned to amplify the advantages of big lots beyond merely property taxes. Those who owned expensive houses nearly always had high incomes, and those with inexpensive houses had low incomes.

A third problem with zoning is the pressure for exceptions. While the favorable aspect is that a board can grant variances, it may do so too easily. Like many facets of politics in a pluralist society, a small group with an intense interest can usually prevail over a large group with a diffuse interest. A further pressure may be that the municipal government itself wants the variance. For example, a supermarket chain may seek to open a new store in a residential zone, so it agrees to pay a hefty property tax and, in most states, to pay sales tax revenues to the town.

New Jersey officials call this a "rateable" because it is rated for taxes. However, local residents are also good at defending their immediate area. Supermarket chains find it hard to locate in a neighborhood of quarter-acre lots. They do find many opportunities where no houses are very close, often beside a river or an undeveloped park since streams and marshes are highly vulnerable to the dollars of commercialism. Zoning generates an entire professional sector of real estate agents, lawyers, and speculators. Critics would also add cynical politicians eager for campaign contributions.

While the zoning movement swept most of the country, some cities chose a different track. Most examples of these are located in Texas and elsewhere in the west. The results of the supposedly opposite method (no zoning) turn out to be much the same. Houston, for example, looks like most other cities of its size. Three factors explain the convergence. First, the variances in a zoned city are so extensive that they disrupt the integrity of plan. The exceptions are everywhere. Second, houses have restrictive covenants in order to protect neighborhoods. And the third factor is that economic logic accomplishes much the same result as zoning. A supermarket chain does not want to construct a new store on a quiet cul-de-sac; it wants a big highway. Heavy industry wants a site next to a railroad or a river and does not want to pay a high price for the land. Moreover, at the time most cities began to zone, after 1920 and more likely after 1945, its pattern for land use was already established. Railroads, canals, and dumps were in place.

The alternative to zoning that has gained popularity in the past thirty years is comprehensive planning. The English began planning and building Greenbelt Towns in the 1920s and 1930s. The concept was to build completely new suburban towns about ten miles beyond the city outskirts and permanently buffer them with a green belt of farms, parks, and nature preserves. The new towns should be self-sufficient with housing, schools, and shops, but most workers commute into the main city. Thus, growing cities do not sprawl, but leapfrog ahead in order to preserve the green buffers. With their more extensive local railways and in the infancy of the automobile, the English anticipated the suburbanites would commute by train. In the United States the New Deal innovators sponsored one outside Washington, appropriately named Greenbelt.

Yet, in the view of many environmentalists, the greenbelt town did not catch on in the post-World War II boom when its impact would have been the greatest. It finally reappeared in the 1960s in two towns, again in the Washington area: Reston, Virginia and Columbia, Maryland. The investors' goals in both cases combined commercial profit with social reform. Reston was supposed to recreate the advantages of a small town where residents walked to the park and to shop, knew each other personally, and participated in the Parent Teacher Association and civic committees. The first units constructed followed a European model with apartments above shops clustered around a plaza and next to a small lake. Farther away, other apartments and town houses clustered together with architecture de-emphasizing automobiles and promoting sociability.

Each unit had a children's playground, a softball diamond, and pathways with woods and lawns separating the clusters.

The Restonites loved their town; they were zealots who bored their coworkers downtown with stories about its glories. However, after a few years, customer demand fell short and the company went bankrupt. After one or two false starts, the new corporate owners shifted toward a more traditional suburb with detached houses on quarter-acre lots. Reston still thrives, while retaining much of the original architecture, parks, and enthusiasm. Retail stores, offices, and light manufacturing provide employment for forty thousand people. Ironically, when the developers polled Restonites to suggest improvements, they found that the residents wanted to have "a real downtown." Always willing to oblige, the company dug up a vacant field to build a two-block crossroads with narrow streets, a bandstand, a skating rink, a fountain, and a movie theater.

Reston's counterpart in Maryland followed a smoother course. Columbia was the dream of James Rouse, who held a similar vision of a community fulfilling a social mission and with architecture compatible with nature. The housing density varied, concentrating townhouses and apartments in clusters with open lawns and woods between them. Rouse gauged the market better, so Columbia did not suffer from bankruptcy and grew to a population of eighty thousand residents.

While the two methods of zoning and comprehensive planning have opposite characteristics—in effect they have merged. Most municipalities plan, and virtually no municipality that adopted planning has abolished zoning. Their plans overlay, enhance, and integrate their zoning. Current assumptions of planning reverse those of twenty to forty years ago. In the older system, the automobile was king. The municipality encouraged wide streets, cul-de-sacs, and three-car garages. Sidewalks were considered unnecessary. The result was a neighborhood where walking was dangerous, and pedestrian routes were longcuts instead of shortcuts. The current layout returns to narrow streets to discourage fast driving with short distances suitable for walking and bicycling. Jogging and bike trails are convenient. Sidewalks cut through the middle of blocks. The town of Davis, California, for example, takes pride in both making life more pleasant and fighting smog.

Although zoning and planning are the major tools by which local governments make decisions affecting the environment, there are others. Construction companies may donate land to the municipality or county in a manner that increases the price they can get for new houses, particularly the more expensive ones. One scheme is to build along a creek, and donate strips surrounding the house on three sides. In this case, the house may have lot dimensions approximating seventy-five by one hundred feet with a buffer between the next house of fifty feet and fifty feet back to the stream. Although the municipality gets a free park, it is not very accessible to the public and may be expensive to maintain. The supposed benefit to the purchaser is not paying taxes on the "parkland" that actually functions as an extended yard. On the other hand, the property tax is based on the assessed value of the house and lot, and this "parkland" enhances the value so the owner pays more tax anyhow.

In recent years local governments have become more sophisticated in dealing with developers. They now require a construction company to build all the roads, sewers, and sidewalks that a new subdivision needs. They may also require the company to construct playgrounds, bike trails, and parks.

Another technique that has come into use is the scenic easement or conservation easement, which has become popular among environmentalists. The standard easement modifies a deed by allowing access, perhaps for the electric company to reach a pole at the rear of a lot. A scenic easement allows neighbors to have a view over a property so they can enjoy the scenery. The owner sacrifices his or her own right to sell the air rights, perhaps to a company that would erect a tall building and spoil the view of a valley or mountain. Making arrangements for scenic easement has been found to work best in a wealthy neighborhood where the residents do not need to ring out the last dollar of their investment. In the Cascade Mountains near Seattle, members of the rock band Pearl Jam donated $400,000 to protect the Alpine Lakes Wilderness Area from development by the United Cascade Mining Company. Near Ithica, New York, the Finger Lakes Land Trust protects property where Cornell University biology students discovered a rare fungus.

The ugliness of urban sprawl has stimulated a number of states to enact programs to preserve farmland at the suburban fringe. A real estate developer who seeks to build a subdivision or a company looking for a new factory site can easily afford to buy farmland. The land's value for crops or pasture is low compared to quarter-acre lots, a retail mall, or a factory. Moreover, the taxes on agricultural land increase when it adjoins a town because of its potential for development. The most expensive farm land in America is in Connecticut and Maryland, between $3,000 to $5,000 per acre, not for its fertility, but for its potential for development. Midwestern farmland, which is far more productive, is worth $800 to $1,500 per acre.

In a typical program, a farmer who wishes to participate grants the state an agricultural easement, which reduces his property tax to 7 percent of his household income. If the farmer ever sells the land for development he must repay all taxes that were deferred. This deferment, however, is the chief failing of the program; when a farmer sells his or her land for development, paying the back taxes is a minor expense compared to the profit. Consequently, the program provides no long-term protection of agricultural land, but merely a tax deferment to the farmer.

LOCAL USE OF NATIONAL PROGRAMS

Highways and waste water treatment are two national programs that are, in many ways, local programs. On the negative side, constructing an interstate highway through a city can do more environmental damage than a dozen other actions. On the positive side, the Clean Water Act requirement in Section 208 has generated regional cooperation extending far beyond water.

Obviously, the overwhelming number of miles of U.S. and interstate highways are rural where routes may well date back to when the pioneers headed west. On the rare occasions where the government needs to find a new route, the logic of topography and the choice of alternative paths de-emphasize the environmental impact. In urban areas a new freeway is likely to require a new route, and when determining the need for that freeway and finding its exact route, the national, state, and local governments cooperate. The Federal Highway Administration in the Department of Transportation determines the general need, specifies engineering standards, and supplies money. For interstate highways, the national government covers 90 percent of the cost, and for U.S. highways, 50 percent. The state highway department selects the specific route and contracts with a private company for the actual construction, while municipalities advise on the route. For the most part, cities are eager to improve their roads, especially when most of the money comes from Washington.

From about 1956 to the early 1960s, highway planners tried to serve the added function of slum removal. Often, the tacit objective was racial since the best engineering path seemed to frequently go through a black neighborhood. Racial bigotry was not the only motivation, however; leveling the "slums" could mean conveniently avoiding middle-class neighborhoods where the citizens knew how to mobilize, lobby, and make their votes count.

A popular route for a new freeway is often through a wetland or across a neglected creek. During the 1950s and 1960s, highways commonly paved over parks along major rivers. The river, after all, was the natural transportation corridor, frequently the original reason for the location of the cities and industry, but amendments to the Highway Act now prevent this aspect of road construction. More recent targets are the lesser natural features. For example, the Ohio Department of Transportation proposed to fill in a tributary of the Ottawa River and its marshland to connect downtown Toledo to Interstate 75. The Buckeye Basin, as it is known, is not a first-class, natural setting because five old factories are adjoined to it. In the past, chemical companies have discharged their effluent, and people have dumped old furniture and garbage within the basin. Even so, neglect protected it from more serious damage. In the summer, egrets and blue herons wade there, and in the spring and fall, ducks and Canada geese rest during migration. Ironically, plans drafted to get a park grant in the 1970s sketched in a road connecting three proposed parks. Once on a map, the road gained a life of its own. The state highway department apparently forgot the original purpose and began to promote it for industrial development. To save the basin from further damage, a local homeowner organized his neighbors to protest the state highway's plans by picketing, seeking an injunction in court, and dramatically chaining himself to a bulldozer.

CONCLUSION

In many ways, the conservation movement at the turn of the century was not a mass movement at all, because its leaders came from professional foresters and timber companies. A major purpose was to conserve timber, coal, iron ore, and other resources for big corporations. It had a practical plan with little emotion. In the 1960s and 1970s, public outrage against coal companies that strip-mined in Pennsylvania, West Virginia, Kentucky, and Tennessee came closer to being a true mass movement. The technological causes were giant electric shovels and augers. Mining had depleted the biggest coal reserves, and emotions about the environmental damage ran high. Most recently, the mass movement affecting land has been right-wing utopians like the Weaver family. Primarily located in the west, their numbers are small and their ideology has not connected with mainstream environmentalists. More moderate activists on the right adhere to the label of "wise use," while earlier activists were Sagebrush rebels. Distrust and dissatisfaction with the national government extends widely in the west, and encompasses more than just greed. At the same time, western independence can be an impediment to an expanding movement. The traditional goal of autonomy contradicts cooperation and networking.

Both developers and environmentalists have organized as interest groups. Timber, mining, and ranching groups are well organized regionally and in Washington. They keep in close touch with their senators and Bureau of Land Management, and although small in size, they raise money and employ professional staff as well as their own political connections. At the other end of the land use spectrum, local zoning blossoms with interest groups. Real estate developers, on one side, and neighborhood citizens, on the other, battle over new factories and stores.

Land policy divides the two parties even more than parks. The Republicans backed the Sagebrush Rebellion and the wise use movement, but they opposed the Surface Mining Act. During the Reagan administration, the Department of the Interior eagerly leased BLM land for coal, oil, and gas. (The GOP proclivity toward development dates back to "Give Away" McKay and earlier.) In many states and municipalities, Republicans tend to favor business development. The Democratic preference for command and control regulations derives from its big government heritage.

Government procedures explain much of land policy. The chronicles of the Surface-Mining Act cannot be separated from its genesis in the House Interior Committee. The bureaucratic tool of planning has played an important role. Since Congress enacted the Federal Land Policy Planning Act, the BLM and the Forest Service have developed plans for nearly all the public domain. At the local level, zoning is nearly synonymous with planning. Yet, beyond planning, the other tools of a bureaucracy do not prove so useful. The expertise needed to make decisions on grazing or logging is minimal. (Mining and oil production do require scientific knowledge, however.) Zoning does not require highly technical skills and the planning professionals have little information that others cannot obtain and understand. Indeed, BLM employees often point with pride to their label of "manager" and tell how they strive to balance different interests.

NOTES

1. U.S. Department of the Interior, Office of the Secretary. "Secretary Babbitt Forced to Sign Four More Mining Patents under Antiquated Mining Law," Press release, June 25, 1997.
2. Jane Fritsch, "Friend of the Timber Industry," *New York Times*, August 10, 1995.
3. *Hodel* v. *Virginia Surface Mining and Reclamation Association* 452 U.S. 264.
4. *Dolan* v. *Tigard* (1994).

CHAPTER 9
CONCLUSION

Environmental politics are now mature—the public has voiced its preferences on many sides, interest groups have developed, and Congress has passed laws. The EPA, the NRC, and the departments of Interior and Agriculture have implemented them. Three issues of environmental politics remain that do not fit the pattern, however. The first is population growth. At present, world population is not an American environmental issue, but it is sure to be soon. The second issue is the comparison of the environmental policy arena to the consumer protection arena, which has not stabilized much. The politics of the two arenas are similar, sharing features like support of a citizens movement, delegated programs, and congressional enthusiasm. Thirdly, the success of the green political parties in Europe suggests a lesson to be learned in the United States. Finally, examining environmental politics of the past and the present in terms of the four approaches gives hints for the future.

POPULATION

Human beings threaten not only nature, but their own existence by pumping chemicals into the air or water, by carelessly discarding hazardous material, and by destroying forests. Yet, even if people were to stop their bad habits of polluting, their normal demand for food, clothing, gasoline, and newspapers would continue to deplete the Earth's natural resources. More people cause more demand. With expanded international trade, everyone in the world competes

Scorecard for POPULATION GROWTH

LAWS
Annual appropriations to U. S. Agency for International Development (AID).

CONGRESS
House and Senate Committees on Appropriations, subcommittees on Foreign Operations

AGENCIES
U. S. AID

INTEREST GROUPS
Zero Population Growth
Population Council
Planned Parenthood
Population Research Institute

WORLD POPULATION

10,000 B.C.	1–10 million
1000	50 million
500	100 million
A.D. 1	300 million
1000	300 million
1400	360 million
1450	500 million
1804	1 billion
1927	2 billion
1960	3 billion
1974	4 billion
1987	5 billion
1998	6 billion
2009	7 billion
2200	12 billion

Source: U. S. Bureau of the Census, International Programs Center, "Historical Estimates of World Population" 1997; and United Nations Population Division, Department for Economic and Social Information, "World Population Growth from 0 to Stabilization" 1997.

against everyone else. Until the mid-twentieth century, most countries were at least moderately self-sufficient. Certainly, this self-sufficiency was true for the larger countries such as the United States, China, India, and Brazil. While this was less true of Britain, Belgium, and smaller European countries, the industrial regions did not place demands on the entire world the way they do today.

At the beginning of recorded history, the world population was around fifty million people, the equivalent of the population of France today. After six thousand years of agriculture and commerce, the population increased to eight hundred million in 1700, slightly less than the population of India today. From the ecological perspective, human population followed much the same constraints as animal populations: food, disease, and predation (chiefly by other humans, not hungry tigers). Peace and improved agriculture caused population increases in the Roman empire and in Europe during the twelfth and thirteenth centuries. In medieval Europe, agriculture expanded because of decreased warfare and of new technology, such as better plows, water wheels, and wind mills, but during the first decade of the 1300s, the climate deteriorated, causing poor harvests and famine. France and England began the Hundred Years War (1337–1453) and, in 1347, the Black Death appeared, eventually killing twenty-five million people— a third of the population. The recovery from the famines and epidemics took Europe two centuries. The population increase remained moderate until the Industrial Revolution. Starting in England two hundred years ago, and spreading to the continent of Europe and to the American colonies, agriculture, technology, and transportation improved. At the same time, sanitation, and later medicine, improved thereby decreasing the amount of diseases that had previously controlled population growth.

Birth control is the other side of the population equation. Prior to "the Pill" in 1960, and, to a lesser extent, diaphragms and condoms in the 1920s, for a couple to limit pregnancies demanded above-average education and discipline. Socially and culturally, there was little pressure for a couple to limit the number of their children below six or seven. This number makes sense on a farm where expenses are low and children can contribute economically by the age of seven. Six or seven children remained the average for Americans, rural and urban, up to the 1920s. Then, the urban rate declined because, in a city, children were more expensive and could not contribute economically. The availability of food and shelter were more direct biological factors. As in other animals, the human birth rate falls during scarcity. The American rate declined dramatically during the Great Depression and then doubled during the baby boom after 1945.

From colonial times to the twentieth century, government policy encouraged population growth in order to settle the frontier. Without birth control options, however, policy had little impact on individuals. In the nineteenth century, Connecticut passed a law preventing dissemination of information on contraception and other states followed their lead within a few years. The pressure came from Protestant clergy and laymen who wanted to control the morals of the working class. The Roman Catholic hierarchy soon joined the campaign. A parallel cause was the increasing professionalization of physicians. Caught up in the general spirit of reform, they campaigned to outlaw "amateur" abortionists. The policy locus at the state level reflected both the unimportance of the national level in that era and the states' traditional role in family law. The Connecticut law against birth control information remained in force until 1965 when the Supreme Court decided that it violated the First, Third, Fourth, and Fifth Amendments. State prohibitions against abortion remained widespread until the Supreme Court decided the bans were unconstitutional in *Roe* v. *Wade* in 1973. New York and a few other states had legalized abortion in the late 1960s. Although the legal changes were done by courts and state legislatures, the underlying reason was improved medical technology, and increasing education about sexuality.

219

While the United States had one policy for population at home up to 1965, it had a conflicting one for foreign countries. The impetus was economic development, and behind that, Cold War competition with the Soviet Union and communist China. American foreign policy assumed that the best way to prevent a foreign nation from becoming communist, or allying with the Soviet Union or China, was for it to develop a prosperous economy. People who were poor and without hope would be prey for the communists. Countries like India realized that their own efforts at economic development were wasted if the population increased faster than the economy. Therefore, in the 1950s, India, as well as other countries, asked the United States foreign aid program to provide birth control supplies, information, and training.

The conflicting policies—opposing birth control at home, while supporting it overseas—were not reconciled, but merely veiled. The foreign aid for birth control was not an official secret; it was just not talked about. Members of Congress considered it sound foreign policy, but feared their conservative constituents. From Eisenhower to Carter, presidents supported the aid sub rosa, while trying to avoid the issue publicly. Conservative members of Congress made speeches opposing it, but had little success. Until Reagan became president and the Republicans won the Senate, the government supported birth control in India and other countries with grants and technical advice.

The program in India started with education and distribution of intrauterine devices. Later on, it switched its strategy to a campaign to sterilize men, because this was the cheapest way to reduce births. Each province and district got a quota from the national headquarters. Although the sterilizations were supposed to be voluntary, the local offices strove hard to meet their quotas, to the point of tricking and bribing the men, most of whom were impoverished and illiterate. Men complained they were not told that the operation would prevent them from fathering children or were told that it was only temporary. Because 80 percent of India is rural, traditional incentives remain. Parents want children to work in the fields and support them in their old age.

Person for person, an American places a harder toll on the environment than an East Indian. For example, the average American consumes thirty-two times as much oil, coal, and gas as the average East Indian. To examine this statistic in a different way, the amount of energy used by one American is the same amount of energy used by 140 Bangladeshis or 284 Tanzanians. Collectively, Americans constitute 5 percent of the world population, while consuming 25 percent of its resources. Although the American population increases only 1 percent a year, while the Indian increases 3 percent a year, its consumption is higher. The addition of 2.5 million Americans each year has the environmental impact equivalent to 80 million additional East Indian citizens. In this light, American population growth is more damaging to the planet than India's growth. Although growth rates of 3 or 4 percent a year may seem small, the cumulative impact is huge— within fifty years, the East Indian population will be 1.6 billion and the U.S. population will be four hundred million.

The worry about population growth came to the forefront in 1972 when the Club of Rome published *The Limits to Growth*. The report argues that, at present rates, the population increase will outstrip resources and pollute the air and water. Based on a computer simulation that treats the factors simultaneously, it predicts the entire world economy will "crash" around 2040. Population will be over ten billion, the farmland will be used up, and oil reserves will be depleted. At this point, industrial production will decline sharply, but population will continue to grow; the strain will cause starvation and wars.[1] The report gained immediate attention and much agreement throughout the industrial world.

The potential for disaster ahead causes many environmentalists to advocate birth control measures to bring the explosion under control. Many consider the present world population of 5.7 billion to be high enough, while others maintain that the earth has the capacity to support more people, although not an infinite number. At some point it must stabilize, perhaps at eight or twelve billion. A simple head count, however, ignores different levels of consumption. Are the eight or ten billion inhabitants expected to consume at the level of the United States or at the level of India? To raise the standard of living for the whole world to the American level is the equivalent of adding twenty billion more people. Yet, are Americans to reduce their standard to that of India? Deep Ecologists advocate less material wealth, while Zero Population Growth association advocates keeping the numbers at the present level. This level would amount to 2.1 children per family in the United States and Europe where infant mortality is low (the present rate is 2.0 children). In less-developed countries where many children die, the replacement rate would be higher.

Some environmentalists propose that if they personally forego having children, their sacrifice will contribute to preserving Planet Earth. Indeed, the next step in the logic is that one less American baby helps the world as much as thirty-two fewer Indian babies. The impulse appears sincere and unselfish, yet environmentalists are supposedly more in tune with biology, and the sacrifice goes contrary to the innate propensity to procreate. The Biophilia Hypothesis maintains that homo sapiens seek to stay close to nature. The human tendency to reproduce would seem even stronger than longing for the East African savanna. Although for a couple to not have children may be altruistic, it can hardly be considered biologically normal.

This raises the issue whether natural controls exist within humans. The pessimistic view came from Thomas Malthus, who wrote in 1798 that the human population would grow faster than agricultural productivity, thus, leading to starvation, crime, and war. Interestingly, one of the first scientists to incorporate Malthus's theory was Charles Darwin in his study of animal evolution. Malthus also stimulated Karl Marx, who disagreed, rebutting that the increase was a symptom rather than a cause—workers who controled production would be able to feed themselves. Only when the ruling class denies them the tools of production does the working class suffer. Once the workers have social justice, they will produce enough.

The modern (not particularly Marxist) version of this issue is that new technology will ameliorate the problem. This theory concedes that Malthus may have been correct for the agricultural age in which he lived, but with the industrial revolution, production was no longer constrained by farming and hand labor. Agriculture is more efficient with tractors, fertilizer, hybrid crops, and irrigation; and factories can manufacture many times as much as the individual craftsman. The third stage in economic development moves beyond agriculture and manufacturing to services. In this sector, people will still consume goods from the first sector of agriculture and mining and the second sector of manufactured products. Then, they will want more services like education, music, computer networks, and medical care (which is the most expensive and fastest growing service). People will also consume inexpensive services like haircuts, lawn care, and restaurants. One implication of this analytical approach is that for the world to progress best, it needs the best-educated people. To reduce the population of the United States or other highly developed countries would be unwise because it would decrease the scientific and technical knowledge that the rest of the world would depend upon.

The People's Republic of China policy on population growth has gone from one extreme to the other. Currently, it has 1.2 billion people, four times as many as in 1945. Between 1950 and 1980 the death rate dropped from twenty to eight per thousand; life expectancy increased from forty-seven to seventy years. China's communist founder, Mao Tse Tung, encouraged the population to grow in order to have a bigger army and to replace those lost in the famine when his Great Leap Forward movement failed. After his death in 1976, his successors first stopped encouraging births, and then introduced a massive program to limit births to one per family. The government asks couples willing to participate to sign a pledge, and if they participate, the government provides birth control, such as pills, condoms, intrauterine devices, or abortions. When the couple is ready for a baby, they ask permission to fit into that year's quota. Approved babies receive free delivery, preference in education, and, eventually, in job placement. The parents receive better housing, longer vacations, and an extra month's pay each year, while non-cooperating parents find their pay cut and their children penalized.

The new birth control policy contradicted Mao Tse Tung's policy as well as the peasant belief that more children was better, and the traditional expectation that a family must have a son to pass on the family name. Therefore, some parents go to cruel extremes to have a son. Parents with access to modern medicine can examine the fetus by ultrasound during pregnancy, then, if the fetus is a girl, they have it aborted. The less technological method is infanticide, where they kill the daughter after she is born. School records for first grade show 18 percent more boys than girls are enrolled. The regulations permit a second baby if the first is crippled or disfigured, so desperate parents have deliberately maimed or disfigured their daughters. The problem is not confined to China. The Indian parliament has found it necessary to pass a law imposing fines on medical tests used to determine a fetus's sex for the purpose of aborting females. School records in

South Korea, a comparatively prosperous country, indicate that parents are aborting girls.

Research on birth control behavior is not all pessimistic. While the general assumption persists that families will not limit their children as long as they remain poor, researchers have found evidence to the contrary. A study of Tunisian women concludes that they begin to practice birth control once they learn about the techniques, regardless of the family income and of the amount of formal education.[2]

The political and economic deterioration of Africa south of the Sahara presents the worst situation. These countries gained independence from Britain, France, Belgium, or Portugal around 1960. At that time their futures appeared bright. Nearly all possessed good farmland, oil and mineral reserves, a rising level of education, and democratic governments. Eventually, most of them encountered problems. The former Belgian Congo soon fell under the control of Mobuto Seko, who maintained a dictatorship until 1997, during which time he looted its natural resources. Nigeria suffered from a civil war and years of army dictators. In spite of hardships and high infant mortality, it is one of the fastest growing countries in the world, expected to double in population in the next twenty-five years. On average, a Nigerian woman has six children.

Because Africa has been so dependent on extractive industries such as mining, petroleum, and agriculture, foreign trade is more important for these countries than it is for industrialized countries. Because of the instability, American and European companies have been afraid of starting new businesses and are closing old ones. The political and economic decline of Africa, however, will not slow its population growth, judging by similar cases throughout history. Impoverished people lack the luxury of protecting their natural environment. The poachers who kill elephants for their ivory and rhinoceroses for their horns are local residents, not animal assassins dispatched from Taiwan or India.

Only a few countries outside Africa are in such desperate straits. Thailand and Malaysia have become two of the "young tigers" (to use the Asian term for a robust economy) challenging Japan. The average number of children for a Thai woman has fallen to 1.9 children, less than the number for an American. South America seemed economically stagnant and dictators ruled many countries twenty years ago. Argentina, for example, had a dictator, astronomical inflation, and thieves stealing telephone lines to sell the copper. After the return of democracy, its inflation ended, its economy grew, and its birth rate dropped. The population of Brazil is growing 1.1 percent a year, scarcely more than the rate for an industrialized country.

During the communist period, the Soviet Union birth rate was close to the lowest in the world, 0.7 percent in 1975. Although the country was poor economically, the people were well educated and the government had successfully stamped out any old-fashioned expectations of large families. Extensive old age pensions made couples confident that they would have money in their retirement. Universal employment for women and a severe housing shortage kept families small. Since the end of the Soviet regime, the rate of population growth has actually fallen to zero, presumably reflecting the hard economic times and devaluation of savings and pensions brought about in the transition to a market system. Once the economy improves, the Russian consumer is likely to demand goods and services at a level more like Europe and America than an underdeveloped country, and while it seems unlikely that Russians will want families of six or eight children like their peasant great grandparents, they may prefer two children as is typical of western Europe and the United States.

Although alarm about the "population explosion" points out a serious future problem, the question remains as to what the world would look like if humanity resolved the problem. A simple end to population growth would be only part of an answer. Rising consumer demand, which appears to be inexorable, portends that topping off the number of people at eight or ten billion would mean nothing if Chinese, Indians, and Africans increased their income to American levels.

THE CONSUMER MOVEMENT

Although perhaps the biggest and most successful, environmentalism resembles other movements of the same period such as consumerism. Both developed in the 1960s and 1970s, had broad popular support, produced a dozen new laws, and evolved into a mature structure of interest groups and government bureaucracies. Today, these movements are less dynamic and fluid than thirty years ago.

A single man, Ralph Nader, epitomizes the consumer movement. His father, a Lebanese immigrant who ran a grocery story in Winsted, Connecticut, was active in community affairs and encouraged his children to do the same. Nader's intelligence and energy pointed him toward Princeton University and Harvard Law School. Study at Harvard and work as a lawyer representing accident victims convinced him that the American automobile was not safe. In 1965, he published *Unsafe at Any Speed*, a scathing critique of the Corvair, manufactured by General Motors. In order to neutralize this critic and potential expert witness, GM hired a private detective. Just before Nader was to testify before the Senate committee investigating auto safety, the chair learned about the detective and turned the tables on the world's largest corporation. The publicity over GM's covert actions elevated Nader to national attention. After he sued GM for invasion of privacy, the corporation gave him $425,000 to settle the case. Nader used the money to set up a dozen consumer organizations, thereby putting auto safety and consumer protection on the political agenda. This dramatic reversal typified the fluid situation.

This was not the first time consumerism had been on the national agenda. Like the conservation movement of the turn of the century, the Progressive era had sparked reform. The Department of Agriculture's Division of Chemistry became alarmed about unsafe preservatives in food. In 1906, Upton Sinclair published *The Jungle*, which described the filth, rats, and worker oppression of the Chicago meat-packing industry. Theodore Roosevelt backed a national law, due

Ralph Nader and picketers in front of the General Motors building in 1969 protesting the company's indifference to automotive air pollution.

to his personal experience during the Spanish American War when his Rough Riders received canned meat that was rotted and adulterated. Congress passed the Meat Inspection and Pure Food acts. As progressivism faded by 1920, so did this first consumer movement.

Franklin Roosevelt's New Deal revived a few aspects. Again, the Department of Agriculture, then the parent department for the Food and Drug Administration, supplied the technical information about lack of sanitation and safety. Tragedy struck when several hundred people died from taking an unsafe medicine, Elixir of Sulfanilamide, prompting Congress to rewrite the Food and Drug Act. In a related consumer sphere, one of Roosevelt's chief objectives in building dams to generate electricity and transmit it to rural areas was to end the high rates the private utilities charged customers. Overall, however, consumer protection was only a minor part of the New Deal and the onset of World War II ended it.[3] In 1927, a best-selling book titled *100,000,000 Guinea Pigs: the Dangers in Everyday Foods, Drugs, and Cosmetics* spawned a testing laboratory that published a newsletter for consumers. In turn, this led to the Consumers' Union, which began *Consumer Reports*.

The sudden growth of consumerism in the 1960s owed a large part of its success to the increasing educational level of Americans. The high employment and

225

wages of the period meant people could afford to examine their situation more critically. The form the consumer movement took fit Americans' declining trust of big business. From 1945 onward, large corporations enjoyed great support from government, and even labor unions, but by the 1960s, the partnership had run its course. The technical factors spurring the movement are less clear since the biggest technical change had occurred sixty years earlier when food processors like Nabisco and Armour began to sell to a national market. In the nineteenth century, customers could judge the quality of the meat, bread, and milk with their eyes, hands, and nose, and by knowing the butcher, baker, or farmer personally.

Nader not only fit the model of a policy entrepreneur, he defined it from then on. He was and remains the leader. Nader's personal resources are his total dedication, his talent for persuasion and publicity, and a good education. After General Motors paid him $425,000 to settle his lawsuit, he had the financial resources as well. The people who rallied to the movement had grievances of unsafe automobiles, high prices, and poor service. If General Motors made safer cars, all its customers benefitted, not just the ones who had helped force the improvements. The movement only succeeded because of a few dedicated advocates. Nader, for example, accepted only a small salary and lived in a modest apartment in Washington. Much of the money came from university students who contributed several dollars of their fees to Public Interest Research Groups.

Consumer advocates often believe the answer to problems is for government to pass laws and regulate. This command and control strategy stands at odds with the recent trend towards deregulation. It focuses on Washington, believing that corporations can circumvent state regulation. Consumerists see the corporations as untrustworthy adversaries. Even so, consumerists favor deregulation in cases like airlines. Congress and administrative action reduced and ended the stranglehold the Civil Aeronautics Board held over airlines, thereby reducing the cost of tickets by about a third. The Department of Justice settlement of its anti-trust lawsuit against AT&T in 1982 and parallel reforms by the Federal Communications Commission deregulated long distance telephone service, resulting in lower costs and advanced technology.

The two movements, environmental and consumer, evolved in tandem. Both arose in the 1960s with broad popular support, and, during the following decade, persuaded Congress to enact many laws for protection. Both allied with the Democratic party and suffered setbacks during the Reagan administration. Viewed as a mass movement, environmentalism has fared better. The total membership in environmental groups is hundreds of times more than in consumer groups. And, in addition to collective benefits, environmental groups furnish individual benefits like magazines, travel tours, and weekend hikes, which consumerism cannot provide. While environmentalism is a mature movement, the consumer movement remains in flux.

Viewing the two movements from the perspective of interest groups, consumerism has evolved into interest groups, even if to a smaller degree than environmentalism. For example, the Center for Auto Safety and the National Consumer Insurance Organization specialize, while the Advocacy Institute and Center for the Study of Responsive Law is more general. Many groups belong to the National Consumers League, an umbrella organization that encompasses over four hundred state and local groups. And Public Citizen, Inc., is an umbrella for groups founded by Nader. Compared to their adversaries, consumer interest groups lack resources to membership, staff, and money. Grass roots membership is thin; in fact, many centers and institutes have virtually no members. Two million members are on the rolls of various groups, although this includes double counting—meaning that a person may belong to two or more groups, and that that person will be counted as a member of both groups. Funds come from philanthropies and government contracts, and their few staff members are often recent graduates of universities and law schools. Supposedly, a major advantage of pluralism is that one interest group balances another. This argument for countervailing forces rings hollow when the Goliath of business confronts the David of consumerism (one of the movement's favorite metaphors). Consumerists do not want the government to be neutral and may not consider opposing interest groups to be legitimate.

Viewing the two movements from the perspective of governmental procedures, consumerism has gained victories that are strictly procedural like the Cigarette Labeling Act, the Truth in Lending Act, and the Energy Act, which required labels rating energy efficiency and expenses for refrigerators, hot water heaters, and other appliances. The public right to present facts under the Administrative Procedures Act gives consumerists the opportunity to intervene. The Food and Drug Administration (FDA) now requires drugs to be effective as well as safe, which bumped a lot of medicines off the store shelves.

Giving consumers the right to sue as a class, not just individually, provides a procedure to encourage attorneys to devote the long hours needed to win. A "class action" permits a plaintiff to sue on behalf of hundreds or thousands of others in the same situation, for instance, all passengers of an airline or all purchasers of an automobile. For an individual consumer, the money at stake is small, perhaps only a few dollars, but for an entire class of thousands and occasionally millions of consumers, the stake may be huge. Plaintiff attorneys may ask for punitive damages, allowing the judge to multiply the amount of money for the actual damages by two or three times as a way to punish a company. Combining this long-standing legal remedy with class action creates a powerful weapon. Moreover, juries often have been generous when weighing the injury to an individual against the profits of a big corporation. In 1997, the combination of state lawsuits, under the leadership of the Mississippi attorney general, against tobacco companies marked a new direction, which was neither regulation nor citizen law suits. A dozen states sued the companies for the expense of treating lung cancer and heart disease for their citizens who were too poor to pay their own medical expenses. This broad attack forced the companies to negotiate a comprehensive, nationwide agreement that was instantly acclaimed as an innovative use of the power of the states, independent of the national government. But within weeks, the agreement unraveled as medical experts and consumer groups assailed it for letting the tobacco companies off too easy. President Bill Clinton and the top officials in the Department of Health and Human Services refused to support the proposed settlement, thereby undercutting a noble innovation.

Congress set up several agencies to look out for consumers. The National Transportation Safety Board received authority to set standards for automobiles. Recalls by Ford, Chrysler, General Motors, and foreign manufacturers are now common. (Cost-benefit analysis shows the dollar savings from improved safety to be $5 billion each year, while the dollar savings of controlling auto emissions to be slight.)[4] The Consumer Product Safety Commission, established in 1973, emphasizes the safety of children. It requires their sleepwear to be fire retardant, cribs to have space between the slats narrower than a baby's head, bicycles to have good brakes, and medicine bottles to be difficult to open. For adults' safety, it requires mattresses be fire retardant, and lawn mowers to be less likely to amputate fingers and toes. Although not a new agency, the FDA has gained more authority. Originally, Congress intended the Office of Consumer Affairs to be located in the White House to coordinate programs throughout the government, but support lagged and now, with low visibility, it makes its home in the Department of Health and Human Services.

Compared to the EPA, the Safety Board, the Product Commission, and the FDA are not as well known because the functions are divided among different agencies instead of one, and because the consumer agencies face constant attacks from industry. Auto manufacturers resist complaints that their cars are not safe, and toy manufacturers defend their toys against the Product Commission. For both of these industries, the costs of recalls and delays eat into profits.

Pharmaceutical companies are less contentious, but they still resist scientific criticism. When the FDA moved to regulate tobacco as an addictive drug, the farmers and cigarette manufacturers mobilized. The FDA's first proposal merely was to regulate sales to children under the age of eighteen. The American Tobacco Institute lobbied on Capitol Hill, sponsored advertisements, and contributed lavishly to Bob Dole and, to a lesser extent, Bill Clinton in the 1996 election. Senators and representatives gained campaign donations too. Although Clinton gave support to the FDA, it was lukewarm because of the political opposition. The FDA faced another problem in its strict standards for licensing drugs for the treatment of AIDS. Groups of victims asked the agency to speed up the process for pharmaceuticals already licensed in Europe. The FDA insisted that American field tests were necessary; its regulations did not permit foreign tests. With enough political pressure, the FDA gave in. As the victims groups predicted, many of the drugs proved dramatically effective. In spite of the opposition to it, the FDA had many bureaucratic strengths of expertise, autonomy, permanency, and specialization. Its scientific and medical mission gave it prestige, although the tobacco and AIDS issues overwhelmed these sources of power. The EPA has never enjoyed the scientific prestige and autonomy of the FDA.

Unlike the dynamic period of consumerism in the 1960s, today's government agencies operate in a stable, mature situation. The bureaus see a series of technical problems, such as a defective brake or a dangerous toy, which they fix by ordering the manufacturer to change the design or repair the automobile or toy. Their concern is to implement the program, not to engage in debate on the overall policy, which has been in place for ten to twenty years. Both the Democrats and the Republicans want to protect consumers. The bureaucrats are aware, however, that Republicans tend to weigh the cost to the manufacturer more heavily. The agency needs to respond to the chair of the congressional committee with jurisdiction by good communication, sensitivity to his or her home district, and seeking advice. Failure to please the chair may reduce annual appropriations or lead him or her to propose unfavorable amendments. Likewise, the agency needs to build bridges to interest groups that can provide support and to industry to inform when it cannot please.

GREEN PARTIES

In the 1996 election, for the first time Americans could vote for a Green party. Much of its inspiration came from the Green party of Germany, which had first won seats in Parliament in 1983 and again in 1994 when it became the third largest German party. Since their establishment in 1979, the Greens have captured world attention due to their idealism, candor, and colorful slogans. Unlike the American situation, German (and other European) politics tend to be ideological on a right to left spectrum. The Greens, atypically, derive from both the right and the left. Its conservative antecedents are romantic and even authoritarian, which are exemplified by scientific forestry (of the sort that influenced Bernard Fernow and Gifford Pinchot) developed in Germany, or the romantic poets and authors (like Jean Jacques Rousseau) who called for a return to nature. An 1815 article by the German patriot, Ernst Moritz Arndt, rails against shortsighted exploitation of woodlands and soil and condemns deforestation, and in 1867, the German zoologist, Ernst Haeckel, coined the term "ecology." On the left of the spectrum, student radicals from the 1960s turned their attention to the environment as they grew older. Many identified themselves as Marxist, Leninist, or Maoist.

Three events during the 1970s stimulated the Green consciousness. The oil crisis demonstrated that West Germany was vulnerable in spite of its "Economic Miracle" since World War II. Publication of the Club of Rome's *The Limits of Growth* publicized the problems of pollution, resource destruction, and world population. The government response to the shortage of energy and resources was to expand its nuclear industry. It planned to build a hundred plants and embraced the plutonium fast-breeder technology. Alarmed, environmentalists feared the radiation and the connections to nuclear weapons (the West Germans realized that their country could be the first battlefield for World War III). The Greens on the left who opposed both war and pollution joined those on the right who wanted to protect nature. Its mottos, derived from necessity, were "Unity in

Diversity" and "Neither Right nor Left but Forward." Electoral success came quickly. In 1983, only three years after its official establishment, the Green party won twenty-seven seats in Parliament, attracting voters who were far younger than the average German. The party had concentrated on grass roots organization, and the effort had paid off.

German election law provides an advantage for ideological parties by its system of proportional representation, whereby voters in a large region vote for a party, rather than an individual, and the representatives are elected in proportion to the total vote. The American "winner take all" system of districts which choose only one senator, representative or council member makes it virtually impossible for a specialized party to win. The Greens claimed to be an "antiparty" to stress that it was a "movement" that did not intend to give in to the unidealistic compromises of politicians. In the early years, it refused to form alliances with other parties as is the custom in Germany. In the 1987 election, the Greens gained more seats to reach a total of forty-two.

American attention often followed Petra Kelly, a leader from the beginning. Kelly embodied multiple influences. Growing up in a conservative Bavarian town and attending Catholic schools, she was raised largely by her grandmother who espoused radical politics. Her parents divorced when she was young and when Kelly was twelve years old, her mother married an American army officer who gave her his Irish name. Her new family moved to the United States. Kelly's college years in Washington, DC, became crucial to her future because that was also when the country was inflamed with the Civil Rights Movement and the anti-Vietnam War protests, which she considered inspirations for her environmentalism, peace advocacy, and feminism.[5] She returned to Europe in 1971 to work for the European Community bureaucracy, and became active in environmental and peace politics. Once elected to Parliament in 1983, Kelly became a celebrity due to her skill as a speaker, radical positions, and American background.

The Green parliamentarians faced the dilemma of how much to compromise and participate. They did not want to be just a "stinking normal party" (as they phrased it). In parliamentary sessions they flouted conventional speech, wore casual clothes, and carried flowers and banners. After their initial unwillingness to cooperate with other parties, they later became more realistic. This in turn estranged them from the grass roots members who wanted the Greens to remain a movement rather than a party.

The 1990 election proved disastrous due to the issue of German reunification following the collapse of the East German Communist regime. The Green policy of pacifism led to the corollary that nationalism was bad. Moreover, the Marxist strain in the party made it favorable toward the East Germans (the joke was that the party was like a watermelon: green on the outside and red on the inside). The Greens advocated that East Germany remain a separate nation, but that both Germanies be neutral. The voters totally rejected this idea and the Green candidates all were defeated. Having learned from their defeat, the party came back in the 1994 election to win forty-nine seats, once again making it the third largest in Parliament. A shadow on the victory was that Petra Kelly had been murdered two years earlier by her intimate companion and fellow parliamentary representative, who then committed suicide.

PAST, PRESENT, AND FUTURE

Speculating on the future tests the four approaches of mass movements, interest groups, partisanships, and procedures. Taken as a whole, the life cycle of the environmental movement is now in its mature phase. Its youthful years have passed, and it has settled into stable middle age. The vague malcontent of the 1960s produced an agenda which evolved into laws and programs. Policies for air and water, the two biggest and most expensive forms of pollution, certainly fit this mold. Hazardous waste, which emerged later, now fits into the Superfund and the RCRA. Nevertheless, when companies or governments propose new dumps, the neighbors usually complain, and grass roots protests are frequent. Radiation dangers no longer generate thousands of citizens objecting. A good deal of the quiescence, however, is due to the moribund state of the industry. If utilities do not build new reactors, the public is not riled, while constructing a waste site at Yucca Mountain and the low-level dumps stimulate vigorous objections. Danger incidental to disassembling weapons has not yet developed as a grievance, although if disarmament proceeds, it seems likely to become an issue. The greatest dangers are overseas in the former Soviet republics. Although Kazakhstan, Ukraine, and Belarus have agreed to turn over their nuclear warheads to Russia for dismantling, not all weapons can be accounted for.

The overseas problem threatening the environment most is population increase, which has the two aspects of the increase itself coupled with higher levels of consumption. Under an optimistic scenario, world population is virtually certain to increase to eight billion, and the pessimistic scenario goes as high as ten to twelve billion. The smaller increase will probably go hand in hand with more prosperity, which increases the demand for oil, coal, lumber, and food, thus straining the environment. Although the global utopias of Deep Ecology seem fantasies, small grass root utopias like the Weaver family or Earth First! seem likely to continue. Overall, the quiescence of environmental politics owes much to the American prosperity of the 1990s. The United States can regulate air pollution without too much harm to industry, and even though an economic recession could change the equation, the threat of rolling back protection would reactivate the movement.

Interest groups are firmly established. Environmentalists have learned how to lobby and have recruited both wealthy sponsors and thousands of members who can finance their programs with dues of $25 a year. Businesses have lost their earlier advantage in lobbying, but have normalized their roles and interaction with the environmentalists. Environmental interest groups are now more professional with experts on their permanent staffs. The groups cooperate among each other and even cooperate with business groups. Washington is the undisputed center for the groups; those based in San Francisco or New York maintain offices in the capital. New issues overseas will not necessarily fit the groups' operations. Some like Greenpeace already have members in many countries; others will probably expand by linking with groups abroad and recruiting directly. To the extent the population issue moves onto the political agenda, new groups will participate, for example the Roman Catholic Church. The controversy between loggers and environmentalists about logging in national forests and the BLM land seems headed for a showdown, and the Tongass Forest appears destined to be the battleground. Citizens are becoming more organized and finding more allies. The timber interests have loyal support from key senators, but with fewer and fewer trees, the environmental side becomes stronger.

As long as the Republicans hew to their conservative line and maintain their links to business, partisanship will continue to determine policy. The Democrats now hold an advantageous position to keep the support of the public. They have carved out the place Nixon hoped to have for the Republicans. After reading the polls in 1996, the GOP backed away from directly assaulting environmental protection, but the party still does not give much support in rhetoric or congressional votes. The Republican goals of balancing the budget and reducing taxes squeeze money away from the EPA. In the past, the two parties have favored different styles of regulation, that is command and control versus market solutions. Now, however, the Democrats have adopted many market-based solutions, stealing the Republicans' thunder. Vice President Al Gore has kept environmental protection at the top of the Democrats' agenda, and his pursuit of the party's nomination for president will keep it there. The possibility of a Green party emerging seems slight; its success in Germany owes much to the voting system of proportional representation. The American system disadvantages a Green candidate. Moreover, the Democrats' success in capturing mainstream environmental support lures away potential third party voters.

After nearly three decades of attention, environmental politics is largely routine. Critics complain it is bureaucratized, which is largely true. The laws on air, water, hazardous waste, and radiation have been implemented and amended once or twice. The EPA is in place, albeit with budget cuts. The Interior Department now favors the environment and the Agriculture Department is heading in that direction. The norm for the present is for issues to be seen as problems that scientists, engineers, and planners can solve, and industry employs thousands of environmental compliance specialists. Environmental organizations themselves have their own bureaucracies. Like government agencies, they enjoy the benefits of specialization, full-time attention, and autonomy.

Of course the future will never be as placid as this projection. Even within the mature and routine arena, issues will break out. Nuclear waste and decommissioning old reactors will provoke storms. At some point after timber companies have sawed down more forests, Congress will address the controversy, and further into the future, the question of world population is sure to set off fireworks.

NOTES

1. Donella Meadows, *The Limits to Growth* (New York: Universe Press, 1973).
2. Nathan Keyfitz, "The Growing Human Population," *Scientific American*, September 1989, 123.
3. Mark V. Nadel, *The Politics of Consumer Protection* (Indianapolis, IN: Bobbs Merrill, 1971).
4. Robert Crandall et al., *Regulating the Automobile* (Washington, DC: Brookings, 1986).
5. Petra Kelly, "Women and the Global Green Movement," Francine D'Amico and Peter R. Beckman, eds., *Women in World Politics*, (Westport, CT: Bergin and Garvey, 1995), 176-177.

SUGGESTIONS FOR INTERNET SITES

The World Wide Web offers huge amounts of up-to-date information from many sources. From the political perspective, nearly every sort of opinion is available. Every site has its bias, however, even if it is only the EPA's bias in favor of its official programs. Because the Internet is so dynamic, many of these sites may have new addresses within a year or two. In these cases, a brief search will probably give the new location. The author maintains a home page for this book at www.utoledo.edu/homepages/ddavis/aep.htm. If the address changes, search for the author's personal home page and link from that or e-mail Nelson Hall Publishers (nelsonhal@aol.com).

Chapter 1
Introduction
Environmental policy may be understood in four ways:

1. Mass movements: Lois Gibbs mobilized her neighbors to fight the toxic dump at Love Canal (www.vida.com/speakout/People/LoisMarieGibbs .html). Current grass roots groups are Stop Landfill Expansion (www.SurfRite.com/soc/), Friends of the Jerome Park Reservoir (members.aol.com/jeromepark/index.html), the Southern Utah Wilderness Alliance (www.seanet.com/~bigsteve/), and the Southeast Alaska Conservation Council (www.juneau.com/seacc/seacc.html).
2. Interest groups: The best known are the Sierra Club (www.sierraclub. org/), the Friends of the Earth (www.foe.org/), the Earth Island Institute

(www.econet.apc.org/ei/index.html), and the Natural Resources Defense Council (www.nrdc.org/). David Brower (www.econet.apc.org/ei/browerbrowerbr.html) has led three of them. Much opposition to environmental protection comes from industry: the American Petroleum Institute (www.api.org/), Exxon (www.exxon.com/exxoncorp/environment/environment.html), the Edison Electric Institute (www.eei.org/), General Motors (www.gm.com/), Chrysler (www.chryslercorp.com/), and the Chemical Manufacturers' Association (www.cmahq.com/).

3. Political parties: the Democrats (www.democrats.org/) and the Republicans (www.rnc.org/).

4. Governmental Procedures: Governmental procedures influence policy, for example, the jurisdiction of the House Committee on Resources (www.house.gov/resources/) and the Senate Committee on Energy and Natural Resources (www. senate.gov/~energy/). The U.S. Environmental Protection Agency (www.epa.gov/) administers most laws in the area. It also delegates programs to state agencies like the Ohio EPA (www.epa.ohio.gov/). The U.S. Department of the Interior (www.doi.gov/) runs programs on land management and surface mining.

Chapter 2
Air Pollution Control

Air pollution control comes under the jurisdiction of the EPA Office of Air and Radiation (www.epa.gov/oar/oarhome.html). The American Lung Association (www.lungusa.org/) is an interest group on one side, and industries like auto manufacturing, such as the Ford Motor Company (www.ford.com/corporate info/environment/) and the American Road and Transportation Builders Association (www.artba.org/advocacy.html), are on the other. The United Auto Workers Union (www.uaw.org/) supports the auto manufacturers. Local governmental agencies include the South Coast District in California (www.aqmd.gov/) and New York City Department of Environmental Protection (www.ci.nyc.ny.us/html/dep/html/about.html). Clean Air Action is a citizens group in Houston (www.cleanairaction.org/). The danger of global climate change (www.eei.org/Industry/enviro/enviss.htm#global).

Chapter 3
Water Pollution Control

Water pollution control comes under the jurisdiction of the EPA Office of Water (www.epa.gov/owow/). The Izaak Walton League (www.iwla.org/) and Trout Unlimited (xenon.prozima.com:880/) are interest groups on one side, and industries like Bethlehem Steel (www.bethsteel.com/) are on the other. The EPA has program for the Great Lakes (www.epa.gov/glnpo/). The Wetlands Inventory (www.nwi.fws.gov/), information (environment.miningco.com/msubwet.htm/) and links (www2.ari.net/kjfrazi/wetland.html). The Everglades (www.florida-everglades.com/Evhono.htm). The American Water Works Association (www.awwa.org/) consists of companies that build treatment plants. The Bureau of Reclamation (www.usbr.gov/) builds dams in the west. Municipal water departments in Chicago (www.ci.chi.il.us/WorksMart/Water/), Atlanta (www.atlanta.org/dept/water/newwside.htm), and Los Angeles (www.ladwp.com/aboutdwp/history/allabout/allabout.htm).

Chapter 4
Solid, Toxic, and Hazardous Waste Control
These types of waste come under two EPA offices: Solid Waste (www.epa.gov/epaoswer/) and Pesticides and Toxic Substances (www.epa.gov/internet/oppts/). The Superfund (www.epa.gov/superfund/). The Environmental Working Group (www.ewg.org/) is an interest group on one side and industries like the Dow Chemical Company (www.dow.com/dowenv/index.html) are on the other. Rachel Carson wrote *Silent Spring* (www.whitehouse.gov/WH/EOP/OVP/24hours/carson.html). Lois Gibbs, who organized opposition at Love Canal, runs the Citizen's Clearinghouse for Hazardous Waste (www.essential.org/orgs/cchw/cchwinf.html). The Recycling Index (www.isd.net/cpm/wwwlinks.html).

Chapter 5
Radiation Control
Radiation Control is regulated by the Nuclear Regulatory Commission (www.nrc.gov/). The EPA Radiation division (www.epa.gov/radiation/) supervises environmental standards. The Department of Energy Office of Radioactive Waste (www.rw.doe.gov/) and its environmental office (www.em.doe.gov/em30/wastdisp.html) are responsible for planning how to dispose of high-level waste, probably at Yucca Mountain near Las Vegas (www.ymp.gov/). States will be responsible for low-level waste (www.inel.gov/national/national.html). The Critical Mass Energy Project (www.essential.org/orgs/public_citizen/CMEP/) and Greenpeace (www.greenpeace.org/cnuk.html) are anti-nuclear interest groups and industries that operate plants at Diablo Canyon (www.pge.com/), Seabrook (www.psnh.com/), and Fermi (www.detroitedison.com/) favor nuclear plants. General Electric (www.ge.com/nuclear/) builds the plants. A directory on radiation protection (www.indirect.com/user/kencoon/rp-hp.html).

Chapter 6
Protecting the Endangered Species and the Wilderness
The Fish and Wildlife Service (www.fws.gov/) is the lead agency for endangered species (www.fws.gov/~r9endspp/endspp.html). Other agencies concerned with endangered species and with wilderness areas are the National Park Service (www.nps.gov/), the Bureau of Land Management (www.blm.gov/), and the Forest Service (www.fs.fed.us/). The Wilderness Society (www.wilderness.org/) began in 1936 to advocate the concept. Opposition comes from ranchers (www.ncanet.org/) and timber companies (www.gp.com/). The Audubon Society (www.audubon.org/) wants protection.

Chapter 7
Protecting the Parks

The National Park Service (www.nps.gov/) manages parks like Yellowstone (www.nps.gov/yell/), Yosemite (www.nps.gov/yose/), and Sleeping Bear Dunes (www.nps.gov/slbe/). Environmentalists organize to protect parks like Yellowstone (www.desktop.org/gyc) and the Indiana Dunes (www.savedunes. org/). Adirondack Park (unix2.nysed.gov/ils/executive/apa/mission.htm) and state agencies in Michigan, (www.dnr.state.mi.us/www/parks/index.htm), Missouri (www.mobot.org/Stateparks/welcome.html) and Texas www.tpwd. state.tx.us/park/). Parks in Boston (www.anaserve.com/~cyndi/boston.htm), Chicago (www.ci.chi.il.us/WorksMart/Parks/), the Detroit area (www. metroparks.com/), Portland (www.parks.ci.portland.or.us/), San Francisco (www.ci.sf.ca.us/recpark/), and Toledo (cs.bluffton.edu/~estell/metroparks/ oakopenings.html). In New York City, citizens support Central Park (www. centralpark.org) and in Oregon they support Silver Falls State Park (www. open.org/slverfall/).

Chapter 8
Protecting the Land

The Bureau of Land Management (www.blm.gov/) is responsible for 270 million acres. The Office of Surface Mining (www.osmre.gov/) regulates coal mining. American Forests (www.amfor.org/) is an interest group that seeks to preserve forests. Corporations like Boise Cascade (www.bc.com/enviro/envmain.htm) and the Peabody Coal Company (www.PeabodyGroup.com/) advocate being good citizens. The Wise Use Movement (www.eskimo.com/~rarnold/ issues.html) defends property rights. Others are concerned about takings (www.webcom.com/~pcj/takings.html). Earth First! (www.imaja.com/imaja/ change/environment/ef/earthfirst.html) is a radical group with many opinions (gopher://gopher.igc.apc.org/11/orgs/ef.journal). In fragile areas, real estate companies (www.traverse.com/envguide/cover.html) may be concerned with protection, or they may not.

Chapter 9
Conclusion and Resources

The United Nations (www.undp.org/popin/) and the U.S. Agency for International Development (www.info.usaid.gov/pop_health/) run programs to limit population growth. Planned Parenthood (www.ippf.org/) and the Population Council (www.popcouncil.org/) are private organizations that favor control and the Population Research Institute (www.pop.org/around.html) opposes it. The population clock at the Census Bureau (www.census.gov/ipc/www/world.html).

Green parties are active in many western democracies. The German party (www.hrz.uni-oldenburg.de:81/~oliver/bg/e.bgindex.html) is the most successful. In the United States, the Green party (www.greens.org/california/), which is primarily active in California, nominated Ralph Nader for president (www.rahul.net/cameron/nader/). An overview of British and European parties (www.barnsdle.demon.co.uk/pol/fundi.html).

Resources from Envirolink (envirolink.org/), Earth Systems (earthsystems.org/ Environment.html) and Asphalt Strawberry (www.imaja.com/imaja/change/ environment/Environment.html).

State environmental agencies in California (www.arb.ca.gov/homepage. htm), Illinois (www.epa.state.il.us/), Michigan (www.deq.state.mi.us/), Ohio (www. epa.ohio.gov/), Pennsylvania (www.dep.state.pa.us/), Tennessee (www.state.tn.us/ environment/), Wisconsin (www.dnr.state.wi.us/news/events.htm), and a list of agencies in all states (www-epin.ies.ncsu.edu/apti/resource/apdln.htm).

SUBJECT INDEX

endangered species, 23, 200
Endangered Species Act, 132, 143,
   147–149, 156, 158
Energy, Department of, 24, 105,
   113–114, 117, 120–122, 127–128
Energy Research and Development
   Administration (ERDA), 114, 118
Energy Tax Act of 1978, 49
enforcement, 39, 41
England, 46, 181
Enlightenment, 187
entrepreneur, 12–13
Environmental Decade, 1, 2, 8
Environmental Defense Fund, 3, 47
Environmental Impact Statement (EIS),
   111, 113, 118
environmental overkill, 113
Environmental Protection Agency, 1, 2,
   7, 18–21, 24, 34–36, 38–39, 47–50,
   53, 60–62, 65–67, 69–70, 77, 79,
   84, 85, 88, 90–93, 95, 97, 104–105,
   125, 127, 198, 201, 228
EPA Enforcement Division, 91
EPA Planning Division, 39
EPA, the two faces of, 48
ERDA. *See* Energy Research and
   Development Administration
Erie Canal, 170
Estes Park, CO, 172
ethanol industry, 49
Ethyl Company, 33–34
Euclid, OH, 210
European Community, 52, 230
Everglades, 136, 203
evolution, 133, 168, 221
expertise, 20
extinctions, mass, 133
Exxon Valdez, 77–78
Fairfax Company, VA, 124
Fairmont Park, Philadelphia, 163
Family Farm Preservation Association,
   207
Farm Act of 1996, 70
farmers, 49
farmland preservation, 213
fascism, 11–12, 15, 107
fashion, women's hats, 138
Federal Bureau of Investigation (FBI),
   88, 206
Federal Communications Commission,
   8, 226
Federal Emergency Management
   Agency, 45, 69

Federal Energy Regulatory Commission
   (FERC), 114
Federal Highway Administration, 12, 27,
   214
federalism, 122–123
Federalist No. 10, 14
Federal Land Policy Planning Act 215
Federal Power Commission (FPC) 114
Federal Register, 19, 38
FEMA. *See* Federal Emergency
   Management Agency
FERC. *See* Federal Energy Regulatory
   Commission
Fermi, Enrico, 107
Fermi I plant, 105, 111, 121, 126
Fernow, Bernhard, 191–192
Fifth Amendment, 203
fire, 134, 191, 199, 209, 207
Fire Island National Seashore, 170
fiscal crisis, 174
fishable and swimmable, 1, 64, 76
Fish and Wildlife Coordination Act, 147
Fish and Wildlife Service, 68, 70, 76,
   84, 132, 148–149, 157
Flathead County, MT, 203
Flathead Indians, 165
flood control, 69, 73
   plain, 203
Florida, 50, 58, 166
Florida Keys, 157
flowers, 162
Food and Drug Administration, 93, 225,
   227–228
Ford, Gerald, 40–41, 84, 113, 198
Ford administration, 114
Ford Motor Company, 30, 31
forest, tropical, 132
Foresta, Ronald, 183n
Forest Service, 9, 52, 140, 159, 180,
   185, 191–193, 200–201, 205
Forest Service Advisory Committees, 19
Forts
   Benning, 149
   Bragg, 149
   McHenry, 60
   Peck, 2, 74, 79, 143
Fort Wayne, IN, 78
fossil fuels, 51–52
Four Corners, 38
Fowler, Robert Booth, 104n
Framework Convention on Climate
   Change, 52

PHOTO CREDITS